$15.95

S0-AIV-524

Visions of a Future

A Study of Christian Eschatology

NEW THEOLOGY STUDIES

General Editor: Peter C. Phan

*

Editorial Consultants:
Monika Hellwig
Robert Imbelli
Robert Schreiter

*

Volume 8: Visions of a Future

Visions of a Future

A Study of Christian Eschatology

by

Zachary Hayes, O.F.M.

A Michael Glazier Book

THE LITURGICAL PRESS
Collegeville, Minnesota

A Michael Glazier Book published by The Liturgical Press.

Cover design by David Manahan, O.S.B.

The Bible text in this publication is from the Revised Standard Version of the Bible, copyrighted 1946, 1952 © 1971, 1973 by the Division of Christian Education of the National Council of the Churches of Christ in the U.S.A., and used by permission.

Copyright 1989 by Michael Glazier, Inc. Copyright © 1990 by The Order of St. Benedict, Inc., Collegeville, Minnesota. All rights reserved. No part of this book may be reproduced in any form or by any means, electronic or mechanical, including photocopying, recording, taping, or any retrieval system, without the written permission of The Liturgical Press, Collegeville, Minnesota 56321. Printed in the United States of America.

2   3   4   5   6   7   8   9

Library of Congress Cataloging-in-Publication Data

Hayes, Zachary.
    Visions of a future / by Zachary Hayes.
       p.   cm.
    "A Michael Glazier book."
    Originally published: Wilmington, Del. : M. Glazier, 1987. (New theology studies ; v. 8)
    Includes bibliographical references and index.
    ISBN 0-8146-5742-7
    1. Eschatology—History of doctrines.   I. Title.
[BT819.5.H38   1992]
236—dc20

                                              92-13827
                                                 CIP

For my beloved nephew
Paul Kulczyk

Table of Contents

Editor's Preface

This series entitled *New Theology Studies,* composed of eight volumes, is an attempt to answer the need felt by professors and students alike for scholarly yet readable books dealing with certain Catholic beliefs traditionally associated with dogmatic theology. The volumes treat of fundamental theology (revelation, the nature and method of theology, the credibility of the Christian faith), trinitarian theology, christology, ecclesiology, anthropology, and eschatology.

There has been, of course, no lack of books, published singly or in series, both in this continent and elsewhere, which are concerned with these central truths of Christianity. Nevertheless, there is room, we believe, for yet another series of texts on systematic theology, not because these offer entirely novel insights into the aforementioned teachings, but because it is incumbent upon Christians of every age to reflect upon their faith in light of their cultural and religious experiences and to articulate their understanding in terms accessible to their contemporaries.

Theology is traditionally described as faith in search of understanding, *fides quaerens intellectum.* The faith to which the contributors to this series are committed is the Christian faith as lived and taught by the (Roman) Catholic Church. It is, however, a faith that is ecumenically sensitive, open to ways of living and thinking practiced by other Christian communities and other religions. The understanding which the series seeks to foster goes beyond an accumulation of information, however interesting, on the Christian past to retrieve and renew, by means of the analogical imagination, the Christian Tradition embodied in its various classics. In this way, it is hoped, one can understand afresh both the meaning and the truth of the Christian beliefs and their multiple interconnections. Lastly, the contributors are convinced that theology is a never-ending quest for insights into faith, a *cogitatio fidei*. Its ultimate purpose is not to provide definite and definitive answers to every conceivable problem posed by faith, but to gain an understanding, which will always be imperfect and fragmentary, of its subject, God the incomprehensible Mystery. Thus, theology remains an essentially unfinished business, to be taken up over and again in light of and in confrontation with the challenges found in every age. And our age is no exception, when, to cite only two examples, massive poverty and injustice structured into the present economic order, and the unprecedented meeting of religious faiths in new contexts of dialogue, have impelled theologians to reconceptualize the Christian faith in radical terms.

Contrary to some recent series of textbooks, *New Theology Studies* does not intend to advocate and advance a uniform or even unified viewpoint. Contributors are left free to present their own understanding and approach to the subject matter assigned to them. They are only requested to treat their themes in an integrating manner by situating them in the context of Tradition (highlighting their biblical, patristic, medieval, and modern developments), by expounding their theological meaning and function in light of current pronouncements of the Magisterium, by exploring their implications for Christian living, and by indicating possible different contemporary conceptualizations of these doctrines. The goal is to achieve some measure of comprehensiveness and balance by taking into account all the important issues of the subject matter under discussion and at the same time exhibit some thematic unity by means of a consistent method and a unifying perspective.

The eight volumes are intended primarily as resource books, "launching and landing bases," for upper-division theology courses in Catholic colleges and seminaries, but it is hoped that they will be useful also to people—priests, permanent deacons, religious, and educated laity, inside and outside of the Roman Catholic communion—interested in understanding the Christian faith in contemporary cultural and ecclesial contexts. We hope that these volumes will make a contribution, however modest, to the intellectual and spiritual life of the Christian Church as it prepares to enter its third millennium.

Peter C. Phan
The Catholic University of America

INTRODUCTION

In the late 1950's, Hans Urs von Balthasar described eschatology as the "storm center" of theology. The situation at that time was such that it was impossible to speak of a unified position among theologians concerning eschatology. To a certain extent, that is still the case today. In no sense are the primary problems of eschatology resolved. Yet it is possible to detect a broad shift in the direction of eschatological thought that points to a significant consensus in a number of important areas.

Taken in its basic etymological sense, the word "eschatology" means "doctrine about the final reality." But that simple definition has undergone significant shifts in meaning during the course of the twentieth century. Roman Catholic theology entered the century deeply immersed in the neo-Scholastic, hand-book style of theology. Here eschatology was seen as the doctrine about those things which awaited the individual person in death and beyond (death, judgment, purgation, heaven, hell) and that which awaited the whole human race at the end of history (the return of Christ, the general resurrection, and the general judgment). This style tended to see the "last things" as objects, predictable events, and places in the world beyond. It was described by Yves Congar as a physical style of eschatology.

The first major shift in Roman Catholic eschatology may be detected in the aftermath of the declaration of the dogma of the Assumption in 1950. This Marian dogma gave rise to reflection on the theology of death. By attempting to shed light on the relation between human life and the experience of death, this shift of emphasis brought a strongly anthropological tone to the understanding of eschatology. This tone was related to the styles of personalist and existential philosophy in vogue at the same time. The anthropological shift gave eschatology a tone decidedly different from that of the earlier physical style. It remains a significant element in eschatology to the present.

Another important shift can be detected in the pastoral constitution *Gaudium et Spes* of Vatican II. In this document, the Council addressed itself to the role of the church in the history of the world. With a strong emphasis on Christian hope, the document orientates Christian reflection to the historical and cosmological context of hope. Here the problem of the relation between Christian hope and the great humanistic and technological enterprises of the modern world surfaces. Does Christian hope have any relation to the specific hopes of humanity? What is the role of the Christian community in the movement of human history? What is the relation between the human, historical activity of building the world which is the concern of human hope, and the divinely given gift of the Kingdom of God which is the object of Christian hope.

Through these developments, the primary thrust of eschatology has shifted from a concentration on the structures of the world beyond to a theological reflection on the nature of Christian hope itself. Its biblical motto might be drawn from the *First Letter of Peter*: "Always be prepared to make a defense to anyone who calls you to account for the hope that is in you. . ." (1 Pt. 3:15). What is the ground and object of Christian hope? How can we give an account of Christian hope in the context of the secular hopes of the modern world? What is the Christian vision of hope for the individual, for the human race, and for the world of God's creation?

Eschatology can be developed in this way only if the hope held out to us by Scripture is allowed to interact with the many forms of hope that make up so much of human life. What is it in human existence that is addressed by the message of hope in the Scriptures? This question is the concern of the first three chapters of this book. The first two offer a survey of the historical, biblical roots of the theology of hope; the third treats the problem of the anthropological root of hope. While the vision of hope mediated through the historical revelation of the Scriptures and the destiny of Jesus Christ is a distinctive vision of human destiny, it does not come to us as something totally foreign to our human aspirations. Indeed, even though the divine promise communicated through the biblical history offers a fulfillment that transcends our fondest human dreams, yet it is addressed to something that lies at the very roots of human existence.

The final four chapters present the understanding of that promise as it is reflected on in contemporary theology. Chapter four charts the course of the contemporary discussion of individual destiny. Here the theology of death is the central question. Chapters five through seven present the discussion of the collective destiny of humanity and the cosmos. It is here in particular that the larger questions about the theology of history will be discussed. Although it is impossible to speak of a unanimous understanding on these broader questions, it is possible to highlight the fundamental elements that must be taken into account in a systematic treatment of eschatology. Issues that are often cast in the form of "either/or" options call for some kind of "both/and" formulation if the elements of Christian hope are to be maintained in their integrity.

Although this book is directed mainly to advanced students of theology, it discusses issues which are of interest to many believers today who find themselves in a situation where their knowledge about matters of religion has not kept pace with their knowledge of the secular disciplines. The primary purpose of the book is to offer a view of the present state of Roman Catholic eschatological thought. It is symptomatic of the present state of theology, however, that Roman Catholic thought has not developed without great indebtedness to Protestant theologians. As the state of Catholic theology at the present would be unthinkable without such figures as K. Rahner and H. Urs von Balthasar, it would be similarly incomprehensible without the work of J. Moltmann and W. Pannenberg, not to mention R. Bultmann, J. Jeremias, O. Cullmann and many other exegetes without whose contribution to our understanding of the Scriptures the present perspectives on eschatology would be simply impossible. While their works are not cited explicitly with great frequency, their presence stands behind many of the views discussed in the course of this presentation.

I have attempted to avoid an excessive use of difficult, technical language in the course of this presentation. Yet, regardless of my intentions, this has not always been possible. Whenever the use of such language seemed unavoidable, I have attempted to clarify it in an intelligible way rather than take it for granted. On certain issues, the explanation of philosophical arguments seemed appropriate so that the more recent theological arguments can be seen as more than a mere change in terminology. This makes for more difficult reading at times. It is my hope that it also makes for a more profitable understanding of the issues involved.

I would like to express my gratitude to the many students at the Catholic Theological Union and the many lay persons in parishes throughout the Chicago area with whom I have discussed these matters in classes, seminars, and workshops over the years. Their response to the issues and their questions concerning the variety of theological viewpoints have been a constant stimulus for reflecting on the matters treated here.

1

THE STORY OF HOPE IN THE HEBREW SCRIPTURES

Christians are people of hope. But they are not alone in this, for hope is a common element in human experience. What distinguishes Christians is not the mere fact that they hope, but the peculiar way in which they hope and the distinctive reasons for which they hope. In the Scriptures, the object of Christian hope is called the Kingdom of God. The ground for Christian hope is that which God has done in Jesus of Nazareth for the salvation of the world. Here, in seminal form, is the heart of the Christian faith. It is from this center that theology attempts to explicate the vision which Christian hope has for the future of the world.

It is impossible to grasp fully the nature of Christian hope without understanding something of the history through which this hope came into being. Christians are people whose hope lives, ultimately, from what God has done in Jesus Christ. If the meaning of Christian hope cannot be understood except in reference to Jesus, then it cannot be understood except against the backdrop of the rich, religious tradition from which Jesus came and which he shared so deeply. In this chapter, we shall investigate the historical roots of Christian hope. This is the question of the historical faith of Israel in its centuries-long development.

1. A Seed of Hope in the Midst of Ambiguity

The opening pages of the bible present a powerful picture of the ambiguity of human life. The writers of these inspired texts have reflected deeply on the centuries-long history of their people. Theirs was a nation that believed itself to be heir to a divine promise. If the promise was from God, would not faith inevitably include the hope that the promise would be fulfilled?

What, then, is this people to make of the fact that their concrete experience never seems to measure up to the expectations awakened by the promise of the Lord? Their history has been a painful mixture of goodness and evil, of glory and treachery, of divine summons and faltering human response. Anything that might be seen as a fulfillment of the promise has been limited at best and extremely fragile. It seems never to have been a secure possession. Yet, the promise was from God. God would be faithful to the word of promise.

In reflecting on this experience of the Hebrew nation, the authors of Scripture are led to reflect not only on the experience of their own people but on the mystery of human life in broader and more universal terms. The experience of the Jewish people may shed light on human experience in general. Thus, the so-called *proto-history* in the opening chapters of the book of *Genesis* presents a moving picture of the ambiguous character of human life.

The Lord of life, in a loving act of creation, brings forth a world of created beings so that creatures might share, at least in a limited way, the gift of life, goodness, and love. With special concern, God offers a fullness of life and love to humanity. The world of creation is good and laden with great potential. Its destiny is tied inextricably into the destiny of humanity. God has created humanity in the very image of the divinity and charged humanity with a responsibility for the good of the entire created realm. The destiny of the world lies in human hands. The fullness of life in a harmonious and perfectly covenanted universe is the gift God offers. Pain and failure is the actual experience of life in what appears to be a deeply broken world. Humanity has been weak and inconsistent in taking up its God-given responsibility in and for the world.

Despite the weakness and inconsistency of humanity, God does not turn the world over to a graceless existence. Banished from a promised Paradise of harmony and peace, humanity is given the seed of a hope.

Throughout its history, human existence will be a struggle with hostile powers, a struggle full of suffering and sickness, evil and tragedy. Life will be difficult for all. But humanity, through the grace of God, will gain the clearer victory over the powers of evil. The curse of the serpent is simultaneously a divine promise for humanity: "I will put enmity between you and the woman, and between your seed and her seed; he shall bruise your head, and you shall bruise his heel" (Gn. 3:15).

Generations of Christian interpreters would see in this text a *proto-evangelium*: the first and most original announcement of the Good News which would eventually find its full expression in the work of Jesus of Nazareth and in the Christian Scriptures. We need not share the exegetical principles which would make this a completely legitimate interpretation for the early Fathers of Christianity in order to recognize in the text a subtle seed of promise that stands in clear relationship to the covenants to follow: those given to Noe, to Abraham, to Moses, and to David. It is no accident that the Christian Scriptures would eventually interpret the mystery of Jesus as a new and everlasting covenant. For the notion of covenant is one of the central Scriptural metaphors through which the bible gives expression to the conviction of God's saving presence in the life of the Jewish people and of the human race as a whole. As a thread that runs throughout the history of the Scriptures, covenant-theology can be seen as an expression of the abiding grace of God's presence promised in this *proto-evangelium*.

But this seminal promise of *Genesis* 3:15 stands in dramatic contrast with the history of human folly that follows. From Cain to the Flood (Gn. 4-8), and again from Ham to the Tower of Babel (Gn. 9-11) the history of sin unfolds. Sin destroys not only the order of human life but the order of the cosmos in which human life is lived. Thus the Deluge emerges as an event of cosmic scope, bringing down the old, broken order and clearing the way for a new act of creation and a covenant with Noe, the scope of which would be as wide as the cosmos, and whose symbol would appropriately be the rainbow that reaches from one end of the horizon to the other and ties the earth below to the heavens above.

These opening chapters of the book of *Genesis* are like the overture to a Wagnerian opera. The skilled composer uses the opening minutes of his drama to introduce, through musical motifs, all the principal themes and characters of the work that is to follow. In a similar way, the writers of the Scriptures employ the opening pages of the bible to present, in theological motifs, the principal themes and characters in the drama of the history that is to follow. The principals of the biblical drama are God and humanity; the themes are grace and sin, divine promise and human infidelity. Human perfidy seems to know no limits. With a Promethean pride, humanity raises its feeble pretenses against God. It is not sufficient to be created in the image of God. Humanity would be God for itself. As often as it raises its towers of unrestrained pride, just as predictably disaster strikes. But the seed of divine promise does not wither and die.

2. A Paradigm of Hope

It is against this backdrop of *proto-history* that the character of Abraham is cast. Abraham is commonly seen as the outstanding model of faith. But religious faith does not take the same form in all religious traditions. It is characteristic of the biblical form of faith that it makes a believer to be simultaneously a person of hope. Thus, the figure of Abraham appears as a significant point of departure for the study of hope in the history of Judaism and Christianity. From Abraham, we can look bakward to discern the connections with Noe and with *Genesis* 3:15, and forward to discover the relations of this tradition with that of the Exodus, the monarchy and the prophets.

a) Call and Covenant

The story of Abraham (Gn. 12:1—25:18) remains one of the moving classics of religious literature regardless of one's personal religious convictions. However one may wish to explain these texts, they mediate the sense of a religious experience which re-orientates the whole of a person's life. The story revolves around a call, a promise and a covenant. God's call is experienced by Abraham as a summons to leave his native home in Ur of the Chaldeans. Abraham's response is the decision to move from his familiar surroundings and to undertake a journey to an unknown land. The call is dramatically presented as coming from God alone. The response is not a verbal confession of faith but a concrete action. Abraham follows the call of God summoning him to

an unknown future. In return for such confidence, God promises the
blessing of a land and numerous progeny. God's blessing will be not
only for Abraham but for his descendants and for all the families of
the earth (Gn. 12:3).

The later chapters of *Genesis* (15:1-20; 17:1-27) recount the renewal
of this promise of progeny and land. This renewal is set in the context
of a covenant-ritual. Much is made here, and later in the text of
Romans 4, of the great age of both Abraham and his wife, Sarah.
From a purely human perspective, there is no reasonable basis for
hope in progeny. Abraham and Sarah are simply too old; and their
marriage has remained barren up to this point. When we first meet
Abraham in *Genesis* 12:1-4, he is said to be seventy-five years old. On
the occasion of the covenant and circumcision, he is said to be ninety-
nine years old (Gn. 17:1) and still without a child from his marriage
with Sarah. There is only the son of the maid, Hagar. Yet once again
God promises fertility. Both the text of *Genesis* and that of *Romans*
drive home a point of deep religious significance. Abraham trusts in
the fulfillment of a promise that could not be realized in human terms.
Trust, in its deepest sense, is not the expectation of something that
could be easily predicted or foreseen by human ingenuity. Rather, it is
a radical trust in a possibility opened solely by God's initiative.

b) A Crisis of Hope

The drama of the Abraham-account reaches its peak in the radical
testing of the Patriarch by the God of the promise. The command to
sacrifice Isaac, the son of the promise, becomes understandable in its
religious depth when viewed against the background of the details
sketched above. The promise is from God. The promise is of progeny
and of a land. Isaac is the child of promise. On his survival the
fulfillment of the promise depends. The dramatic Hebrew text places
great emphasis on how greatly Abraham loved his son, thus highlighting the radical nature of the test:

> "Take your son, your only son Isaac, whom you love, and go to the
> land of Moriah, and offer him there as a burnt offering upon one of
> the mountains of which I shall tell you" (Gn. 22:2).

Under any circumstances, such a trial would be severe. But Isaac is more than the beloved son of Abraham's old age. He is the only concrete clue to the fulfillment of the promise. That far-off, future goal which God had held out for so many years and toward which Abraham believed himself to be traveling! How could it be fulfilled if this one last concrete basis for its realization were to be wiped out?

What is the meaning of this remarkable account? M. Eliade suggests that the Abraham-tradition opens a fundamentally new level of religious awareness in the history of the human race. Religions in the Middle East at the time in which the Abraham-tradition is situated were fertility religions of agrarian people. In such agrarian cultures, fertility was sacred. The mystery of birth, death, and rebirth could be seen in the natural rhythms of vegetation and in the cosmic cycles. In such religions, the sacrifice of the first-born child to the god of fertility was a common practise. If the god poured out his very substance in the maintenance of the cycles of life in the world, there is a certain logic in the idea that the sacrifice of the first fruits of the harvest, and above all the first fruits of a marriage would replenish the dwindling power of the god.

In this context, the Isaac-tradition stands out. There really is nothing of logic in Abraham's decision to sacrifice his first-born. Nor does Abraham decide to carry out the sacrifice in order to accomplish some specific, concrete end. He simply acts because his God asks him to do so. What God asks of him must be right. At this point, the Jewish tradition breaks out of the common religious conceptions of the ancient Middle East. Here is opened the possibility that God may be encountered not in nature but in events, that is, in history. Here is opened, also, the sense of religion as a personal relation to a personal deity. In brief, the Abraham-tradition opens a new dimension for the meaning of religious faith: faith as a radical trust in God.[1] Soren Kierkegaard interprets this episode as a paradigm of radical existential trust in the absence of any positive, empirical basis for trust. It is, for Kierkegaard, a model of "credo quia absurdum." Abraham is stripped of every humanly understandable reason for faith and trust. Yet he trusts nonetheless.[2]

[1] *Cosmos and History: The Myth of the Eternal Return*, tr. W.R. Trash (N.Y., 1959), pp. 108-110, 160.

[2] *Fear and Trembling*, p. 30ff in: *Fear and Trembling and Sickness unto Death*, tr. W. Lowrie (Garden City, 1954) p. 30ff.

It would be easy to make too much or too little of the Abraham-tradition. But if we recognize it as containing the reflection of editors and redactors of a late period of Jewish history, it would not be fanciful to suggest that the present form of the story expresses the mature awareness of later history that the faith-vision which lay at the basis of Israel's history would be tested over and over in the most painful ways. Indeed, it had been so tested. The story of the ordeal of Abraham focuses on the radical nature of his trust in the divine promise and the divine purpose. It is one thing to move through life with a naive, starry-eyed belief that all is good and beautiful. It is quite another thing to have been stripped of all human possibilities and yet to trust. In whom or in what can one trust when experience shows over and over that no finite thing can bear the weight of our ultimate trust?

c) Hope and History

In Eliade's interpretation of the Abraham-tradition, the story not only presents a paradigm of radical trust, but contains the seeds of a distinctive vision of history as well.[3] This is not to say that there is anything like an explicit theology of history in these ancient texts. But in the religious experience expressed in these texts there is implied a vision of human life that breaks out of the fatalistic cycles characteristic of the religious and philosophical thought of the ancient world. In the classical vision of antiquity, there is nothing new or different to be expected from the future. On the contrary, if there is hope at all, it is the hope to return to the Golden Age of the beginning. Or one hopes to discover and cling to the lost but unchanging center of reality. It has become commonplace to symbolize this experience of time and history by a circle which, as a geometrical figure, closes back on its beginning. The circle was recognized as the perfect figure precisely for that reason. It ends where it began. Nothing happens in between.

In contrast, the biblical sense of human existence locates humanity in an open-ended history which remains incomplete down to the present. The Fates are replaced by a living God who is both personal and free. Determinism is replaced by the sense of human freedom and

---

[3]Eliade, *ibid.*

responsibility. History is being directed to the ultimate end which God has for it. The vagaries of history and the unpredictable course of human events reflect, among other things, the mystery of human freedom in its response to God's purpose. History is a movement to a mysterious future promised by God. While the heroes of classical antiquity were filled with nostalgia to return "home" to the Golden Age, the heroes of the Scriptures are turned with trusting confidence to the future which God has opened to them. They are pre-eminently people of hope.

d) Ambiguity and Hope

For many of our contemporaries, the word "hope" is associated with a sort of romantic inability to see and to deal with the pain and tragedy of human experience. If the biblical tradition of Abraham is seen as a paradigm of hope, it is clear that the sort of hope suggested here is far removed from such *naiveté*. Biblical hope does not emerge out of a sense that all in life is light and clear. On the contrary, Abraham's hope emerges out of great ambiguity. Above all, in the Isaac-tradition, the sense of ambiguity borders on the mystery of absurdity. Paul Ricoeur's analysis of hope helps clarify the dynamic of hope in the Abraham story.[4] Hope springs not out of clarity, writes Ricoeur, but out of the deepest ambiguity where one senses the threat of absurdity. Hope sees the real threat of absurdity. But it refuses to allow absurdity to have the final word about reality. Looking back at the Abraham-tradition with this in mind, we discover that the ambiguity is almost tangible. The threat of absurdity at Moriah is unmistakable. But, the Lord has promised. The positive signs in human experience may be weak or almost non-existent, but the Lord will be faithful.

In speaking of the opening chapters of *Genesis*, we tried to draw out some of the principal motifs that appeared there: God and humanity, grace and sin, divine promise and human infidelity. In the biblical account of Abraham, all these motifs are given a concrete form, with the exception of human infidelity. For here infidelity is replaced with the powerful model of a faithful response to God. Here the structure of

4"Science humaine et conditionnement de la foi," *Dieu aujourd'hui* (Paris, 1965) pp. 141-142.

a spiritual journey is set out with graphic clarity: promise, covenant, journey, testing, and a God-given future. Individual though he was, Abraham's story is more than the history of an individual. It is the history of a nation as well. In the final analysis, that individual history becomes a model for understanding human existence universally. It is not surprising that Abraham should appear as the Father of faith not only for the Jewish tradition but for the writers of the Christian Scriptures as well (Rm. 4; Hebr. 11). We will trace the historical development of these motifs in the following reflections until we see them flow into the specific form they take in the Christian Scriptures.

3. The Mosaic and Davidic Covenants

a) The Exodus Experience

As we have seen above, in Eliade's view of the Jewish religion, Israel's God is recognized more in events of history than in the cycles of life and death in the world of nature. It was especially in the events of its own national history that the Jewish people came to know its God and deepened its growing awareness of God's salvific presence and intent. If the faith of Abraham was hope-filled and future-oriented, the same can be said of the faith of the tribes made into a nation through the creative action of God in the events of the Exodus and the covenant of Sinai. The God of the Exodus-Sinai experience, like the God of Abraham, is a God of promise. The divine summons calls forth a people from slavery, puts them on the way through a wilderness, enters into a covenant with them and gives them the promise of a land. When asked to express its faith, Israel responds by telling its history as a nation (Dt. 6:20-23). At the outset of this history stands the promise that God would ". . . bring us in and give us the land which he swore to give to our fathers" (Dt. 6:23).

Here, as in the Abraham-tradition, the object of hope lies in the future. But it is a very concrete reality that is hoped for. In the case of Abraham, it was the reality of progeny and a land. Here, the object of hope is just as earthy: a land flowing with milk and honey (Ex. 3:8; 13:5; Lev. 20:24; Nm. 13:17; 14:8; Dt. 6:3; 11:9). This theme is expanded in other sections of the Pentateuch (Gn. 49:8-12; Nm. 23ff.; Dt. 33:13-17). We could hardly expect a more concrete expression of hope: a fertile land with abundant rain, fertility of humanity and of the beasts, and victory over one's enemies. But above all, at the center of this hope is the conviction that the divinity itself will dwell in the midst of the people:

> I will take you for my people, and I will be your God; and you shall know that I am the Lord your God, who has brought you out from under the burdens of the Egyptians (Ex. 6:7).

The Exodus-Sinai event would become a point of reference for the religious leaders of the Jewish people down through the centuries. But at this early stage, Israel's hope seems to have little in common with what later theology will recognize as an "eschatological future." It is concerned with her identity as a people chosen by God. There is no vision of the future of humanity at large nor of universal history. There seems to be no noticeable concern for the survival of individual persons. The principal object of Israel's early hope is the future of this fledgling nation with its land, a nation that enjoys the peculiar favor of God. The hoped-for future apparently would be a period of material prosperity which the nation would soon enjoy through God's victory over Israel's political foes.

The story of her birth as a nation would be told over and over. Not only would it be retold, but it would be reinterpreted as well. Historical details would fade to allow the fundamental structure of the event to emerge in stark clarity. Life is a journey to a divinely promised future. Much of the later history of revelation can be seen as a series of re-interpretations of the nature of that future. When, where, how that future would be brought into being is not clear. But what is clear is the fact that, throughout the many centuries of painful political experience that followed the Exodus-event, Israel preserved her hope for the fullness of life in a God-given future. This is crucial to any understanding of the theology of salvation and eschatology as these eventually develop in the Scriptures.

b) The Monarchy

The development of Israel's hope for salvation is inseparable from the political experience of the nation. Indeed, ideas about salvation and eschatology may be seen as the inspired interpretation of the political history of Israel with all its hopes and frustrations. From the experience of judges, kings, and prophets would come the shaping of hopes for the future and metaphors for expressing those hopes. Especially the experience of the monarchy with its hopes and its disappointments would give rise to a number of themes and metaphors that would play a basic role in the later development of eschatological hope.

First, there is the notion of the Kingdom itself. From the time of the Exodus, Israel believed that God alone should rule among the people. God was thought to exercise his kingship through the instrument of the human king; and the king himself was responsible to God for the good of the entire realm. As long as the political scene was marked by order, harmony, and justice, it was possible to think that God truly ruled among the people. But when the monarchy fell upon evil days and eventually collapsed, there would emerge the hope for a future time in which God would again rule among the people. Out of this experience would emerge the metaphor of the Kingdom or the Rule of God. As a metaphor rooted deeply in the historical experience of the Jewish nation, the Kingdom-metaphor would eventually crystallize the hopes and aspirations of later generations of Jews in a powerful way. As is clear from the Christian Gospels, the same metaphor would play a central role in the preaching of Jesus of Nazareth.

Second, the experience of good times under the rule of David would lead in times of decline to a nostalgic idealization of the Davidic age and specifically of the figure of David himself. David, like Abraham, is seen to receive a promise. God would bless him with offspring and establish his royal line forever (2 Sm. 7).

Third, the custom of anointing kings would lead to the expectation of a future anointed one (a messiah) who would be instrumental in the realization of God's kingly rule among his people. The idea of a future messianic king—a concretization of the blessing given to Abraham— would become basic in the development of the future-expectation of Israel, and this figure is closely bound to the Davidic dynasty from which the savior-king was to come (2 Sm. 7).

The monarchy, begun with Saul and David, reached a high point under Solomon only to go into decline under his successors. Its Golden Age was relatively brief. The division of the people into a northern and a southern kingdom, and the development of the pretensions of the

Solomonic era led to serious difficulties as these two small kingdoms came under threat from the great nations that lay to the east. Internal court intrigues, apostasies and external military threats tore at the vitals of the nation. Viewed from our vantage point, this early history of Israel is hardly a glorious history. Despite the promise of God, the experience of this people seems to be permeated by tragedy. Their possession of the land was fragile from the start. After the division of the kingdom, the north would fall victim to Assyria in the eighth century, b.c.e., and the south would experience the trauma of the Babylonian Captivity some two centuries later. In the great moments of its history—in the glorious days of David, for example—the people could see some degree of fulfillment of the promise. But that fulfillment was always very limited, and always threatened by extinction. As long as the promise lived on, there would be hope for a full and permanent fulfillment of the promise. For the promise was of God, and God is faithful. As long as there is hope for a future fulfillment, the spring-board of eschatological hope is present.

In view of the ambiguity of this political experience of Israel, weighty challenges to the developing religious tradition would have been un-avoidable. At this juncture, we turn to the prophets who played a key role in the development of biblical hope.

4. Prophecy

a) Prophecy in the pre-Exilic Period

While prophecy is often thought to involve ecstatic experiences and predictions of the future, the central function which lies at the core of Jewish prophecy is that of discerning, mediating, and interpreting the divine will for the people.

Since the history in which the Jewish people believed that God was acting was their own political history, it is understandable that the pronouncements of the prophets would be charged with political real-ism. Especially in the pre-Exilic period, the message of the prophets centers around the failure of Israel to live up to the requirements of the covenant. Because of this failure, Jewish society is in need of a funda-mental reform. If the nation refuses to hear the word of the prophet and be converted to the God who has acted in their past history by entering into covenant with them, God will need to discipline the people. This disciplinary action of God could come either through the instrumentality of natural forces or through the agency of international politics. But come it will. Thus, in both the north and the south, pre-Exilic prophecy was emphatically a prophecy of social-political judgment, proclaiming a "Day of the Lord" from which no one would escape (Amos 8:9; Is. 2:12; Zeph. 1:15).

But divine judgment is related to hope. Even in the most dire circumstances, God never leaves the people without hope. Judgment and divine discipline are not aimed at the destruction of the people. On the contrary, God desires to bring about the rebirth of the people in their covenant-relation with God. If God's judgment points to the failures and limitations of their past and present experience, that same judgment holds open the hope of a future that transcends the limitations of the present. While there are indications of a hope for the future in these early prophets, this theme is not developed with the power and consistency that it will assume in the later prophets.

b) Development of the Theme of Hope

P. Hanson argues that the pre-Exilic prophets maintained a balance between two poles of reflection. On the one hand, they were concerned with the universal sovereignty of God. On the other hand, they were distressed by the contemporary political situation of the people. The primary emphasis of these early prophets was not so much on the future as on the religious interpretation of the present in the light of God's sovereignty.

Yet, the great prophet of Jerusalem, Isaiah, offers one of the classic visions of Israel's hope for a future event of salvation. For later Christians, this material has been so thoroughly appropriated and re-interpreted over the centuries that it is difficult to read it without automatically seeing it in its familiar Christological ramifications. The mysterious savior-figure to be born of a young woman and to be named Immanuel (Is. 7:14), the moving description of the ideal king (Is. 9:2-7; 11:1-5), the vision of paradisal peace (Is. 11:6-9), and the desert blooming with abundant life (Is. 35:1-2): all these have left an indelible impression on later Christian generations. Poetic as these descriptions may be, they nonetheless express a concrete sort of hope. Isaiah looks forward to a time of justice, freedom, and peace; a time of abundant fertility and paradisal harmony. It is not to another world that Isaiah looks, but to the liberation of this world from the pervasive results of sin that distort all human relations and make life a tissue of pain and suffering, of warfare and destruction. If God's salvific act means anything at all, it must mean the reversal of the lethal effects of human sinfulness.

This eschatological condition will be ushered in by judgment on Israel and on the other nations. Isaiah suggests also that the final experience of salvation may not be the lot of all of Israel. It may, in fact, be limited to a "Remnant" who will be distinguished not by their numbers but by their faith and holiness (Is. 4:3; 6:13; 11:11; 37:31ff). The Remnant will become the bearer of the election and the promise of the Jewish nation.

If judgment is an important element in the tradition of prophecy, judgment need not be seen to mean the end of things. On the contrary, it can now be seen as a turning-point for the inauguration of a transformed existence in a new heaven and a new earth (Is. 65:17; 66:22). The Kingdom of God will appear in the form of a new and eternal covenant (Jer. 31ff) which will bind humanity to God in the deepest way possible. This will be a covenant of peace not only for Israel but for the nations as well (Is. 2:2ff; Mic. 4:1-4). Unheard-of fertility will enrich the life of the people. War will be no more. The animals will live in peace. Sin will be healed. The nations will live in peace with one another. Israel and the nations will enjoy unprecedented grace and mercy from God. The entire cosmos will be filled with the knowledge of God.

In its final stages, Jewish prophecy gives rise to a vision of the Kingdom of God in which the divine salvific activity embraces the whole of created reality and draws it into supreme harmony. The vision of the future is not merely a restoration of a lost beginning. It is rather a fundamentally new reality that has not yet existed in human experience. It is pre-eminently the object of hope.

5. Late Developments of Jewish Thought

a) Wisdom Literature

The style and concerns of the Wisdom literature differ greatly from those of the historical and prophetic traditions of the Hebrew Scriptures. Here the reader is no longer confronted with weighty theological reflections on the great saving actions of God in Israel's past history. In its search for insight and guidance in the conduct of human life, the Wisdom literature spreads a wide net with which to catch insights from human experience far beyond the specific history of the Jewish people.

More than in the prophetic and historical traditions, the Wisdom literature turns its attention to the life and destiny of the individual human person. Death is a theme to be reflected on. The early belief of the Jews concerning personal death is shrouded in clouds of historical obscurity. But it is safe to say that, at least in the patriarchal tradition, death was seen in a very matter-of-fact way. Death that comes at the end of a long and full life is perfectly natural; it comes as a friend to an aging person who has lived life fully and who leaves behind children and a family to carry on his name (Gn. 25:7-11). The breath of life comes from God, welling up from deep within the mystery of God himself. A living being comes into existence when God breathes the breath of life into lifeless dust (Gn. 2:7). When God withdraws that breath, the living creature ceases to live.

Death is seen in very different terms in the Wisdom literature. Here it is seen as a tragedy to be suffered and as a problem to be reflected on. *Ecclesiastes* wrestles with the enigma of death (8:16—9:10). Death is the great leveler; it is the lot of all humanity, and indeed of all living creatures. Those who have died have nothing. Those who remain among the living have the advantage of realizing that they must die. Even to single this out as an advantage highlights the absurdity of life and its inevitable nihilistic outcome:

> ...the dead know nothing, and they have no more reward; but the memory of them is lost. Their love and their hate and their envy have already perished, and they have no more forever any share in all that is done under the sun (Eccles. 9:5-6).

While such a text seems to reflect little expectation of an after-life, it may be taken as one of the outstanding achievements of the Wisdom literature that it reflects seriously on the possibility that the individual person might conquer death in some way. One might hope to live on in the memory of others (Wis. 4:1) or in one's posterity (Sir. 44:10-14; Job 18:17-19). In the long run, it was inevitable that Israel's sages would be influenced by the notions of immortality in the surrounding nations. Reflections on the dignity and responsibility of the individual person led to some expectation of an after-life. In some of the psalms we find ideas from the Wisdom tradition developed even further. A person who is truly faithful to God in this life is assured of community with God even in death, for true community with God transcends the limit of death (Ps. 49:8ff.-16; 73:23-26). While there is no unanimity of viewpoint concerning the destiny of the individual in death, this litera-ture does, indeed, raise the question of individual destiny, at times with a strong sense of the tragic character of death. While it may not even be possible to speak of a dominant viewpoint in the Wisdom material, the possibility of a life beyond death is raised here.

It is impossible to raise such a possibility without, at the same time, asking: In view of the fact that life in the world is so closely associated with the human body, and the body is left in the world after death, what is it about the human person that continues to exist? And in what condition does it exist? In response to the first question, the idea of an immortal soul was available in the world of Hellenistic thought and religion. The idea of the soul as a spiritual reality that could survive the death of the body offered one possible way of identifying that element of the person that lived on in communion with God after death (Wis. 2:22-24; 3:1; 8:19ff; 9:15). Although this is not a fully developed notion of the soul as we find it in later Christian theology, it represents an important basis for the kind of anthropology that will emerge when theology attempts to treat the problem of the after-life in a more developed way.

b) Sheol

If something of the person survives death, where and in what condi-tion do they survive? For the Jews as for most ancient people, the notion of survival after death is associated with the underworld. In the

Homeric literature of Greece, the underworld is known as *Hades*. In the world of the bible, it is known as *Sheol*. In both instances, it serves the same purpose: it provides a location for the existence of those who no longer exist in the world of ordinary experience. In the case of the Greek underworld, *Hades* is not a place of joy and pleasure but a "mouldering house of chill" inhabited by sickly phantoms. Similarly in the biblical literature, the state of those in *Sheol* is not a happy lot. The dead lead a shadowy existence in which they neither thank nor praise God, for in *Sheol* there is no communion with God (Is. 38:18; Ps. 6:6). In the earlier levels of biblical tradition, not even God has power over the underworld. This awkward theological conclusion was met later in the Wisdom literature which extends God's power and judgment even to the realm of the dead. Since God alone is God, he has power over life and death. God's knowledge and power reach even to *Sheol* (Job 26:6-14; Prov. 15:11; Wis. 16:13-15; Ps. 139:7-12; Tob. 13:2).

While originally *Sheol* was seen as the common lot of the dead, in the intertestamental period, it became customary to distinguish between a situation of reward and a situation of punishment, since God's justice seemed to require this. Now *Sheol* came to be seen as a provisional condition to be followed by *Paradise* for the elect and *Gehenna* for the lost. The notion of *Paradise* as a place of reward is grounded in the growing conviction that true communion with God transcends even the limit of death. For the wicked, punishment is found in a place called *Gehenna*. The name, *Gehenna*, refers originally to a valley in the area of Jerusalem. It was a place with an unsavory reputation over the generations, since it had been the site of a cultic shrine where human sacrifice was offered (2 Kg. 23:10; 2 Chron. 28:3). In *Isaiah* 66:24 it is referred to as a place for the disposal of those who rebel against God. It is described as a place of inexstinguishable fire and undying worms. From this tradition, later generations would develop much of the imagery surrounding the dire fate awaiting the wicked after death.

c) Apocalyptic

1) The Problem of Apocalyptic

In view of the present state of biblical studies, any attempt to unravel the problem of apocalyptic must remain provisional. Yet we can gain important insights into the meaning of this literature if we distinguish between apocalyptic as a literary genre and the theological vision mediated by this genre.

J.J. Collins offers the following provisional, working definition of apocalypse from a literary perspective:

> "Apocalypse" is a genre of revelatory literature with a narrative framework, in which a revelation is mediated by an otherworldly being to a human recipient, disclosing a transcendent reality which is both temporal, insofar as it envisages eschatological salvation, and spatial, insofar as it involves another, supernatural world.[5]

Such a description helps to see what elements the diverse apocalyptic writings have in common and to recognize more adequately the distinction between the theological intention of the writings and the literary form and devices employed. It appears that many of the specific elements often thought of as characteristic of apocalyptic pertain not to the theological content but to the list of literary devices of a particular form of apocalyptic. The principal theological concern of apocalyptic is the communication of the reality of a truly transcendent, eschatological salvation; that is, a salvation that transcends our space-time experience in this world. Collins suggests that, in general terms, the intent of apocalyptic literature may have been to provide a view of the world that could serve as a source of consolation in the face of distress, to provide legitimation for whatever course of action is suggested by the literature, and—in general—to invest this world-view with the status of a supernatural revelation.[6]

While many of the conclusions drawn from the recent study of apocalyptic material are still tentative, the overall course of the discussion will be helpful in understanding more adequately the context for the emergence of Christianity, both in its earliest stages and in its later developments. Not only did apocalyptic sources exert an influence on Jesus and the early community, but they remained a rich source of material for the development of many specific eschatological themes in later Christian history.

---

[5] J.J. Collins, "Towards the Morphology of a Genre," in: *Semeia*, vol. 14 (1979) p. 9.

[6] J.J. Collins, *Daniel. With an Introduction to Apocalyptic Literature. The Forms of Old Testament Literature.* (Grand Rapids, 1984) p. 22.

Hanson's study of prophecy and apocalyptic offers a strong argument against all those theories which affirm a basic dichotomy between prophecy and apocalyptic and have tended to deal with apocalyptic as a sort of aberration. Since Hanson's argument focuses specifically on the eschatological aspect of apocalyptic, it is of particular significance for our reflections.

Hanson argues that there is a clear and continuous thread that goes back to the pre-Exilic period and unites prophecy and apocalyptic in a way that is often overlooked. What prophecy and apocalyptic have in common is an eschatological vision. What distinguished them from each other is to be found in the nuances of that vision. In Hanson's view, apocalyptic can be seen, in its basic theological content, as a form of eschatology just as much of later prophecy reflects an eschatological vision. While much of the literary style of apocalyptic reflects non-Jewish sources, still the fundamental eschatological vision is thoroughly Jewish in nature. The heart of the vision that unites prophecy and apocalyptic is, in Hanson's view, the vision of God's universal rule among his people.

In apocalyptic, therefore, we are dealing with a theology of history. It is a theology that is less likely to be concerned with changing the present world-order and more likely to look expectantly to a future, God-given fulfillment in a transcendent realm. As the movement of history became increasingly dark and unintelligible, it is understandable that the prophetic expectation of a liberating act of God within history would be transformed into the apocalyptic hope in a divinely ordained end "in the latter days" (Dn. 2:28). This old world-aeon would be transcended by a new aeon of salvation.

Ironically, it is precisely when Israel's situation seemed most hopeless from a human perspective and when the visionaries recognized that salvation could come from God alone that the truly universal vision of salvation, embracing not only the Jews but also the Gentiles within the context of God's action, came most emphatically to the fore. Only in the frame-work of a universal vision of salvation does the fate of the dead become a significant theological issue. If salvation is to be truly universal in scope, then even those who have died in the past must somehow partake in it. If judgment is to inaugurate universal justice, then it is not only the just who will rise, but at least some of the evil as well. The just will rise for their reward; the evil for their punishment. Thus, the universal scope of the apocalyptic vision of God's rule is the context from which the notion of a resurrection of the dead would emerge, to be developed further in the Christian era.

In the apocalyptic literature it becomes increasingly clear that it is necessary to speak of a transcendent eschatology in two distinct senses. First, the eschatological vision transcends the destiny of the Jewish people and becomes universal and cosmic in scope. Second, the fulfillment is no longer expected to take place within historical experience as we now know it. It is placed in a transcendent realm the nature of which is never clearly defined. This *new aeon* may be seen as the radical recreation of this world and not necessarily as a transposition to a heavenly realm. But wherever it is to be, the apocalyptic imagination seems consistently to see a fundamental cleavage between the present order of reality and that future order in which salvation is to be found. Around this cleavage it is possible to cluster a number of typical apocalyptic features. If the present reality is characterized by a pervasive evil, the future is seen as the victory of the good over evil. Thus, apocalyptic literature sees history as a mighty struggle between forces of good and evil. This struggle will reach a climactic point of confrontation in the final, cataclysmic struggle in which the power of good will definitively strike down the power of evil. History as the arena of the struggle will come to an end. The dominant pattern in this sense of history is the three-fold pattern of: crisis—judgment—vindication. The confrontation between good and evil culminates in critical situations; evil is called to judgment; and the just who have suffered for the cause of good will be vindicated by God.[7]

What is most commonly thought of as apocalyptic literature is the tendency often found in apocalyptic writings to focus strongly on these end-events in which history will reach its climactic moment. If that is the goal toward which the whole of history is moving, it is not surprising that it should ignite the imagination and give birth to a wide range of calculations as to the precise time at which we might expect this cosmic struggle to reach its climax. Neither is it surprising that the imagination should indulge itself in vivid descriptions of these world-shaking events. Thus, apocalyptic literature both within the Scriptures and outside them commonly contains elaborate interpretations of the

---

[7]B. McGinn, "Early Apocalypticism: The Ongoing Debate," in: *The Apocalypse in English Renaissance Thought and Literature,* ed. C.A. Patrides, J. Wittreich (Cornell University Press, 1984) pp. 10-12.

various stages of world history and empires in the movement toward the end. In as far as history is thought of as a unified whole, each person and event can be subject to an appropriate interpretation within the flow of history. This tendency to pin down precisely the time of the future act of God and to trace where human history is in relation to that moment gives rise to the highly imaginative "apocalyptic" images, metaphors, and mathematical calculations that first come to mind when we hear the word "apocalyptic."

In the light of the above reflections, we can now see the need to distinguish between *apocalyptic eschatology* and *apocalypticism*. Apocalyptic eschatology represents a particular form of eschatology that is deeply rooted in the earlier prophetic tradition and is expressed in a particular theology of history. Apocalypticism, on the other hand, may be seen to refer to particular ways of focusing on the end-events and of interpreting the ages of history as it moves toward the end. From here, we may suggest an evaluation of Rahner's tendency to distinguish between "true eschatology" and "false apocalyptic." Rahner's distinction is motivated, no doubt, by the embarrassment that all main-line Christian traditions have felt over the centuries in the face of the fundamentalist tendency to see the descriptions of the end-times as objective, literal descriptions of actual events that lie in the future. Rahner argues that it is important to distinguish between the fundamental religious message of a text and the metaphors and images through which the message is communicated. To read these speculations about the end-times as a literal preview of coming attractions is—in Rahner's view—indulging in "false apocalypticism." To see the dramatic imagery as a form of expression that calls the reader to take the concreteness of the eschatological future with radical seriousness is quite another matter. This is to refuse to identify the medium with the message, and to open the possibility of communicating the message in other terms.[8] The tendency to objectify the images and metaphors of the apocalyptic genre and interpret them to refer to real

---

[8]K. Rahner, "The Hermeneutics of Eschatological Assertions," in: *Theological Investigations* 4 (London, 1966), pp. 323-346. Rahner's original essay on the interpretation of eschatological statements seemed to deal with apocalyptic as an aberration with no saving features. This early formulation was rightly subjected to criticism. In a later attempt to reformulate his position, Rahner speaks of apocalyptic in more kindly terms: "...apocalyptic can be understood as a mode of expression through which man really takes the concreteness of his eschatological future seriously..." *Foundations of Christian Faith: An Introduction to the Idea of Christianity* (N.Y., 1982) p. 433.

future events is what Rahner originally meant by "false apocalyptic." But it is now clear that apocalyptic literature involves far more than that. Any sweeping condemnation of apocalyptic as false appears to be indefensible. In response to the criticism of his original formulation, Rahner modified his view in a way that brings it into greater harmony with the actual textual tradition and makes it possible to deal with the religiously significant theological vision of the apocalyptic writers in a serious, eschatological manner.

2) Apocalyptic in the Hebrew Scriptures

The question of apocalyptic is not merely a question concerning a body of literature that stands, by and large, outside the biblical canon, between the two Testaments. It is important to note that there is apocalyptic material also within the presently recognized canonical literature of both the Testaments. The book of *Daniel* is a clear example in the Jewish Scriptures. But there are apocalyptic passages inserted in the writings of the older prophets such as Isaiah, Ezekiel, and Zechariah. Since these texts played a significant role in later Christian eschatology, we shall present some brief comments on them.

The book of *Daniel* is commonly recognized as the most influential apocalyptic material in the canonical Scriptures. In its literary form, it represents what Collins calls an "historical apocalypse." Situating the history of Israel within the framework of universal history, *Daniel* reflects not only on the final judgment, but above all on the eschatological rule of God that is to come (Dn. 7:13-14; 9:24; 12:1-3). The rule or kingdom of God can be interpreted in two ways. It can be seen either as the definitive restoration of the national kingdom of Israel on earth (Dn. 7:13-14), or as a heavenly kingdom that will be in no way commensurate with space and time (Dn. 12:1-3). Since *Daniel* sees the reign of King Antiochus Epiphanes as the very consummation of human pride and rebellion against God, it stresses the basic chasm that separates the present experience of the Jewish people under this arrogant foreigner from the eschatological age of God's rule.

This book presents a number of specific themes that were to become important in subsequent Christian theology. The symbolic beasts (Dn. 7:1-28) and the seventy weeks of years (Dn. 9:1-27) would feed the fancy of generations of Christians interested in calculating the end of the world. The figure of the Son of Man (Dn. 7) would play an important role in the early Christian reflections on the identity of Jesus of Nazareth. The expectation of the resurrection of the dead is clearly expressed (Dn. 12:2), although it is not clear precisely how this is to be understood. While prophets such as Ezechiel saw a resurrection in the restoration of the nation (Ez. 37: the vision of the dry bones), Daniel clearly suggests the resurrection of individuals, including both the just and the wicked. The just will rise to join the ranks of the angelic hosts and will become like them. The evil shall awaken to everlasting shame and contempt.

The Isaian apocalypse (Is. 24-27) is replete with apocalyptic themes such as universal judgment and heavenly portents. A picture of pervasive desolation and judgment that shakes the foundations of the earth (Is. 24) is juxtaposed with the vision of the rich banquet which the Lord will make for all peoples. There the Lord will destroy the veil of ignorance that has covered all the nations of the earth. God will swallow up death and wipe away the tears from every face (Is. 25). The psalm that brings chapter 26 to a close looks forward to a resurrection of the dead:

> Thy dead shall live, their bodies shall rise. O dwellers in the dust, awake and sing for joy! For thy dew is a dew of light, and on the land of the shades thou wilt let it fall (Is. 26:19).

Universalism resounds loudly in the apocalypse that now stands at the conclusion of Trito-Isaiah (Is. 66:5-24). While Israel is judged by God, missionaries will be sent to remote coasts to nations who have never heard of Israel's God. God will reveal the divine glory to all the nations, and together with Israel, all will gather in the new Jerusalem. The dire description of judgment is juxtaposed with a climactic picture of the "new heavens and the new earth" which the Lord will create (Is. 66:22) in which "all flesh shall come to worship" before the Lord (Is. 66:23).

Zechariah reflects apocalyptic concerns particularly in the latter chapters (Zech. 9-14). The vision of the arrival of the King of Peace (Zech. 9:9) will provide detailed material for the account of Jesus' entry into the city of Jerusalem. As the oracles of Zechariah come to an end, we hear intimations of universal warfare. All the nations shall rise against Israel. In this context, the author presents a vision of a time when the Lord will be king over all the earth (Zech. 14:9). Jerusalem shall dwell in security (Zech. 14:11), and all the survivors of Israel's enemies "shall go up year after year to worship the King, the Lord of Hosts, and to keep the feast of booths" (Zech. 14:16). Those who fail to do so will suffer drought and plague (Zech. 14:17-19). This vision of the end brings us not to another world but to a new order in this world with Israel as the center of the nations. We see here a universal vision in as far as it involves all the nations. But this universal view does not automatically embrace every individual within the nations. Nor does it reflect the Isaian vision of cosmic peace and harmony, for drought and plague will still be the lot of those who stand against God.

3) Theological Significance of Apocalyptic

In the light of this discussion of apocalyptic, we can now give a definition of eschatology in terms of the vision of history that is shared by prophetic eschatology and apocalyptic. In this broad sense, eschatology is any vision of life that sees history to be moving toward a God-appointed end. Initially, we can say, it is irrelevant where that end is located. History is viewed as open to a future held out to it by God. Faith in God expresses itself in trust and confidence for the coming of the future. If we interpret apocalyptic not as an aberration but as an authentic development of the future-consciousness of biblical faith, we can now argue that one of the most significant aspects of apocalyptic is that it raises the question of the limit of hope more radically than it had been raised in Israel's past by holding out the prospect of a future that truly transcends human expectations and human experience within space and time. If eschatology orientates us with hope toward a transcendent future promised by God, then the measure of the fulfillment is not to be drawn from mere human expectations. In the final analysis, the fulfillment of the promise can be measured only in terms of the infinite mystery of the God of the promise.

For apocalyptic, the eschatological question is no longer that of the destiny of an individual, a family, or a nation. It is now the question of the ultimate destiny of the world of God's creation. Apocalyptic raises the question of ultimate destiny both for the collective body of the human race and for the individual person. If the question of ultimate destiny is at root the question of what we may ultimately hope for in life even in the face of our inevitable death, then it can be said that apocalyptic raises the question of the ultimate limit of human hope in a more radical way than any other body of biblical literature.

What may we hope for as individuals and as a human community when we are aware that every future we create for ourselves within the world can be taken from us? If hope springs from experience within the world, does it not eventually point questioningly beyond our experience of the world? And if hope is eventually directed to a transcendent object not of human making, does the very object of hope presented to us by apocalyptic raise serious questions about the nature and meaning of human involvement within the world? Prophecy had issued a call to a form of conversion that would lead to a transformation of the political-social order within the world. Apocalyptic likewise issues a call to conversion. But because of the transcendent nature of the future to which it summons us, the meaning of conversion can readily be seen as a call to withdrawal from involvement in the concerns of the present aeon. Because of its pessimism concerning worldly possibilities, apocalyptic takes the significant move to the notion of a transcendent future. But by holding out this vision of the future, it raises difficult questions about the relation between such a future and the historical processes which make up the greater portion of human life in society. These questions, which apocalyptic itself does not answer, will become important in the development of Christian eschatology.

6. Conclusions on the Hebrew Scriptures

From this review of the development of the Hebrew Scriptures it is possible to draw some conclusions concerning the theological significance of this development.

1) While the Hebrew Scriptures do not offer any clear teaching about the topics which hand-book theology usually treated in the tract called *eschatology*, there is a sense in which it is possible to speak of eschatology even in the early levels of the Scriptural tradition. This is largely a question of the definition of terms. If eschatology is thought of solely as doctrine about death, judgment, heaven, and hell, the term can hardly be applied to most of the pre-Christian, biblical tradition.

If, however, the term is taken to refer to the conviction that this world of human experience is destined for a goal set for it by God, toward which God is leading it, then there is good reason for speaking of the emergence of eschatology in the history of the future-consciousness in the Hebrew Scriptures. In this sense, eschatology involves a theology of history. History is fundamentally incomplete until that time when God's eternal plan is actualized fully in human reality. Ultimately our future, wherever and however it comes about, is the gift of God to creation. An eschatological sense of history emerges out of the development of future-consciousness which is present already in the Abraham-tradition and is developed more throughout the centuries of Jewish history that follow.

2) The development of eschatological awareness arises from two poles. On the one hand, Israel lives from faith in the God of the promise. On the other hand, Israel's concrete experience never lives up to the measure of the divine promise. When, where, how will Israel experience a fulfillment which corresponds in depth and richness to a promise which is of God? Each attempt to pin down an answer to this question is frustrated. Each experience of frustration leads to further attempts to define the fulfillment. From the destiny of one man and his family, the Scriptures lead us to reflect on a destiny that is universal and cosmic in scope. What will be the final condition of the world that God has created, and of the human race which God has placed in the world to be the responsible steward of the gift of creation? This is truly the eschatological question.

3) Christians are accustomed to reading the Hebrew Scriptures from a Christian viewpoint. Consequently, Christian interpretations lay on these texts meanings which are clearly not the original, historical meanings. Christians have been inclined, therefore, to see the entire development of the bible as the evolution of a "messianic promise" which finds its fulfillment in the person of Jesus, the Christ. An immediate reaction to a more critical, historical reading of the Hebrew literature, however, would suggest that such a view is unfounded. A closer look at the evidence is necessary. It is fair enough to say that the original, historical meaning of the prophets could hardly have had Christ or Christianity in mind when these texts were first written. Therefore, the common tendency to search for specific predictions of the future in its Christian form and to see these as the genuine historical meaning of the texts can hardly be sustained.

The relation between the Jewish and the Christian tradition is best seen in terms of the continuous process of reinterpretation of traditions which is so central to the development of the Hebrew Scriptures. There is no *a priori* reason for claiming that this process of interpretation and redefinition ended or had to end with the work of the last Hebrew prophet. As long as the promise remains unfulfilled, the process of redefinition can continue. In fact, the history of interpretations continued beyond the work of the prophets into the history of the intertestamental period, and beyond that into the writings of the Christian Scriptures. When Christians give to Jesus the title of *Christ* they not only relate their experience of Jesus to the ancient Jewish traditions, but they bring those traditions to a new level of interpretation. The process of interpretation that leads to the specifically Christian concerns acquires its distinctive characteristics from the critical role assigned to the person and ministry of Jesus of Nazareth in that reflection.

From this we may conclude that there is a well-grounded sense in which the Christian reading of the Hebrew Scriptures with reference to subsequent Christian history can be seen as a legitimate procedure. The writers of the Christian Scriptures were carrying out procedures well established in the literary history of the Hebrew Scriptures. This does not mean that today Christians ought to reject the historical meaning of the prophetic texts in order to maintain detailed and explicit predictions of the person and ministry of Jesus. The meaning of the history of promise in the Hebrew Scriptures may be seen in terms of the shaping of a future-consciousness which, for the Christian community, took a particular form because of the events centering around the experience of Jesus of Nazareth. For us as for the writers of earlier Christian generations, the entire history of the Jewish people is, indeed, a history of prophetic promise which finds a new and decisive level of realization in the history of Jesus, the Christ.

Readings

Bergant, D., *Job, Ecclesiastes* (M. Glazier, Wilmington, Delaware, 1982).

Charles, R.H., *Eschatology: The Doctrine of a Future Life in Israel, Judaism and Christianity* (Schocken Books, N.Y., 1963).

Collins, John J., *The Apocalyptic Imagination: An Introduction to the Jewish Matrix of Christianity.* (Crossroad, N.Y., 1984).

_____ *The Apocalyptic Vision of the Book of Daniel.* Harvard Semitic Monographs, #16 (Scholars Press, Missoula, Montana, 1977).

Eliade, M., *Cosmos and History: The Myth of the Eternal Return,* tr. W.R. Trask (Harper Torchbooks, N.Y., 1959).

Hanson, P.D., *The Dawn of Apocalyptic. The Historical and Sociological Roots of Jewish Apocalyptic Eschatology.* (Fortress Press, Philadelphia, 1975, 1979).

_____ (ed.) *Visionaries and Their Apocalypses. Issues in Religion and Theology #4 (.*Fortress Press, Philadelphia/London, 1983).

Stuhlmueller, C., *Creative Redemption in Deutero-Isaiah. Analecta Biblica, 43* (Rome, 1970).

Von Rad, G., *Old Testament Theology,* tr. D.M.G. Stalker (Oliver & Boyd, Edinburgh, 1962) Vol. 1.

_____ *Wisdom in Israel* (Abingdon Press, Nashville, 1972).

2

THE STORY OF CHRISTIAN HOPE

If the history of hope in the Hebrew Scriptures is a complex matter, the continuation of this history in the Christian Scriptures is no less difficult to recount. On the one hand, the historical development of the specifically Christian sort of hope is incomprehensible except with reference to its historical roots in the history that we have recounted in the previous chapter. On the other hand, the Christian development is decisively shaped by the historical ministry of Jesus of Nazareth and his disciples' reaction to him both during his ministry and after his death. As the early Christians attempted to shed light on their experience of Jesus before and after his death, they looked back to the earlier traditions of their people where they found rich resources at their disposal. The process that gave birth to the writing of the Christian Scriptures was not a mere repetition of existing traditions, but a new level of interpretation of the expectations found in the prophetic and apocalyptic literature.

In 1964, the Pontifical Biblical Commission issued a document with the title *The Historical Truth of the Gospels*.[1] Since the Gospels are of primary significance for our understanding of the historical origins of Christianity, this document of the Biblical Commission is of great importance in orientating our critical reading of the Scriptures. Our approach to the Christian Scriptures will attempt to follow these guidelines of the Biblical Commission in dealing with the Gospel materials. The questions raised by other writings such as the Epistles and the

[1] *The Historical Truth of the Gospels: The 1964 Instruction of the Biblical Commission*, with commentary by J.J. Fitzmyer, S.J. (Glen Rock, N.J., 1964).

Book of Revelation are of quite a different sort, and will be discussed at the appropriate place. In view of our discussion of the Hebrew Scriptures in the previous chapter, the most appropriate place to begin our reflections on the Christian meaning of hope is with Jesus' preaching of the Kingdom of God.

1. Jesus and the Kingdom of God

We have seen how the metaphor of the Kingdom of God emerged out of the Jewish experience of the Davidic monarchy, and how it eventually became a metaphor of truly eschatological significance in the prophetic and apocalyptic traditions. The metaphor of the Kingdom of God in the later Jewish generations expressed the hope of a restoration of the Davidic kingship through which God's rule would become effective among his people as it had been under the kingship of David in the past. All the longings of the Hebrew nation for freedom, peace, justice, and the fullness of life contained in the ancient covenant-promise were crystallized in this metaphor. Only when God rules will the blessings of final *shalom* be realized. God will inaugurate a new aeon, the final state of salvation, peace, and prosperity for the people and for the world.

One of the most certain results of generations of critical exegesis is the awareness that the central factor in Jesus' historical ministry was the preaching of the Kingdom of God. In taking up this metaphor and placing it in the center of his concern, Jesus was taking up the hopes and expectations of his people. But in preaching the coming of the Kingdom in the precise way he did, he transformed the meaning of the metaphor in the light of his own experience of God.

a) The Centrality of the Kingdom

There can be no serious question about the fact that Jesus set about his mission by proclaiming the coming of the Kingdom of God (Mk. 1:14-15; Mt. 4:17; Lk. 4:14-30). If one were to speak of the eschatology of Jesus, surely the Kingdom-metaphor would have to stand at the center of it. The term *Kingdom of God* (or *Kingdom of heaven*) appears some 122 times throughout the Christian Scriptures. In 99 of these cases, the usage is found in the Synoptic Gospels; and in 90 instances the phrase is placed in the mouth of Jesus himself. From this we can see how firmly the usage is rooted in the ancient Jesus-tradition. Not only do the Synoptic Gospels present the primary impulse of his mission in these terms, but a wealth of material from the parables and from the miracle-tradition points in the same direction. This is to state a fact. It is not to explain the meaning of the fact. And it is precisely there that many of the questions about Christian eschatology have their point of departure.

As the history of this metaphor shows, the Kingdom is not susceptible of a clear definition. This is annoying to modern Christians who tend to think of theological concepts in terms of the precision of the familiar Scholastic definitions. But whatever is said of the Kingdom-metaphor, it is quite clear that it cannot be equated directly with the later Christian, Scholastic concept of heaven as beatific vision. As a metaphor of salvation, it is part of a much larger metaphorical structure pertaining to the final salvific action of God with regard to the world of creation.

b) Nuances of the Kingdom-Metaphor

One of the striking features of Jesus' Kingdom-preaching emerges clearly when we compare his usage with that of the Hebrew Scriptures. The Jewish traditions had looked to a *future* act of God that would inaugurate the Kingdom. To speak of the Kingdom, in those terms, is to draw the hearer's attention away from the bleakness of the present to the glorious future of God's Rule. Jesus, by way of contrast, associates the breaking in of the Kingdom immediately with his person and ministry. Without directly denying the future orientation of the traditional understanding, Jesus gives it some new accentuations. There is, in some of Jesus' preaching, a sense of the future coming of the Kingdom. But that future does not seem to be a far distant point of time. On the contrary it appears to be very imminent. The Kingdom will come *soon* and *surely* (Mk. 4:3-8; 13:28; Lk. 12:54ff). That sense of imminence is even more intense in those sayings of Jesus in which the imminent future seems to yield to the present moment of Jesus' ministry (Mt. 12:28; Lk. 22:20). The time of the coming of God's Kingdom does not lie in the distant future; it is at the door even *now*

(Mt. 10:32ff; 11:21-23a; Lk. 10:13-15; 12:8ff).

As Jesus appears in the Gospel-tradition, he is deeply convinced that the Kingdom of God was drawing near to humanity in a manner unprecedented in the past. There is an unmistakable sense of urgency in his preaching. The summons to conversion and the call to discipleship are radical, for renewal of the human heart and single-minded discipleship are necessary to make possible the final dawning of salvation. In this sense, the core of Jesus' ministry—his preaching of the Kingdom, his call to conversion, and his summons to discipleship— can be seen as an event of the End-time. Thus, Jesus gives the hope of the previous generations a new dimension. What they had hoped for as a future reality is being fulfilled now in his ministry. The New Age which earlier prophets had hoped for is not an unreachable future but is beginning already in the immediate present. The crucial signs of the New Age are taking place in the words and deeds of Jesus (Lk. 10:23ff; 4:21; Mt. 11:5).

This understanding of the present-character of the Kingdom is confirmed by the miracle-tradition as it now appears in the Gospels. The miracles are themselves parables of the Kingdom in miniature. Miracles of forgiveness, of healing, and of exorcisms indicate that the power of God is breaking into history in the experience of Jesus' ministry, bringing with it a wholeness and integrity to human life. "But if it is by the finger of God that I cast out demons, then the kingdom of God has come upon you" (Lk. 11:20). They indicate, further, that the meaning of the Kingdom cannot be limited to the realm of the interior life. Body and soul are the objects of God's loving concern, for God wills the salvation of creatures in their entirety, not only in one part of their being. Sins are forgiven. But limbs are healed, hungry stomachs are fed, blinded eyes regain sight. There is nothing in creation that cannot be drawn into the salvific, life-giving power of God. If the Servant of God heals and reconciles in body and in soul, his activity indicates that the Kingdom of God reaches to all that goes to make up human life. Even though there is a strong sense of the immediacy of God's Kingdom, this seems to be limited to particular situations during the ministry of Jesus. The Kingdom is breaking in; but it is clearly not present in its fullest, universal realization. There is a clear tension between the Kingdom as present reality and the Kingdom in its future, full realization. As long as human beings fail to make a serious and personal decision for the Kingdom of God, there are still serious impediments to the realization of God's Kingdom.

The tension between near-expectation and the obvious delay of fulfillment, to which subsequent Christian history gives abundant testimony, becomes more understandable when it is viewed in the light of human freedom. God offers the grace of the Kingdom to human beings. The divine offer must be freely accepted and responded to. God never bypasses the human, nor does God do what human beings are called to do. Therefore, the Christian experience of grace involves an ongoing polarity between the present and the future, between the already and the not-yet. Grace is already the experience of the eschatological mystery of God. But as long as the human response to grace is not full and unreserved, the reality of God's gracious presence is not fully efficacious in human experience.

c) The God of the Kingdom

While it is virtually impossible to give an adequate and precise definition to the meaning of the Kingdom-metaphor, a wealth of parable material offers significant insight into dimensions of the Kingdom as Jesus understood the term. The parables may be seen as important exegesis of the central metaphor. Even further, they may be taken to offer crucial insights into Jesus' own experience of God as this is reflected in seminal form in the so-called Abba-tradition.

It is one of the assured results of critical exegesis since the studies of Joachim Jeremias[2] that the use of the term *Abba* to designate God is one of the most authentic words of the historical Jesus. Jesus addresses God not simply with the title *Father* but with the Aramaic term *Abba*. *Abba* is a diminutive form that expresses a sense of respectful familiarity. In a religious context where the mere mention of the divine name was forbidden, such a usage on the part of Jesus is significant. When Jesus called God his *Abba*, he stood in a long tradition that had seen God as a loving Father or a loving spouse in relation to his people. The prophetic notion of *hesed* (=loving mercy), which played such a significant role in the prophet Hosea (Hos. 2:1-23), is a moving

[2] *The Central Message of the New Testament* (London, 1965) pp. 9-30; *The Prayers of Jesus* (Naperville, 1967) pp. 11-65; *New Testament Theology* (New York, 1971), pp. 61-68. Cfr. also: Robert Hammerton-Kelly, *God the Father. Theology and Patriarchy in the Teaching of Jesus* (Philadelphia, 1979).

testimony to the Hebrew perception of God as a loving, merciful power who enters into a marriage with his people. What is distinctive about Jesus' understanding of God is not the mere fact that he could call God his Father, but the fact that he sensed the presence of this loving Father in such intimate and personal terms.

Whether one agrees with E. Schillebeeckx in seeing the Abba-experience of Jesus as the springboard for the whole of his mission,[3] it certainly provides a vantage point for drawing many elements of the Scriptural portrait of Jesus into a coherent unity. If the Abba-tradition is taken as a point of departure for understanding the nature of God's Kingdom, the conclusion that God's rule is one of love rather than one of raw power lies close at hand. The direction set by the Abba-tradition is developed with moving power in the great parables of the fifteenth chapter of *Luke*. There is joy in heaven over one repentent sinner (Lk. 15:3-7, 10). The parables of the lost sheep and the lost coin lead quickly to the dramatic story of the generous father and his wayward son (Lk. 15:11-32). The sheer prodigality of the father's love and forgiveness stands in the center of the story. As a story about God and the Kingdom of God, this parable mediates the image of the tireless, accepting, forgiving love of God, who does not wait until we come and knock at the door to plead our cause but runs out to meet us on the way.

If these parables suggest that God is a mystery of indiscriminate love, this is not only a peculiarity of the theology of Luke. In quite a different way and in other circumstances, the Gospel of Matthew suggests the very same insight, but goes on to draw explicit conclusions from this mystery of God for the practical conduct of human life. In what is perhaps the most radical statement of Christian ethics, Matthew writes:

> You have heard that it was said, 'You shall love your neighbor and hate your enemy.' But I say to you, Love your enemies and pray for those who persecute you, so that you may be sons of your Father who is in heaven; for he makes his sun rise on the evil and on the good, and sends rain on the just and on the unjust. For if you love those who love you, what reward have you? Do not even the tax

[3]E. Schillebeeckx, *Jesus: An Experiment in Christology*, tr. H. Hoskins (New York, 1981 [reprint of 1979 translation copyrighted by Crossroad Publ.]), pp. 256-271.

collectors do the same? And if you salute only your brethren, what more are you doing than others? Do not even the Gentiles do the same? You, therefore, must be perfect, as your heavenly Father is perfect (Mt. 5:43-48).

The ethical imperative to love even our enemies is grounded in the nature of God's indiscriminate love. If God is indiscriminate love, can a Christian be satisfied with less than a similar love for all those whom God loves so lavishly? If the rest of the ethical teaching of the Christian Scriptures finds parallels in the Hebrew Scriptures and in other religious systems, this radical demand—which Christians themselves find so difficult to accept and to live—is deeply rooted in Jesus' perception of God. Jesus' preaching is pre-eminently *theo-logical*. It provides the basis for re-defining the mystery of the sacred. The Good News of Jesus is the offer of the merciful forgiveness of the Father and the joy of encountering the boundless and undeserved mercy of God. To experience God's love in this way is to experience that one is absolutely accepted, affirmed, and loved by the Lord of the universe. It is likewise to know that because one is thus accepted by God, one can and must accept oneself and other human beings.

Viewed against the background of the preaching of Jesus, the Scriptural tradition of his actions presents him as one who acts out God's mysterious love in his relations with others. Viewed superficially, Jesus' provocative association with the outcasts of Jewish society might appear as a piece of social criticism. But when viewed from the perspective of Jesus' image of God, this troublesome piece of the tradition appears as a profound theological statement about the nature of God's activity in the world. The merciful love of God cannot be contained or controlled by humanly constructed boundaries. It reaches to all freely and graciously. Jesus' table-fellowship with public sinners and tax-collectors (Mt. 9:10; 11:19; Mk. 2:15-17; Lk. 7:31-35), his openness to the despised Samaritan (Lk. 10:10-37; 17:11-19; Jn. 4), his free association with women (Lk. 7:36-50; 8:1-3; Jn. 4:27), his free attitude with regard to foreigners (Mt. 8:5-13; Mk. 7:24-30; Mt. 11:20-24): all this is of one piece with the message of his central proclamation. The God who moves in Jesus leads his listeners beyond the familiar boundaries of exclusion. The ministry of Jesus, both in word and in act, is a challenging statement about the nature of God and of God's ways of dealing with the world.[4]

d) A Kingdom of Love

This vision of the sacred must enter into the interpretation of the Kingdom-metaphor as Jesus used it. God's rule is a rule of a love that is overwhelmingly generous, forgiving, tolerant, and accepting; it is a love that delights in reconciliation. The metaphor of God as Father has its historical roots in the sociological structure of a patriarchal society. But, as this metaphor is transformed through the experience of Jesus, it loses all overtones of domineering power.

Similarly, as the Kingdom-metaphor is reinterpreted in this light, it loses the national and political overtones which it had in the Hebrew prophets. It no longer means a liberation from the political yoke of Rome or from any other political oppression, at least in any direct sense. It symbolizes, principally, a liberation from the limitations of human self-centeredness. God's rule can become actualized only where human beings are open to such love and responsive to it. In as far as God's gift is accepted and responded to in human life and all human relations, there God's love comes to rule in human life and shapes human relations in a decisive way. The conversion to which Jesus calls us is, in essence, a conversion from self-centered existence to a God-centered existence. The meaning of a God-centered existence is expressed in the mystery of the indiscriminate love of God which is the model after which human life is to be lived.

e) The Death of Jesus

The execution of Jesus on a cross is among the most certain historical facts concerning Jesus of Nazareth. When this execution is viewed from an historical perspective, it is clear that a mixture of religious and political motivations played a central role in Jesus' condemnation. Details concerning the arrest and trial of Jesus are uncertain. Yet, exegetes commonly hold that Jesus' execution was a

---

[4]D. Senior & C. Stuhlmueller, *Biblical Foundations of Mission* (Maryknoll, N.Y., 1983) p. 147ff.

direct result of his ministry. He died because of his preaching and because of his manner of acting. The systematic treatment of Jesus' death, therefore, should not view that death in isolation from the style of life that preceded it. They belong together as a unity.

The death of Jesus has stimulated Christian reflection on the nature of his message and on the meaning of death over the centuries. Why does his ministry for the sake of the Kingdom of God's love lead to such a violent end? Certainly, Jesus himself would have had to wrestle with this question, as the Gethsemane-tradition seems to indicate. The Scriptures indicate a wealth of traditions to which Jesus could reach to come to some understanding of his own impending death. The Scriptures indicate that Jesus employed some of the resources of the Jewish tradition to reflect on his fate, and that he came to accept his death out of a sense of fidelity to the will of God and with a profound trust that, despite all signs to the contrary, God would vindicate this faithful witness.

For the early disciples, the death of Jesus would have been an experience of severe crisis. During his life, Jesus had lived from a deep sense of unique closeness to God and had given himself totally to the service of that God. "He trusts in God; let God deliver him now, if he desires him; for he said, 'I am the Son of God'" (Mt. 27:43). Jesus died abandoned by his disciples, but apparently by God as well. How could one trust in the God for whom Jesus stood if this was the outcome? Was the death of Jesus indeed the end for him and for the cause of the God for whom he had stood throughout his ministry?

Christian reflection on his death takes place only from the perspective of the Easter-experience of the early disciples and makes use of a wealth of traditional material in the Jewish religious context to search for deeper insight into the meaning of Jesus' death.

The Scriptures indicate a variety of directions in this reflection. It was possible to see Jesus in the context of the prophetic tradition and to interpret his death in terms of the common fate of the prophets (Mt. 23:34-39; Lk. 13:32-35). This could be readily related to the tradition concerning the suffering righteous one whose suffering would be vindicated by God (Wis. 2-3; Ps. 22). These traditions play a major role in the shaping of the passion-narratives of the Gospels. Jesus could be seen as the righteous one whose obedience to the will of God brought him into that conflict with the religious and political authorities that eventually led to his death.

Such a line of reflection is not far removed from the Suffering-Servant tradition which would play a significant role in early Christological reflection. Here Jesus' death could be seen to have a distinctly salvific meaning. The suffering and death of the innocent one can be a beneficial source of life for others. Readily related to this is the Old Testament theology of sacrifice. As a sacrifice, Jesus' death is the expression of the inner attitude of reverent obedience and faithfulness to God that had governed his life from the start. His death, then, is not an unfortunate appendix to an otherwise beautiful life. On the contrary, it came to be seen as the consummate expression of what that life was about (1 Pt. 2:21-24; Hebr. 6ff).

Thus, while the death of Jesus was at first a scandal and a moment of crisis for his followers, over a period of time Christian reflection eventually came to attribute genuine salvific meaning to that death. But this was possible only when the death was viewed in retrospect from the experience of Easter. Easter provided the vantage-point from which the disciples could look back and come to ever deeper understanding of the meaning of his life and death.

2. The Resurrection

What is common to Christians over the centuries is their belief in the resurrection of Jesus. But the meaning of that faith is no longer as self-evident as it may have seemed in the past. Historical-critical studies of the Scriptures have led to a wide range of viewpoints concerning the origin and original meaning of this faith-confession. Honesty must lead us to admit, however, that many of the current interpretations are motivated not only by textual problems but by other convictions of a broader philosophical sort. Thus, if one believes, for whatever reason, that there is no such thing as life beyond death, and if one still wants to give some meaning to the texts of Scripture, there is a natural inclination to exclude any continued existence of Jesus as a possible meaning of the resurrection-texts. In view of the obvious role played by such subjective biases, questions of methodology become basic. Since such questions are dealt with extensively both in Scriptural studies and in systematic studies of Christology, we will not treat them here in detail but only in as far as they are necessary to highlight and lend legitimacy to the interpretation of the resurrection which we intend to present.[5]

It is sufficient at the beginning of this discussion to point out that the notion of resurrection is a metaphor which had already gained currency in the time between the Testaments as a part of the apocalyptic scenario of the turn from this historical aeon to the final aeon of God's Kingdom. As a metaphor, it expressed a deep faith in the fact that God would vindicate the great martyrs of faith. When the Christian Scriptures make use of this metaphor, they are operating within a religious, apocalyptic framework which includes the aspiration of life-with-God beyond death, at least for the just; for God can create life even out of death.

When the question of the meaning of the resurrection is asked in the light of the historical context from which the metaphor came and in which Christians came to use it, it becomes clear that the Scriptures offer no single, clear, unified definition of the meaning of the metaphor. The resurrection-metaphor does not affirm one particular thing, but draws together in a suggestive manner a number of insights and experiences. Its meaning cannot be limited to its function as a reward for Jesus' suffering and death. It may be that, but it is much more besides. As P. Perkins says, it is part of a much larger story: the story of God's dealing with Israel and through Israel with humanity at large. The metaphor is situated in the context of hope for the radical renewal of creation and the coming of God's Rule.[6]

To see the resurrection as a metaphor of apocalyptic eschatology is to say that it affirms a transcendent destiny for Jesus that differs from any return to space and time experience. Jesus, with all that he was about in his ministry, has been vindicated by God and has been accepted into the stream of God's life-giving power. Resurrection is an act of God in Jesus, bringing Jesus into God's dimension and filling his humanity with the fullness of the gift of the Spirit. Viewed in this way, the resurrection is—by definition—not an historical event but the transcendent act of God in Jesus. It is in no way equivalent to a return to life, or a near-death experience. Neither have we even come close to

---

[5]W. Kasper, *Jesus the Christ*, tr. V. Green (London/N.Y., 1976) pp. 124-160. Schillebeeckx, *op. cit.*, pp. 41-104 offers an extended treatment of problems of hermeneutics by a systematician. The explicit treatment of resurrection on the basis of the principles set out in the first part of the book is found later, pp. 399-571.

[6]P. Perkins, *Resurrection: New Testament Witness and Contemporary Reflection* (Garden City, 1984) p. 21; 26.

the meaning of the resurrection in the philosophy of the power of positive thought. To say that the resurrection is not an historical event is not to say that it is not real but merely to say that we ought not confine the limits of reality *a priori* to the way we experience reality in the space-time framework of our present existence.

As a part of the apocalyptic scenario of the end-time, resurrection is not something one expects for an individual in isolation from the collective and cosmic renewal of the new age. This fact suggests that the experience of the disciples, both during the ministry of Jesus and after his death (in the appearances) must have been an experience of great spiritual power; for it led them to affirm of one man, and as a realized fact, what was expected as the collective destiny of the redeemed at the end of history. Even if one might argue that they could have come to such a view simply from subjective, psychological mechanisms, it is difficult to explain the persistence of this claim in the light of their subsequent experience. The variety of traditions reflected in Scripture and the wide range of people attesting to the resurrection make any reduction of the resurrection to some form of projection-mechanism in the disciples quite unconvincing. What all such psychological interpretations fail to take into account is the fact that the message of the early followers of Jesus is not a message about their own experience but a message about what God has done in Jesus.

Because of the apocalyptic-eschatological significance of the resurrection-metaphor, the Christian claim has universal significance. This may be expressed in a number of ways. Basically, what is implied in the resurrection-affirmation is that the end of the old age has arrived and the new age of God's final gift of salvation is inaugurated. What has happened in Jesus is the anticipation of what God wills for humanity as a whole and for the world. The resurrection of Jesus, while it is his personal destiny, is not only that. It is the beginning of the recreation of the world.

When the resurrection is viewed in this way, it can be seen also as a decisive disclosure of God as one whose final word to the world is one of acceptance, forgiveness, and reconciliation. God may now be described simply in the words of St. Paul as a God "who gives life to the dead" (Rm. 4:17). God is revealed as one whose power transcends life and death and whose fidelity is stronger than death. Resurrection-faith is not a belief in a supposedly natural immortality of the soul, but a faith in the creative power and fidelity of God's love.

Finally, the corporality of the resurrection implied in the expression "resurrection of the body" is consistent with the apocalyptic context. However, in as far as we are now dealing with a transcendent dimension of being and meaning, this corporality should not be understood in terms of materiality as experienced in space and time. It may be seen as related to the historical hope for the salvation of the whole person in all its dimensions. Bodily resurrection is a way of saying that Jesus, in the wholeness of his being, is with God.

In brief, when we interpret the meaning of the resurrection in its historical context, the intent of the metaphor is to express the conviction that Jesus lives in a new and transformed way in his own individual reality in the presence of the God whom he served so faithfully in his ministry. In this destiny of Jesus is anticipated the destiny of humanity and of the world. This sort of claim about Jesus with all its anthropological and cosmic implications may seem foreign to many modern Christians who are inclined to think of salvation in far narrower terms. From a Scriptural perspective, it is too limiting to think that the resurrection is nothing but a reward for having suffered in life. Similarly, it is too limiting to think that resurrection is simply the assurance of some form of immortality for the human soul. What may be even more disturbing is the fact that the Scriptures make a salvific claim about Jesus that does not seem to bear any clear relation to the typically contemporary questions about human well-being in our psychological and technological culture.[7] One has to ask what the original Christian claim about salvation through God's act in Jesus has to do with the modern quest for justice and peace and the humanization of the world. Here the problem is no longer one of reconstructing the world of Jesus and the early community so as to come to a responsible historical judgment about the initial intent of the Christian claims about Jesus, but the further and unavoidable problem of relating those claims to human experience in a fundamentally different cultural context. This sort of question will be taken up in later chapters.

[7]Perkins, op. cit., pp. 21-28.

3. Early Christian Expectations

As we have seen in the section on Jesus' preaching, there are clear apocalyptic overtones in his use of the Kingdom-metaphor. We have argued that one of the particular nuances which Jesus gave to the metaphor was the association of the Kingdom with his person and ministry. At the same time, we pointed out that there is an unmistakable element of the future in his preaching, indeed, of a very imminent future. If this is the case with the ministry of Jesus, it should come as no surprise that the post-Easter community of disciples would have shared this near-expectation in some way. Not only the impact of Jesus' ministry but even more so the power of the Easter-experience make it easy to understand that there should be a strong sense of tension between present and future in the early community. The emphasis which Jesus had placed on the present offer of the Kingdom would have been decisively reinforced by the experience of the presence of the Risen Lord and the gift of the Spirit. If the present is already seen as an experience of eschatological grace, the universal manifestation of this eschatological gift cannot be far off. If the collective destiny of the human race has already begun in the resurrection of Jesus, it is difficult to envision an extended time between the realization of that individual destiny and the collective destiny of the human race. Consequently, it is not difficult to understand that there would have been an intense near-expectation of the end of history and a hope for the return of the Lord in the near future.

This becomes particularly clear in Paul's two epistles to the Thessalonians and the first epistle to the Corinthians. Paul clearly expresses the expectation that he will be living at the time of the parousia, or the return of the Lord (1 Thess. 4:15; 1 Cor. 15:51-52). These writings of Paul, dating from about 51 c.e. to 57 c.e., contain some of the earliest extant apocalyptic texts of the New Testament canon. Not only does Paul express the unmistakable expectation that the parousia is not far off, but he makes use of other significant apocalyptic material. While he does not attempt to specify a date for the return of the Lord, he offers a partial description of the parousia in which he employs many familiar apocalyptic themes:

> For the Lord himself will descend from heaven with a cry of command, with the archangel's call, and with the sound of the trumpet of

God. And the dead in Christ will rise first; then we who are alive, who are left shall be caught up together with them in the clouds to meet the Lord in the air; and so we shall always be with the Lord (1 Thess. 4:16-17).

The apocalyptic tone is unmistakable. The spatial image of heaven located above the earth, the cry of the coming judge, the archangel, and the trumpet are all familiar elements of the apocalyptic scenario. The clouds represent the veil traditionally involved in theophanies. The apocalyptic tradition associates the clouds with the coming of the Son of Man. Paul sees the clouds as the place of the meeting with the Lord. While these elements are all well known in the traditional literature, the object of hope is decisively changed for Paul. Now the object of hope is clearly resurrection and a life of sharing in the glory of Christ. The goal of God's salvific activity is the union of the believers with the Risen Lord (1 Thess. 4:14). Paul's teaching reaches its climax in those poignant yet hopeful words: "We shall always be with the Lord" (1 Thess. 4:17).

The theme of conflict emerges with particular clarity in *2 Thessalonians.*[8] Here Paul introduces a mysterious figure called the "man of lawlessness" (2 Thess. 2:3), thus providing the basis for the figure of the anti-Christ which would play such an important role in later speculations about the end of history.

The Pauline material provides interesting clues as to the role of apocalyptic thought in the early Christian community. Their understanding of Jesus' preaching and their experience of the Risen Lord clearly produced a form of near-expectation. How can this kind of expectation be kept alive as time continues, and as the world does not seem to be noticeably changed? Is something essential lost when an intense near-expectation declines? Is an authentic Christian eschatology possible without such expectation? These questions are difficult to answer with any degree of satisfaction. Even a comparison of the two epistles to the Thessalonians indicates the possibility that the intense near-expectation of the first letter is replaced by an indeterminate future in the second.

There can be little disagreement about the fact that the early Chris-

---

[8]B.S. Childs, *The New Testament as Canon: An Introduction* (Philadelphia, 1984) p. 350-372 for the current state of the question on the relation between the two epistles to the Thessalonians.

tian community shared in the imminent apocalyptic expectations of Judaism. To what precise degree this was the case, however, can be debated. N. Perrin seems to overstate the case in his claim that the early church was originally an apocalyptic sect within Judaism.[9] There can be no serious doubt that the apocalyptic tradition was a critical factor in the development of early Christianity. But the claim that the total meaning of early Christianity can be found in apocalyptic, or that there was a purely apocalyptic Christianity which represented only one form of apocalyptic goes far beyond the evidence at our disposal.[10]

The history of Christian theology indicates that near-expectation comes and goes, and that—most commonly—when it is experienced intensely, it is the concern not of the main-line theological traditions but of sectarian groups. We will come back to this issue later. For the moment, we shall turn to other elements in Paul's eschatology.

In the late Pauline epistles, the contrast between present and future reality shifts to a contrast between that which is "above" and that which is "below" (Cfr. 1 Cor. 15:35-50; 2 Cor. 5:1-10; Phil. 3:20-21). Since the contrast between the present and the future is characteristic of the historical framework of apocalyptic, this change in usage may reflect a lessening of the apocalyptic sense of the imminent end. The Pauline baptismal theology (Rm. 6; 2 Cor. 5:17; Gal. 6:15) sees the present experience of Christians as already a participation in eschatological reality. In baptism, the believer has already "put on" the Lord Jesus Christ as a suit of armor. What is begun in baptism must become a lived reality in Christian life. Personal identification with the light of Christ overcomes the power of darkness. In the life lived from the grace of baptism, the power of Christ's light emanates into the world of human experience. There is, then, in this Pauline eschatology both a present and a future dimension. The present or realized dimension includes two realities: that which God has done in the death and resurrection of Jesus, and that which happens in the Christian through baptism and an appropriate living out of the meaning of baptism. The future dimension designates the full working out of the power of resurrection which remains to be accomplished. The primary point of

---

[9]N. Perrin, "Apocalyptic Christianity," in: *Visionaries and their Apocalypses*, ed. P. Hanson (Philadelphia/London, 1983) p. 121. This chapter is a reprint of a portion of Perrin's *The New Testament: An Introduction* (1974) pp. 65-85.

[10]McGinn, *The Apocalypse...*, p. 19.

reference for Paul's eschatology is that which has already happened for human salvation in the death and resurrection of Christ. But the true life of faith has an open-ended quality; the power of God's act must yet work out its inner dynamic throughout the life of the believer. The full establishment of God's rule remains the hope for the future.

4. Eschatology in the Gospel of John

The Gospel of John brings its own peculiar set of problems. The immense literature on this Gospel leaves most of the biggest questions about the origin, nature and purpose of this text with no definite answers. Concerning the literary history that lies behind the present text, most agree that a variety of sources were used by the author of the final text. But there is no universal agreement as to precisely what sources are involved, or as to exactly how the sources were used. Many are convinced that the Gospel reflects considerable disunity in style and in theology. Others feel that the Gospel reflects a very strong linguistic and stylistic unity. However one may eventually resolve such questions, it is possible to discern at least two approaches to eschatology in the Gospel. Precisely how these two types are related is not clear. Because of the complexity of the textual problems, we will limit ourselves to a short statement of the eschatological dimensions of the Gospel and some remarks as to their significance.

The two types of eschatology reflected in *John* can be described in a variety of ways. R. Brown distinguishes them as "vertical" and "horizontal."[11] By the horizontal, Brown understands that which is generally found in the Scriptures; that is, the idea of the movement of history under God's providence toward a point at which God's final salvific act will transform reality. By vertical, Brown means any view that operates in terms of the contrast between a transcendent world and the empirical world, usually expressed in the spatial metaphors of above and below, or categories of time such as eternal and temporal. Such vertical views of salvation may be found commonly outside the biblical tradition. Salvation can be seen as an escape from history, or as the presence of the eternal to the believer in time. While the vertical view is not the common view of the bible, it is found at times, particularly in

[11] R. Brown, *The Gospel according to John*, vol. 1 (Garden City, N.Y., 1966) pp. CXV-CXXI.

the Christian Scriptures. We have seen an instance of it in the Pauline epistles treated above. The difference between these two types of eschatology may be pin-pointed in the following way. The horizontal model places emphasis on the future point at which salvation will be actualized while the vertical model emphasizes the importance of the present as a place of salvation.

It is commonly agreed that the theology of John places great emphasis on the present experience of salvation. It can be said, therefore, that John presents a form of "realized eschatology." Indeed, John may be the clearest example of such a realized eschatology in the whole of the Scriptures, although Paul also knows a realized eschatology, as we have seen above. The typical metaphor with which John speaks of the present experience of salvation is that of "eternal life" (Jn. 3:36; 5:24-27; 11:24-27; 17:3). Eternal life is experienced even now, in the present. Similarly, judgment (3:18; 9:39) and resurrection (5:21.24.26) are associated with the present experience of the believer.

Although the emphasis on the present experience of eternal life is a characteristic of John's message, the Gospel retains remnants of apocalyptic eschatology. There is a clear sense of futurity in Chapter 12:25 and 12:48. The text of chapter 14:2-3 refers to a transcendent realm to which Jesus must go in order to prepare a place for his disciples. Is this, perhaps, an allusion to the traditional concept of parousia? This possibility becomes clearer when such texts are compared with 14:18, 28,29 where the reference to the return of Jesus is explicit. Chapters 15 and 16 speak extensively of tribulation and sorrow, a common theme of apocalyptic with respect to the end-time. Chapter 16:21-22 uses the metaphor of a woman in labor, which takes its inspiration from the apocalyptic tradition. In the light of such texts, it can be convincingly argued that John's Gospel contains elements which can only be construed as a futurist eschatology. One may hesitate to describe this as an eschatology and prefer to interpret it as remnants of a tradition which have not been fully appropriated by the Gospel of John. This view is held commonly by exegetes since it seems to harmonize with the dominant concern of the Gospel which focuses so strongly on the eschatological dimension of present experience.

What is to be said of the Johannine view in relation to the other Christian Scriptures? Does John represent a radical departure from previous Christian writings in this regard? There is no doubt that the Gospel of John seems different in many ways. But in terms of its eschatology, it seems to reflect a shift of emphasis rather than a radical departure from the previous writings. John's realized eschatology is in harmony with his doctrine of the Spirit. For John, the Spirit is seen as the one who continues and completes the mission of Jesus among believers. Yet the primitive expectation of a future return of Jesus as Messiah and Judge is reflected not only in the Gospel of John (5:28) but also in *1 John* 2:28. Such future expectation is found in early texts such as *Acts* 3:12-26 as well as in late texts such as *2 Pt.* 3:1-13. The shift of emphasis found in John from future to present is noticed already in Paul, as we have seen above. The Pauline writings do not hesitate to speak of the present gift of the Spirit as a "down payment" against the future (2 Cor. 1:22; 5:5; Eph. 1:14). Such a shift of emphasis may well be related to the delay in the return of the Lord. In this respect, it would correspond to the development in the Christological reflection of the Scriptures which moves from a concern with the future functions of Christ to a more immediate concern for what he is doing at the present in the life of the community. Whatever the case may be, for Paul and more so for John, the old prophetic and apocalyptic notion of a future salvation has become inadequate because of what has been experienced in Jesus Christ: in his life, death, resurrection, and continued activity in the community. Therefore, salvation can no longer be described totally in future terms. What is experienced now in the present life of faith and grace is already "eternal life." Yet, John can continue to speak of hope (14:18.28; 17:1-26), for the possibilities of eternal life are not exhausted in the present experience. Clearly the term *eternal* as used here no longer has a directly temporal significance, but points to the quality of life as experienced in faith and grace. That qualitative dimension can be and is experienced at least in an initial way in the present life of the believer. In a context charged with a sense of the final hour and of the power of the antichrist, *1 John* writes in a manner that expresses this polarity:

> Beloved, we are God's children now; it does not yet appear what we shall be, but we know that when he appears we shall be like him, for we shall see him as he is. And everyone who thus hopes in him purifies himself as he is pure (3:2-3).

When this polarity of present and future, found so strikingly in John, is viewed in relation to the preaching of Jesus, it becomes clear that the evangelist is not creating "from nothing." Neither present nor future eschatology is a new product of the early Christian community. Both have their antecedent in the ministry of Jesus. If John may be taken as the best example of a "realized" eschatology, it must be pointed out immediately that this realized eschatology does not see the experience of salvation to be exhausted in our spatial-temporal experience. John's realized eschatology cannot be identified with any sort of immanent, this-worldly eschatology.

5. Other Apocalyptic Materials

a) The Synoptic Gospels and the Petrine Epistles

N. Perrin has argued that the pre-Synoptic Q-source is dominated by a certain kind of apocalyptic expectation in which the text of *Daniel* 7:13-14 served to interpret the person of Jesus as the Son of Man (Lk. 11:30; 12:8-9; 12:40; 17:26-30; Mt. 12:32; 12:40). It is not clear precisely how this identification of Jesus came to be made. Perrin holds that it very likely does not go back to a specific claim on the part of Jesus but to the community interpreting the resurrection in the light of *Psalm* 110:1 and *Daniel* 7:13-14. However it came about, the title served to express the hoped-for return of Jesus as Son of Man with power to execute eschatological judgment, thus lending this Christology a strongly apocalyptic tone.

In *Mark* 13 (par. Mt. 24; Lk. 21), we come nearer to the actual literary form of apocalyptic in the Synoptic Gospels. Somewhat lengthy speeches put into the mouth of Jesus provide detailed descriptions of the events to be expected before the coming of the end. Employing apocalyptic materials and style, these speeches attempt to explain what Jesus meant for Jerusalem, for his disciples, and for humanity in general. Together with predictions of coming perils and persecution, the evangelists exhort their readers to vigilance. It is possible to unravel the complexity of these texts by keeping in mind the two perspectives from which they seem to speak. On the one hand, they look to the coming of the Son of Man, whose arrival is not far off. In all the Synoptic Gospels, these highly apocalyptic speeches are presented as the final discourse of Jesus to his disciples before the tragic events of the final week of his life. Thus, his ministry is brought to a close by each of the Synoptists with warnings of the end.

The coming of the Son of Man refers to something that transcends the historical destruction of Jerusalem. The description of this and of the dire events which will precede it draws extensively on the imagery of the Hebrew Scriptures and the intertestamental apocalyptic tradition. The appeal to traditional cosmic metaphors of apocalyptic literature elicits the sense of the coming judgment. It is impossible to fix a time for this:

> But of that day or that hour no one knows, not even the angels in heaven, nor the Son, but only the Father. Take heed, watch; for you do not know when the time will come (Mk. 13:32-33).

Therefore, the urgent exhortation to vigilance:

> "And what I say to you I say to all: Watch" (Mk. 13:37).

The eschatology of the Q-material includes not only the warnings of judgment, but statements of consolation and hope as well (Mt. 10:28-31; Lk. 12, 2ff; Lk. 12:8-12). The so-called Q-apocalypse reflects some of the confusion that presumably affected the community when the parousia failed to materialize. Reports of false parousias are rampant, but Christians should not fall into deceptive certainty. The coming of the Son of Man will take place suddenly and will affect the entire world. Therefore, Christians should remain open to his future coming (Mt. 24:26-28; Mt. 24:40ff; Lk. 17:26ff).

Both the epistles attributed to Peter provide further instances of Christian apocalyptic material. In *1 Peter*, a strong baptismal theology (2:4-10; 3:21) stands together with a sense of the impending end. This epistle is the only Scriptural text which speaks of Christ's preaching to the "spirits in prison" (3:18-22). This text became the basis for the traditional idea of Christ's descent into hell. The tone of *2 Peter* likewise is strongly apocalyptic. This epistle contains the only Scriptural passage that speaks of a final conflagration of the universe (3:10). The idea of cosmic destruction is apparently taken from Persian sources which influenced the Greco-Roman world and the world of Judaic apocalyptic.

If the end events are so certain, why the delay? By appealing to

Psalm 89:4, the author shows how the mystery of divine transcendence can be used to deal with the problem of the delay of the parousia. If the realization of the promise seems to be coming very slowly, that is only a human perception of what, from the divine side, is the mystery of divine forbearance or patience. It is because God wishes that all should come to repentance that he has not acted as yet (3:9). In view of the fact that this world is to be dissolved and replaced with "new heavens and a new earth" (3:13), Christians ought to live in a way that is appropriate to that new order of things.

b) Revelation

The book that now stands at the end of the Christian canon, the *Revelation to John*, is the only book of the Christian Scriptures which is, in its entirety and consistently, apocalyptic in nature. Its acceptance into the canon has had its own strange history, probably because of the literary peculiarities of its apocalyptic style. And even though it is recognized as canonical and its texts have fed the Christian liturgical tradition over many centuries, yet the book remains a puzzle.

Probably more than in any other canonical Christian writing, this book rivets the attention of the reader on the crisis and judgment that is to come. But for all its concern with the end-time and the wealth of symbolism with which that is treated, the author never suggests a precise temporal calculation of those climactic events. Here as elsewhere in the Scriptures the emphasis is on the suddenness, inevitability, and surprising character of the end. This is usually suggested by the simple statement that the Lord "will come like a thief" (Rev. 16:15).

The mysterious figure of the "Son of Man" from the book of Daniel (7:13) is identified with the Christ of the parousia and the final judgment. The use of this figure is explicit in *Revelation* 14:14. It is developed further in chapters 19 and 20 where the parousia is described as a massive conflict in which Christ is victorious over the Beast and the false prophet. The Christ of the parousia is depicted as warrior and judge (19:11-16) whose victory involves the defeat of all powers inimical to the rule of God, up to and including the final enemy—death and Hades (20:14).

The final battle is divided into two phases. The first is followed by a thousand years in which Satan will be chained and Christ will reign with those who had been executed for their witness to him (20:2-6). Drawing on the apocalyptic tradition, John sees their sacrifice to be vindicated by a resurrection. This is the first resurrection and refers only to the martyrs of the faith. It is distinguished from a second resurrection which involves "the rest of the dead" (20:5), and which is placed after the thousand years. Here for the first time there is an unambiguous reference to the general resurrection of the dead.

The final battle between the power of good and the power of evil (19:11—20:10) and the final judgment (19:11-12) issues in eschatological salvation (21:1-8). As presented by John, this is a vision of life centered around the throne of God and the Lamb. When the final enemies have been overcome, God will create a "new heaven and a new earth" (21:1); for God alone "will make all things new" (21:5). There will be a new Jerusalem coming down from above (21:2). Adding metaphor to metaphor, John moves to a play on the Mosaic covenant-formula:

> Behold, the dwelling of God is with men. He will dwell with them, and they shall be his people, and God Himself will be with them; he will wipe away every tear from their eyes, and death shall be no more, neither shall there be mourning nor crying nor pain any more, for the former things have passed away (21:3-4).

Thus the final book of the Christian Scriptures envisions the eschatological fulfillment of the ancient covenant. The new and glorious Jerusalem, the hope of the exilic and post-exilic prophets, is here described in all its splendor, reflecting the glory of God (21:9—22:5). Through a rich variety of allusions, the Mosaic and prophetic traditions are here transformed in the light of the conviction that God has acted with eschatological decisiveness in the person of Jesus Christ. The judgment is the final and decisive realization of God's victory over evil through his Servant, Jesus. The parousia is the expression of the final vindication of God's eschatological act in Jesus. History will find its consummation in God, in the saving presence of Christ, and in the completion of that which was begun in the resurrection of Jesus of Nazareth. Far from being a message of despair, the book of Revelation is, above all, a summons to hope in God's ultimate victory.

6. Conclusions on the Christian Development

From this survey of the Christian Scriptures, it is possible to draw a number of conclusions of basic importance for the systematic understanding of Christian eschatology.

1) The central factor in the Christian understanding of human life and destiny is the life, death, and resurrection of Jesus Christ. It is from the perspective of this mystery that the Christian community reinterprets the tradition of Judaism in the creation of the Christian Scriptures. The unity of the life, death and resurrection of Jesus is the point of departure for the distinctively Christian revelation. It is, therefore, of normative significance for Christian eschatology. The analysis of this point of departure makes it clear that Christian eschatology must embrace the questions about human destiny both at the individual and at the collective level. It must deal with the question of human hopes in relation to all that makes up human life in its spiritual and corporal dimensions.

2) Christian eschatology, from the beginning, has been characterized by a tension between the present and the future. The experience of faith and grace in the present is already an experience of eschatological reality. But the mystery of grace is not completely realized in any historical experience. There remains a future fulfillment which is the object of hope. This tension between the present experience of grace and the future fulfillment of grace in the Kingdom must remain as a dimension of Christian eschatological awareness throughout history.

3) It would be a caricature to envision the early Christian community as nothing more than a Jewish apocalyptic sect whose members simply sat waiting for the final events that would bring history to an end.[12] That apocalyptic expectation was an influential factor in the development of Christian consciousness cannot be doubted. But to argue that all of Christianity can be accounted for in those terms is to take a step not warranted by the textual evidence.

---

[12]McGinn, *op. cit.*, pp. 30-31. Against such monolithic views as those of Käsemann, Werner, and Perrin, McGinn points out that the textual evidence supports the claim that early Christianity was "highly complex, socially and intellectually, from the start." As we have seen in our study of the texts, apocalyptic elements are found both early and late. Likewise, non-apocalyptic views are found in the thelogy of the synoptic Gospels at an early stage and in the late Johannine literature. If the dictum of Käsemann that "apocalyptic was the mother of all Christian theology" is to be given any credence, it must be significantly modified. K. Koch agrees with this assessment in *The Rediscovery of Apocalyptic* (Naperville, 1970) p. 73ff.

4) The Christ-mystery, taken in its fullness, is the basis for the Christian vision of a future that transcends historical experience. The future which awaits humanity lies ultimately in the hands of God. This vision of a transcendent future, which has historical roots in Jewish apocalyptic but is determined decisively by the resurrection of Jesus, can be distinguished from apocalypticism with its tendency to speculate on the details of the end-events of history. Christian eschatology lives from the conviction that the history of the world can reach its fulfillment only in communion with God and that it will be brought to this fulfillment by its incorporation into Christ who embodies God's promise to the human race.

•

In his perceptive summary of the biblical vision of history, D. Senior argues that the Scriptures communicate a dynamic view of world history. In this view, God leads history forward to a fulfillment, not backwards to a Golden Past nor pointlessly in circles. This sense of history and of eschatology becomes gradually more inclusive in nature. It includes not just Israel, and not just the Church of the Christian dispensation. The nations and even the cosmic powers will be caught up in the saving events of the end-time. Senior's summary remarks may serve as an appropriate synthesis of the developments we have followed during the course of these reflections on the Hebrew and Christian traditions:

> The biblical view of history is, in the final analysis, decisively optimistic. The final word is life, not death. The final action is gathering and fulfillment, not dispersal and frustration. This view of history, as apocalyptic literature made clear, is not naive. The march to the end-time involves bitter suffering and cataclysmic transformation. But the end is without doubt salvific, because God will have the last Word.[13]

[13]Senior-Stuhlmueller, *op. cit.*, p. 340.

Readings

Barrett, C.K., *The Gospel according to St. John* (SPCK, London, 1955, 1978²).

Brown, R., *The Gospel according to John,* 2 vols. (Doubleday, Garden City, N.Y., 1966, 1970).

Fiorenza, F.S., *Foundational Theology: Jesus and the Church* (Crossroad, New York, 1984).

Hamerton-Kelly, R., *God the Father: Theology and Patriarchy in the Teaching of Jesus* (Fortress Press, Philadelphia, 1979).

Jeremias, J., *The Prayers of Jesus* (A.R. Allenson, Naperville, 1967).

Kasper, W., *Jesus the Christ* (Paulist Press, London/Naperville, 1976).

O'Collins, G., *Interpreting Jesus* (Paulist Press, London/Ramsey, N.J., 1983).

Patrides, C.A., & Wittreich, J., *The Apocalypse in English Renaissance Thought and Literature* (Cornell University Press, Ithaca, N.Y., 1984).

Perkins, P., *Resurrection: New Testament Witness and Contemporary Reflection* (Doubleday, Garden City, N.Y., 1984).

Perrin, N., *The Kingdom of God in the Teaching of Jesus* (Westminster Press, Philadelphia, 1963).

Schillebeeckx, E., *Jesus: An Experiment in Christology,* tr. H. Hoskins (Crossroad, New York, 1981; reprint of 1979 translation).

Schnackenburg, R., *God's Rule and Kingdom* (Herder & Herder, New York, 1963).

Senior, D. & Stuhlmueller, C., *Biblical Foundations of Mission* (Orbis Press, Maryknoll, N.Y., 1983).

3

PHILOSOPHICAL BASIS FOR SYSTEMATIC ESCHATOLOGY

In the two previous chapters, we have outlined the development of hope as it is found in the biblical tradition. Our attempt was, first, to uncover the historical roots of Christian hope in Jewish history and, second, to study the form that hope takes in Christianity itself because of the impact of the person and ministry of Jesus Christ on Christian faith. Our concern was principally with the history of a religious form of hope. As such, it is a hope that is ultimately grounded in God and not in the power of positive human thought. It is a hope that the final outcome of human life and history will be positive not because of any particular convictions about the nobility of humanity but because of convictions about the fidelity of the God of life.

Four decades ago, Yves Congar spoke of the shift from a physical style to a more anthropological style of eschatology.[1] By this he meant that the older form of Scholastic and neo-Scholastic eschatology was largely concerned with depicting the last events of history and the geography of the world beyond this one, whereas the tendency of contemporary theology is to see eschatology principally in terms of the fulfillment of God's creative intent in humanity and in the world of God's creation. The primary focus of such reflection is not on the

---

[1] Yves Congar, "Fins derniers," in: *Revue de Sciences Philosophiques et Theologiques* 33 (1949) pp. 463-484.

nature of the final "things," but on the final, life-giving, fulfilling relation between God and humanity, and through humanity, with the
world.

Since this is the case, the primary concern of this style of theology
becomes the problem of anthropology, that is, the problem of human
nature in itself, in its relation to the rest of the created order, and in its
relation with God. If there is something in the very structure of human
nature that serves as the basis for hope in its human forms, then that
element may be seen as the deep point to which the word of divine
promise is addressed. To the extent that this may be established, it
would become possible to see the biblical hope in a divinely promised
fulfillment as a religious horizon within which we can more appropriately understand and interpret the ordinary human hopes from which
we live on a daily basis.

That there is a profound difference between the hope to which the
Gospel summons the believer and a human person's hope for success
in a career cannot be denied. The question is whether there is any
positive relation between them. If there is such a positive relation, then
it would be possible to see in what sense Christian hope sheds meaningful light on our common human experience of hope. If, on the other
hand, no such relationship can be ascertained then the message of the
Gospel does not resonate with the deep desires of the human heart,
and Christian eschatology will be nothing other than a collection of
arcane information about another world, or apocalyptic speculations
about the end of this world. Raising this sort of question forces us to
probe more deeply into the human source of the phenomenon of hope.
For most forms of contemporary theology, if we can speak of the
human source of hope in any form, that source is to be located in some
understanding of human self-transcendence. It is to this question that
we now turn our attention. We shall pursue this question by discussing
the following points of anthropology: The phenomenon of human
self-transcendence; the temporal-historical context in which human
self-transcendence is carried out; the relational character of human
nature expressed in the actualization of human self-transcendence.

1. Anthropological Reflections

a) The Phenomenon of Human Transcendence

It has long been a conviction of Christian theology that the human person is, in its deepest reality, a radical openness to the mystery of God. Augustine gave this conviction classical expression when he wrote: "Thou has made us for Thyself, and our hearts are restless until they rest in Thee."[2] For Augustine, the whole of life appeared to be a search for the mystery of God carried out in the search for the truth, goodness, and beauty of reality in the created world. Since created beings are but limited participations in the mystery of being, the desire of the human heart is never stilled by them. No matter how much we may be filled with created goods, the dynamism of the human heart impels us beyond them to the mystery of God. In his *Discourses on Psalm 127*, this master of the spiritual journey distinguished between the more superficial desires reflected in human experience and the deeper, perhaps even unconscious desire that impels us on our journey through life. Imagine that God said to you that you could have anything you want in the world. You may have all the pleasure, honor, power, and wealth that you want. Nothing would be forbidden to you, and nothing you do would be a sin. You may have all this not only for a brief time, but forever. Only one condition is attached to this. You will never see God's face. "Why is your heart struck when you hear 'You shall never see my face'?" If you abound in the goods and pleasures of this world, what more do you desire? Augustine answers: "One thing I ask of the Lord, and only this do I seek: that I might dwell in the house of the Lord all the days of my life."[3]

We can easily recogize the fact that there are desires which impel us to seek human fulfillment in the world. It is when we become aware that there is a more profound desire that leaves us unsatisfied regardless of the human satisfaction we may find in wealth, power, or success that we recognize what Augustine sees as the hidden desire for God. In our deepest heart, we are made for God and desire God, even though we may not be consciously aware of this. Following the direction

[2] *Confessions*, I, 1 (PL 32 661).
[3] *Enarratio in Ps. CXXVII*, 9 (PL 37 1682).

indicated by our superficial desires may give us a sense of meaning in the short run. But it does not make our lives meaningful in the long run. We are created for God, and the emptiness of our spirit can be touched most deeply only by the mystery of God. Humanity is engaged in a search for meaning and fulfillment, but it can never reach this goal unless it moves out of itself and beyond itself to God. Transcendence beyond the limiting world of the self and beyond the limiting world of created goods which we tend to gather around ourselves is the indispensable condition for finding the fullness which our heart desires most deeply.

This religious, theological conviction expresses a truth about human nature which is reflected in a number of diverse ways in contemporary thought, though it is given different forms of interpretation. Jean-Paul Sartre sees a movement of human transcendence emerging out of human freedom. Through its power of self-transcendence, humanity invests a meaningless world with some degree of meaning. Sartre sees the entire human effort to create a world of meaning as a human attempt to become God. Since, for Sartre, the existence of God is impossible, he concludes that the phenomenon of human self-transcendence reveals that human nature is but a useless passion.[4]

Where the philosophy of Sartre differs fundamentally from the religious understanding of humanity is not in any denial of self-transcendence but in the interpretation given to this phenomenon. Sartre's thought is indeed a philosophy of the absurd. On the one hand, in recognizing the movement of human transcendence, Sartre detects a dimension of human experience that is remarkably similar to the dynamic which theistic faith sees as the basis for speaking of God and of hope. On the other hand, because of the interpretation given to this dynamic, human existence for Sartre must remain forever without meaning. Human beings do, indeed, hope. But hope is forever doomed to frustration.

Sartre's compatriot and contemporary, Gabriel Marcel, analyzes the human situation in dramatically different terms. Rejecting any form of mechanistic determinism or pure empiricism as a fatal error,[5]

---

[4]J.P. Sartre, *Being and Nothingness*, tr. H.E. Barne (New York, 1956) p. 566ff.

[5]For the following reflections on Marcel, cfr. G. Marcel, *Homo Viator: Introduction to a Metaphysic of Hope*. tr. E. Crauford (N.Y., 1962). This is a reprint of a translation originally published by Victor Gollanz, Ltd., London & Henry Regnery, Chicago, in 1951.

Marcel concentrates his thought on the mystery of personal relations. The mistake of empiricism is the belief that human existence is so completely determined that its future course can be charted exactly on the basis of the accumulated "wisdom" of the past. In contrast with this, Marcel points out that it is precisely in the context of human relations that we discover the reality and the unpredictability of freedom. Since unpredictability makes it impossible to know the future in any real sense, freedom is the basis for the expectation that something "more" and something "new" might emerge out of the creativity of human relations. Because of freedom, reality is unpredictable. And because reality is unpredictable, there can be hope and expectation. Hope, then, is grounded in freedom. Hope is born of the realization that the true potential of human existence cannot be known simply on the basis of past experience. On the contrary, hope is the living conviction that past and present reality are laden with the potential for something more and unpredictable. While Sartre saw freedom as a useless passion, Marcel sees it as the revelation that reality is open-ended. This open-ended character of reality is the home of genuine hope.

Marcel's analysis begins with the experience of individual human relations. In such relations we discover the meaning of fidelity, trust, and hope. As qualities of human relations, these are first directed to particular persons. But the deeper such qualities are experienced, the less they can be understood in relation to specific objects and goals. What does one truly expect from a loving relation with another person? This is not simply a question of rights and demands that I make on a person. Nor is it simply a question of what I hope to get out of a relationship for myself. It is above all a question of what can be expected for both people involved in the relationship. As Marcel writes, the most adequate expression of the act of hope is: "I hope in thee for us."[6] What emerges out of a deep human relationship is more than two people standing side by side. It is the experience of a communion of persons that is both more intimate and richer in quality than a mere juxtaposition of persons. It is, indeed, a new reality, a new level of being. It is to this new depth of being that hope is directed.

The possibility of hope may be seen in every experience of com-

---

[6]*Homo Viator*, p. 60.

munion and renewal in human life. Such experiences strike sympathetic vibrations deep in the human heart where there is rooted the desire for something completely new. Thus, the movement of hope, first experienced in a one-to-one human relationship, pushes beyond this level to define our relation to reality as such. Marcel writes:

> We might say that hope is essentially the availability of a soul which has entered intimately enough into the experience of communion to accomplish in the teeth of will and knowledge the transcendent act—the act establishing the vital regeneration of which this experience affords both the pledge and the first-fruits.[7]

At this point Marcel makes an important distinction between specific acts of hope and what he calls an absolute hope. Although hope is first experienced in specific acts directed to particular objects, it pushes beyond this, as we have just seen. Hope begins to define our relation to reality as such. When we ask about the ground of particular acts of hope, we can point to experiences of renewal in human life. But when we ask about the ground of absolute hope, we cannot answer this question in terms of specific experiences, since each experience of renewal pushes beyond itself in hope for more. Absolute hope is not a specific act of hope but a fundamental attitude that expresses itself in each specific act of hope. Absolute hope is hope for the meaning of life as such. Can there be hope for the renewal of life as such? To ask about the ground of hope at this level is to inquire about absolute hope as a response to an infinite Being, for the ground of absolute hope can only be a deathless source of power and meaning that can be trusted absolutely.[8]

With this, the relation between the question of hope and the question of God becomes explicit. If particular acts of hope are based in a deeper and absolute hope, then the question of hope is the question of the final meaning and validity of human life. That question is implied in every human act of hope. And that is precisely the question of God. Is there a ground of the absolute hope for meaning? Or is that hope itself the ultimate illusion? The parallel between this analysis and the Abraham-tradition is clear. The hope of the biblical hero is directed to

---

[7] *op. cit.*, p. 67.
[8] *op. cit.*, p. 47.

a shifting array of specific objects, but that hope is ultimately grounded in the promise of God. Each specific act of hope is the expression of a more radical religious attitude: hope in the infinite source of life and goodness. Thus, Marcel's analysis points to the possibility of a positive relation between the common experiences of human hope and the radical hope of the biblical tradition. Only if the specific acts of human hope are seen in relation to the underlying attitude of which they are the concrete expression are they seen in terms of their deeper meaning.

Placing the thought of Sartre and Marcel side by side reveals important aspects of human experience and human hope. How is it possible that two people so close in place and time can arrive at such fundamentally different visions of human life? It is clear that both philosophers are reflecting on the same phenomenon of human self-transcendence. Why does one arrive at a philosophy of the absurd and the other at a metaphysic of hope?

This dramatic difference in understanding points to the basic ambiguity of human experience. Is reality basically good and trustworthy? Or is life pointless and meaningless in the final analysis? There are no definitive answers to such questions. Human experience is a web of good and evil. There are positive signs that might lead one to believe that, at root, things are in good order. There are, just as truly, negative signs that incline one to wonder whether, in the final analysis, it really makes any difference what we try to make of our lives. Sartre places primary emphasis on the negative signs; Marcel on the positive. In either case, we are dealing with a form of philosophical faith since experience is never clear enough to make a decision that can be fully justified in terms of reason. In the case of Sartre, philosophical faith takes the form of atheistic nihilism. Human self-transcendence is the final irony. For Marcel, self-transcendence expresses itself in hope. But hope itself can be seen as meaningful only within the context of a theistic world-view. For only if hope opens human life to a deathless source of being and meaning is absolute hope a viable position rather than a mere psychological mechanism that makes life appear to be more bearable. Is human transcendence ultimately open to Nothingness or to life-giving Fullness? The polarity of Sartre and Marcel is a polarity that lies within each human being. No fully rational answer can be given to this question. Hence, if there is hope—and there is—hope arises not out of clarity and unassailable evidence but out of deep ambiguity.

No name in contemporary philosophy appears with such frequency in discussions of hope as that of Ernst Bloch. This is fully understandable, for Bloch, more than any other philosopher, has placed the phenomenon of hope in the very center of philosophy. Bloch's work is inspired by the Marxist understanding of religion as the "opium of the people." It is from this perspective that Bloch undertakes a phenomenological study of the world of human dreams, fantasy, and imagination as this is reflected in the personal world of day-dreams and night-dreams and in the public world of literature, art, and culture.[9]

From these rich resources which express so much about humanity in its historical struggles, Bloch concludes that the phenomenon of hope reaches into the very depths of human reality and reveals to us the most profound nature of human existence. The human person is one who dreams of a future, who hopes for it, and who strives to attain it. Hope reveals the nature of human existence as a "being on the way." Human nature, in its inner depths, is open-ended; it is directed to a future which does not yet exist. Hope is the expression of the incompleteness of humanity. It is that attitude which refuses to let the past and the present define the limits of human existence. Hope breaks open the present and drives humanity to the future. The most fundamental truth about human existence is, in Bloch's view, the fact that we are beings who hope. Humanity, in its empirical forms, is incomplete. What it is to be must be brought about in history.

If this anthropological insight is taken as a clue concerning the nature of the world, it means that the whole of created reality is incomplete. Humanity and the world in which it lives must be brought to completion. To speak of incompleteness in this sense means that in its concrete form, human nature is alienated from its truest essence; for its essence lies in the future as something that has never existed up to now. Hope is grounded, in Bloch's analysis, in the real difference between that which humanity now is (=existence) and that which it is

---

[9]The major work of Bloch is his massive, three-volume study, *The Principle of Hope* (Cambridge, Mass., 1986). Although not available in English until recently, it has been an influential source for those interested in Bloch's thought, particularly in the context of the Christian-Marxist discussions during the 1960s. For other English material, cfr. E. Bloch, *Man on His Own: Essays in the Philosophy of Religion*, tr. E.B. Ashton (N.Y., 1970). Here Bloch treats the central themes elaborated in *The Principle of Hope* such as apocalypse, utopia, the mystery of humanity, death and transcendence.

to be in the future (=essence). This alienation can be overcome only through human action in history, action which is an aggressive participation in the process of building the world. Humanity is alienated not from its eternal origin in God, nor from some Golden Age of the past, but from its true essence which does not yet exist. It is through hope in its myriad forms that humanity expresses its active desire to overcome its historical alienation. Hope is the seed-bed of social revolutions.

Hope may be basic to human existence, but hope can take two quite different forms. In its most authentic meaning, as Bloch argues, hope is active and aggressive. The painful disproportion between reality as it now is and as it could be ought to impel people to make every effort to change the world in which they live. In this sense hope directs people to active participation in the cultural, social, and political processes to make the world more suitable for human life.

It is possible, however, that hope can have precisely the opposite effect. It can readily become the rationale for passivity and resignation in the face of the pain and tragedy of human experience. This happens particularly when hope is related to a transcendent God who is thought to be the source of fulfillment. This is the problem referred to by Karl Marx when he called religion the "opium of the people." In Bloch's view, this, indeed, is a problem with the historical form of Christianity as it has been known at least in Western Europe. The God of the familiar Christian churches keeps his distance from any genuine revolutionary tendencies in society. Historical Christianity has betrayed its own initial inspiration. The true significance of Christian hope lies in its original explosive messianism. This has been lost by too much lip-service and ecclesiastical compromise. When Christianity created a transcendent, divine being and took this to be the ground of its hope, it undercut its own power for social change and became the reinforcement of human alienation. Since this sort of heavenly transcendence is an impediment to achieving an authentic sense of human responsibility, it must be done away with. The essential meaning of that so-called "heavenly being," as Bloch sees it, is nothing but the unknown future of humanity. Human transcendence must be directed to this world and not to some other world. Human hope expresses the awareness that the present world is open to a better and more humane possibility. To make that possibility a reality is the project of hope.

As a Christian theologian, K. Rahner employs the entire arsenal of transcendental philosophy to analyze the meaning of human self-transcendence.[10] In Rahner's analysis, the human person is seen to have an innate power to move outward from the center of individual existence to draw other persons and things into a living relation with itself. Self-transcendence is experienced in an ongoing dialogue between the individual human person and the world of persons and things surrounding the individual. Through his analysis of the questioning that undergirds the human quest for meaning and fulfillment, Rahner sees human nature to be a dynamism that places us on a journey of discovery and meaning. But in every specific goal reached on the journey is present the seed of something more. The human person, with its mind and will, is not a neutral potential capable of finding meaning and fulfillment in anything at all. On the contrary, it is dynamically oriented to the mystery of the Absolute and can find its genuine fulfillment only in that mystery. In every experience by which we move out to the world of finite reality in search of truth and goodness, we are drawn by the magnetic pull of the Absolute, which Rahner identifies with God. The experience of life as a journey in search of meaning and fulfillment reveals the unfinished nature of human reality. Because we experience ourselves as incomplete, we can hope for completion. In Rahner's analysis, hope is encountered empirically whenever we turn our expectation of fulfillment to some particular object, person, or project. Such empirical hopes, he calls categorical hopes. But, if it is ultimately the Absolute to which we are drawn, it is the Absolute that is the ground of that abiding hopefulness that undergirds all specific acts of hope. This abiding attitude is called transcendental hope. Thus, from a different point of departure and through a different form of philosophical analysis, Rahner arrives at a distinction similar to that of Marcel. Hope is not limited to specific acts directed to particular objects. On the contrary, all specific acts of hope flow from a deeper level of what Rahner calls transcendental hope, and what Marcel calls absolute hope. In both instances, the most basic meaning of hope is related to the hope for the fulfillment of our existence as such, and not

---

[10]Rahner's original philosophical analysis is available in his early work, *Spirit in the World* (N.Y., 1968) and *Hearers of the Word* (N.Y., 1969).

For background on the question of transcendental method and on Rahner in particular, cfr. A. Carr, *The Theological Method of Karl Rahner* (Missoula, Mont., 1977); R. Kress, *A Rahner Handbook* (Atlanta, Ga., 1982); O. Muck, *The Transcendental Method* (N.Y., 1968); L. Roberts, *The Achievement of Karl Rahner* (N.Y., 1967); K.H. Weger, *Karl Rahner: An Introduction to his Theology* (N.Y., 1980).

hope for success in specific projects or human programs.

Each of these philosophers has reflected on human self-transcendence. Each raises the issue of hope as a human phenomenon. That human beings hope is an undeniable fact. If we allow for the distinction made by Marcel and Rahner between every-day hopes and a deeper, abiding hope, it is not necessary to argue that all human beings experience hope at the every-day level, or that all people hope at that level to the same degree and at all times of their lives. A quality of hope may exist in the background of a life, which—on the surface—appears to be a hopeless existence. Hope is a human phenomenon before we ever raise the question of the bible and its particular vision of hope.

Whether hope is merely a mechanism that functions to make a painful existence somehow bearable as might be concluded from Sartre, or whether hope is a dynamism that opens human life to a fulfillment that transcends present experience, as suggested by Marcel, Bloch, and Rahner remains an issue of radical faith, either of a philosophical or of a religious sort. It is impossible to take up one's life and live it in any way without saying—at least implicitly and at an existential level—that one hopes to gain something from the endeavor. Yet the evidence of life-experience is never sufficiently clear to render a judgment on the matter that can be fully validated rationally.

Hope is a human phenomenon that needs to be reflected on. Hope appears as a fundamental attitude, a way of transcending the limits of present experience. It lends itself to a range of interpretations among which the biblical tradition is one of great religious and human importance. If the great metaphors of biblical hope can be seen in relation to the deeply human forms of hope, then theological eschatology can become a way of interpreting human hope in its deepest and most radical dimensions. The question of hope becomes a truly eschatological question when we ask: What can we hope for in the face of death for ourselves as individuals, and for the human family as a whole? Is death the final limit to human hope? Or can we hope for a fulfillment that transcends even the limit of death? This is the question of hope that emerges from human experience in the world.

We may describe human life as a questioning hope, a hope for fulfillment that is never finally answered within our historical experience. There is good reason to conclude from this that human nature possesses an inner ear which is ready and waiting to hear a word of divine promise such as that spoken through the biblical tradition. The fact that there is an inner organ ready to receive a message does not mean that we could have devised the message by ourselves. It is truly a word of God. But because we possess a receptive organ for that word, when the word is spoken in history, it does not come to us as something totally foreign to our human experience. Instead, it speaks to the deepest roots of what we are as human beings in history.

b) Time and Historicity

This analysis of the quest for meaning in human life is based on the conviction that, as human beings, we are capable of knowing and loving reality, but that we do not do so from the start. We can choose to become a particular sort of person, but we are not that sort of person from the beginning. To exist as a human person is to be engaged in a process of becoming. To experience ourselves as "becoming" is to realize that we are not in full possession of our complete reality. We are spread out on a time-line of past—present—future within a world of persons and objects that interacts with us at a number of levels.

This complex structure of factors that condition us—time, persons, things—may be called simply *historicity*. Our quest for meaning and fulfillment is essentially a process carried out in time. Time and historicity, therefore, are intrinsic to our existence as incomplete beings in the world. Human transcendence is essentially a transcendence experienced within time. Some reflections on time and historicity, therefore, are important in understanding the deeper roots of hope as a human phenomenon.

What is time? This question has puzzled philosophers over the centuries. Augustine is an interesting case to the point.

> What, then, is time? If no one asks me, I know; if I want to explain it to someone who does ask me, I do not know. Yet I state confidently that I know this: if nothing were passing away, there would be no past time, and if nothing were coming, there would be no future time, and if nothing existed, there would be no present time.[11]

[11]*Confessions*, XI, 14:17ff (PL 32 815ff). For a challenging analysis of the text of Augustine,

How is it possible to speak of time? The past no longer exists, and the future does not yet exist. Only the present moment seems to exist in reality. And it is the very nature of the present moment that it must pass into the past; for if it did not, then it would no longer be time but eternity. Faced with the paradox of time, the sceptics of antiquity denied the very existence of time. This Augustine could not accept. On the other hand, the ordinary perception of time at the level of everyday experience cannot be accepted at face value.

In his reflection on time, Augustine set out on a path that would be taken by many later philosophers, including Husserl, Heidegger, Merleau-Ponty, and Rahner. This reflection on the nature of time is important for our understanding of the historicity of human existence as well as for our understanding of the dynamic of eschatological language. Therefore we will look in some detail at Augustine's analysis and at its relationship to contemporary eschatology.

Paul Ricoeur speaks of Augustine's insight into the puzzle of time as a "stroke of genius."[12] In what does this insight consist? This may be best illustrated by pointing out that Augustine is keenly aware of the inadequacy of the ordinary understanding of time which sees it in very physical terms, or which follows Aristotle in defining time as the measure of motion and change. There is such a thing as objective time which can be measured by clocks and calendars. But as long as we think of time exclusively as an objective reality outside human experience, we have not come close to understanding its nature as a philosophical problem. At this level, as we have seen in the quote above, the past does not exist in any physical sense. Neither does the future. There is only the present moment. There is always only the present moment in physical reality. This is why the sceptics could reject the experience of time as an illusion.

Some insight into this problem appears when, with Augustine, we turn to the interior world of human experience. Rather than think of time as a quantitative reality, we now think of it more as a quality of human experience. For it is primarily in the world of interior human experience that we experience the flow of time as a movement from past to present to future.

cfr. P. Ricoeur, *Time and Narrative*, vol. 1, tr. K. McLaughlin & D. Pellauer (Chicago/London, 1984) pp. 5-30.

[12] *Time and Narrative*, p. 16.

If it is true to say that, in terms of physical time, only the present moment really exists, the same does not seem to be true in the human, psychological experience of time. In the psychological realm, human experience makes it clear that, in some way, an event which is physically past truly lives on in the human spirit. The present moment of my experience does not exist independently of the past events of my experience. In a very significant sense, the past is present to me even now. The physical reality of the past is converted into the spiritual reality of *memory*. In the form of memory, the past becomes present reality in the human subject. The past is not simply gone in its physical reality. Its real impact on the soul lives on in my present experience. The soul is, as it were, stretched out beyond the present physical moment to embrace within itself all the present moments that have become past. The experience of past and present as a flow of time is, for Augustine, a sort of "distention" of the soul. The soul is present to itself *now* in terms of the *past* retained in it in the form of memory.

But what of the future? It does not yet exist in any physical sense. Therefore, it cannot be dealt with in the same way as the past is dealt with, that is, in terms of memory. We cannot retain in memory something that we have not yet experienced. Augustine deals with the future in terms of *expectation*. As the past impinges on present experience in the form of memory, the possibilities of the future impinge on the present in the form of expectation. As memory distends the soul "backward" to embrace the past, expectation distends the soul "forward" to anticipate future possibilities. As the past is present in the form of memory, the future is present in the form of expectation.

Memory and expectation, then, are dimensions of present experience. The experience of time, in Augustine's analysis, might be described as the experience of a three-layered present. The present moment is never simply the present as this can be measured on the clock. It is a present that is internally shaped by the past that lives as present in the spiritual power of memory. But it is a present that does not allow the past to be the final measure of what can be; for then the past would become a prison from which no escape is possible. By opening itself to a future in expectation, the soul opens itself to the possibility of moving beyond the limitations of the past to something new and unpredictable. Human existence, then, is an existence in the present, from the past, and for the future.

Augustine uses one, simple technical term to express this understanding of time. Time, he writes, is nothing other than a *distentio animi*. In this way, he shifts our attention from the cosmological dimensions of time and views it as a distinctly human phenomenon.

> ...it seemed to me that time is nothing more than distention: but of what thing I know not ... if it is not of the mind itself.[13]

This insistence on the fact that time includes both past and future in the present is an important step in the history of Christian thought. It represents a decisive break from the ancient Greek notion of time and history as basically cyclic in nature. It creates a frame-work within which Augustine, as a theologian, would be able to deal with some of the most basic concerns of the Judaeo-Christian tradition: that humanity is not merely the victim of fates but the creator of history; and that within history, there are distinctive historical events which bear ultimate meaning for humanity. Such events, which have happened "once for all" (Rm. 6:9), still can be said to have universal significance. Important both for philosophy and for theology, this movement into interiority allows us to understand time in its distinctively human qualities, and to understand that time and historicity are intrinsic to the very nature of humanity.

This excursion into the thought of Augustine is not only of historical interest. It also gives us an important key into the meaning of modern philosophies of time and historicity. As we have seen in the philosophical reflections above, the experience of human transcendence from which the reality of hope emerges is intrinsically tied into the human experience of being in time. To be in time is to be engaged in a movement toward completion. It is this movement from incompletion to completion that is carried out in the search for meaning which we have analyzed above. It is not only a search for cognitive insight, but a quest for the fullness of being which we do not yet possess.

As in Augustine's analysis, so in Rahner's the human person is the subject of time in a distinctive way. Not only are we in time, but we are conscious of being in time. Viewed from this perspective, the basic task of human life is to make sense of our present experience—for that is where we find ourselves—and to live authentically in the present. But, echoing the Augustinian analysis, Rahner argues that we cannot come

---

[13] *Confessions*, XI, 26 (PL 32 822).

to terms fully with the present without a two-fold extrapolation. There must be an extrapolation backward through which we become consciously aware of the real impact of the past on our present reality. Only when we see our present in terms of our past which has made the present can we come to terms with the present. This backward extrapolation Rahner calls *anamnesis*. This, of course, is the Greek term for memory. As Rahner uses the term, it designates not just the retention of abstract concepts drawn from past experiences, but the living presence of the past in the present. Similarly, there must be an extrapolation in the direction of the future, for neither past nor present can be seen adequately unless they are seen in terms of their potential for fuller and deeper existence and meaning. The present of human experience—made by a past—is open to a real future. Humanity can become something that it has not yet been. Thus, future possibilities bear on the present, and the future becomes essential in coming to terms with the meaning of the present. Therefore, Rahner concludes that, just as there must be a backward extrapolation from the present to the past, there must be a forward extrapolation from the present to the future. This projection he calls *prognosis*. Although it is not a genuine knowledge of the future, it is a form of anticipation of the possibilities that lie before us in the present. It is this forward projection that becomes basic to the understanding of hope and eschatology.

Time and history cannot be simply identified with the sort of temporal duration found in all the physical or biological phenomena of the world. Certainly time must be understood in a broad sense to include these cosmic dimensions. But in a particular sense, which may be derived from the Augustinian analysis and which is basic to Rahner's theology, time and history take on a distinctive significance precisely as human phenomena.

In this more specific sense, time might be described as the place in which human freedom exists, for it is in our relation to the past and the future that we discover the reality of human freedom. Conditioned by a past, we are yet not totally determined since we can take a position with respect to the past. This means we are capable of transcending the limits of the past, for we have already transcended them in taking a position about the past. Open to a future which is not predetermined, we have the task of freely choosing what kind of human being we shall become. We are ultimately responsible for ourselves. Our freedom to choose from among different courses of action is, in essence, the power to choose what sort of identity will be ours.

History as a human phenomenon is the space in which human freedom is worked out. In fact, history is precisely what comes to be through the exercise of human freedom. Humanity is a freedom poised between past and future. The past need not be a prison. It can become a spring-board from which we move into a future which, though rooted in the past, can yet bring forth something new which is not simply predictable from the past.

When we first think of the past, it appears to us in terms of the concrete persons and events that have preceded us. We have parents, grandparents, great-grandparents, etc. We have gone to this or that school. We have been influenced by some particular teacher. In this sense, the past is a chain of secondary causes that have influenced us for better or worse. But as we reflect on the past from a theological perspective, the question of the past is ultimately the question not about secondary causes but about the mystery from which we derive our existence as such. It is a question of our transcendental origin in God. Thus, theologically, the question of the past becomes the doctrine of creation. In a parallel fashion, the question of the future first appears as a series of particular projects, plans, and goals to be worked out in space and time. These are the categorical futures of which we have already spoken. The question of the future moves to yet another level when we ask: to what are we ultimately moving in all the day-to-day projects with which we fill our lives? Is human openness to the future something more than an openness to tomorrow and to next week? Is it finally an openness to a mystery of absolute fullness which both triggers and yet transcends all our human hopes? The question of the future, therefore, becomes the doctrine of eschatology. The Augustinian and Rahnerian analysis of time in terms of a triple-layered present corresponds to the ultimate theological interpretation of human, temporal reality which takes place in the theological symbols of creation and eschatology, the symbols of absolute origin and absolute future.

This reflection on the temporality of human existence might be taken as a response to the question raised at the beginning of this chapter. What is it in human nature that gives rise to hope in its variety of forms? To view human nature in terms of its temporality is to suggest that humanity as we experience it in the present is fundamentally incomplete. What we are at any given moment is a potential to become something more. It is the dynamic desire for the completion of our being that expresses itself in human dreams, hopes, and expectations. But hope presumes that we experience our present existence as something good. We would hardly be inclined to desire more of something that we experience as totally bad. But the good of the present is limited. There would be no reason to hope for more of what is essentially full and complete already. Because the good of the present is limited, we can envision removing the limits and maximizing the good.

To say that we are temporal beings is to affirm that we are really open to and actively inclined to a real future. Something lies ahead of us that does not really exist for us as yet. And that future reality is not just something external to our nature. It is, in fact, the full realization of the potential that our human nature is. The future-projections with which we fill our lives have as their real purpose the actualization of our full potential as human beings in the world. The categorical projections so familiar to us in our scientific, technological culture are the concern of what we know today as "futurology." The question of the ultimate and absolute future is the concern of the theological discipline known as "eschatology."

Standing before the mystery of its own existence, humanity is confronted by two radical options. Either the question of the ultimate meaning of human existence finds no answer, and human life empties into nothingness and annihilation; or the question finds an answer, but the answer cannot be identified with success in particular, categorical projects or human futures. Each of these represents a fundamental decision about the nature of reality which cannot, ultimately, be verified logically. In this sense, each position represents a form of faith. The first is a nihilistic form of faith similar to that of Sartre. It must eventually conclude that, even though human persons hope, ultimately reality is not trustworthy and it makes no sense to hope in anything but the success that can be found in day-to-day existence. And since finite things seem so often to betray us in our search for fulfillment, it may be that, finally, hope is the ultimate illusion. The second is a theistic form of faith. It believes that, even though our search for meaning may be frustrated over and over again in the course of our day-to-day life, ultimately the quest for meaning can open human life to a fulfillment that transcends all human projects. When asked to name the ground of confidence in the trustworthiness of reality, the theist will name that ground God. The question of God and the question of radical hope are inseparably intertwined. They are, in fact, two sides of the same question, that of the ultimate meaning of existence.

These philosophical reflections on human hope serve to indicate in what sense it is possible to say that hope is a profoundly human reality before we ever ask the question of biblical hope and Christian hope. In as far as hope springs from the incompleteness of human reality, it is a human expression of a hoped-for fulfillment. In as far as particular religious traditions hold out specific visions of such fulfillment, those traditions offer specific interpretations of a fundamentally human phenomenon. The biblical and Christian tradition, then, can be seen as that specific form of hope that has been awakened and shaped in human consciousness through God's interaction with the biblical people during the centuries of their history. The future that it holds open to human hope speaks to the deepest roots of what we are as human beings: incomplete, temporal beings who actively seek the completion of our being through our human, historical journey in search of meaning and fulfillment. The biblical tradition offers a word of divinely inspired revelation that is not at all extrinsic to our human aspirations but offers a larger framework within which we can interpret our more mundane hopes.

Modern critiques of religion are inclined to see the concepts of God and the symbols of eschatology as the alienating products of a projection-mechanism in immature human beings. These criticisms raise a serious question about the psychological dimensions of religion and about the intimate relation that exists between images of God and self-images of humanity. These questions must be reflected on seriously by theologians. But the projection-theories do not seem to give an adequate explanation of the deeper grounds of faith and hope. Even if one were to grant that hope is a pure projection-mechanism, it would still be necessary to ask why human nature is equipped with such a mechanism, and why such a mechanism does not disappear with the technological maturity of modern society. The answer to that sort of question would lead us to decisions about the fundamental nature of reality such as we have just discussed.

c) Relation

While it is true that we are individual persons, each with a personal, individual history, it is just as true to say that no person is totally his or her own creation. The search for meaning and fulfillment which constitutes the human, historical journey can be carried out only by an ongoing dialogue with other persons and things in the world around us. While it is true that there is an inner zone of personal consciousness that is inaccessible to any other human being, it is just as true to say that we cannot develop as individual persons without entering into relations with the world around us. The past, of which we have spoken above, is not merely an individual past. It is, in fact, the past that has been created by generations of humans before us. It is a world of human meaning that is mediated to us in our present reality as the collective history of humanity comes to bear on our present moment and profoundly conditions the kind of persons we are. The past of the individual includes and is included in the past of others. Similarly, the future of the individual includes and is included in the future of others.

This is but a way of saying that not only are we individuals, but we are profoundly social beings as well. In fact, we can find our true, individual identity only through the actualization of our social nature. The fulfillment of our individual existence is dependent on the way in which we attempt to live with this fact of our nature. Those who recognize their social nature and freely live in accordance with it freely accept and live out of that dynamic which is indispensable in achieving a full and authentic human life. Those who refuse to accept this as a fundamental truth of human nature opt for the myth of "rugged individualism." To believe that we can and must carry out the human quest for meaning and fulfillment by ourselves in isolation from others is to live an illusion. It is to attempt to live at the conscious level in a manner that is in fundamental contradiction with our nature.

If the eschatological issue is finally a question about our ultimate human destiny, then it must be seen not only in reference to individual destiny but in reference to the collective destiny of the human race as well. If there are grounds for arguing that Scholastic eschatology tended to over-emphasize the individual dimension of human destiny, the tendency to go in the opposite direction may well be a major temptation at the present time. The relational nature of humanity and its hope for the future can be brought to full expression only when eschatology deals both with the individual and the collective.

2. *Language of the Future and Eschatological Symbols*

If eschatology has to do not only with God and not only with the world, but with a future relation between the world and God which does not yet exist, the question of the referent of eschatological language is unavoidable. The point of this question can be seen more readily if we think of it in terms of the analysis of time given above. If the future is, by definition, something which does not yet exist, how can we *know* anything about it? And only if we can explain the knowledge-claims involved in any attempt to speak of the future can we come to a better understanding of the nature of eschatological language. For, in its own way, eschatological language intends to speak of the future.

This question takes on particular significance when it is viewed against the background of the modern critiques of Christianity. In a variety of ways, modern thought has seen religion in general, and Christianity in particular, as some form of projection which alienates humanity from its truest and best reality. Feuerbach had seen the Christian God as a projection of human goodness into a transcendent, untouchable being. When this sort of projection is made, humanity is left only with its evil and sinfulness to deal with. In as far as this God becomes the object of religion, religion is the expression of alienation from that which is best in humanity. Directly pertinent to the question of eschatology is the critique of Marx, who could describe religion as the opiate of the people largely because of the alienating impact of belief in life after death. One cannot be aware of the nature of these critiques without asking whether eschatological language is, after all, nothing but a chimera-like projection of a "nowhere."

a) *The Nature of Eschatological Language*

In the first section of this chapter we have attempted to deal with the dynamism from which human hope springs. Our concern was with the reality of human self-transcendence as this is actualized in history through dialogue with the world. We shall now attempt to draw out some of the implications of this analysis for our understanding of eschatological language.

As a very concise statement of the epistemological situation implied in this understanding of time, we suggest: We *know* the present in itself; we do not know the past in itself, but we *remember* it in the images of memory; we do not know the future in itself, but we *anticipate* the future in images drawn from past and present. The anticipation that undergirds language about the future draws its resources from the power of imagination which strives to break beyond the limits of past and present experience to a new level of realization.[14] In this sense, we can see how language about the future lives from past and present experience. The present, in which the past is gathered together, is the spring-board for the future. Any positive content in visions of the future is derived from the positive content of the present and is expanded to a better and fuller condition in the future. The good we experience in the present, stripped of all its limitations, commonly becomes our dream of the future.

Rahner has suggested a helpful key for a better understanding of eschatological language. It is a key that relates the issue of eschatological language directly to this understanding of time. "Eschatology is a forward look which is necessary to man for his spiritual decision in freedom, and it is made from the standpoint of his situation in saving history as this is determined by the Christ-event."[15] If this is taken as a fundamental principle, as Rahner suggests, it would have significant implications for the interpretation of eschatological language.

First, it is clear that this principle harmonizes fully with the analysis of time we have suggested above and with implications of that analysis for our understanding of human knowledge about the future. Any attempt to talk about the future can be carried out only from the present experience of humanity. We cannot "know" the future in the way we know the present. The language and images by which we speak of the future, whether a purely human future, or the eschatological future promised by God, can be drawn only from the present experience of humanity, which, as we have seen, is rooted in the history of the past. The sources from which eschatological language is drawn are to be found in the past and present experience of humanity,

---

[14]Cfr. J. Macquarrie, *Principles of Christian Theology* (N.Y., 1966), p. 219ff. Working with the concept of "heuristic anticipation," Polanyi sheds helpful light on this issue. Cfr. M. Polanyi, *Personal Knowledge: Towards a Post-Critical Philosophy* (Chicago, 1958) p. 195ff.

[15]K. Rahner, "Eschatology," in: *Encyclopedia of Theology: The Concise Sacramentum Mundi* (N.Y., 1975) p. 437. Also, the full *Sacramentum Mundi*, II (N.Y., 1968) p. 244.

and particularly in the history of revelation, which opens a specific form of hope to humanity.

Next, it is clear in Rahner's statement that he conceives the present experience of faith and grace as the *now* from which the believer looks to the future for the fulfillment of that grace which is experienced only in a limited degree in the present. Eschatology, therefore, is concerned with the redeemed person as that person is *now*. It is from this base that the believer "knows" what is to come. In as far as that which is to come is the final relation between the creature and God, it remains something fundamentally incomprehensible as the divinity itself is incomprehensible for the human mind. Viewed in this way, eschatology is not so much "knowledge" about future things as it is the "hopeful projection" of fulfillment of the mystery of grace experienced already now in human history.

A final point concerning this principle must be made. The present experience of grace is the experience of the mystery of salvation mediated by God through Jesus Christ. It is at this point that the eschatological question takes on a specifically Christian dimension. The Christian is conscious of the reality of grace as grace has been embodied in the life, death, and resurrection of Jesus Christ. Therefore, the projections of future fulfillment in Christian eschatology must be made in the light of the Christ-event. The eschatological future has been opened to us through the mystery of Christ. It is the explicit recognition of this that makes eschatology specifically Christian. From this it follows that the Christ-event in all its dimensions becomes normative for any understanding of the eschatological future.[16]

b) Eschatological Language as Non-Literal Discourse

As a general observation concerning eschatological language, it can be said that such language stands under the general principle of analogy operative in theology as a whole. Analogical language, as understood in the theological tradition, involves both a similarity and a dissimilarity between the terms of the analogy. At the very least, this means that eschatological language cannot be understood to be a literal description of the future.

[16]E. Schillebeeckx, "The Interpretation of Eschatology," in: *Concilium* 41 (1969) p. 53.

It has long been recognized that when we attempt to express our very deepest experiences and our primal relations with reality, human language begins to operate in strange ways. Classical theology had dealt with this peculiarity in terms of various theories of analogy. Modern philosophy of language has made us even more aware of the fact that, when we are dealing with the most fundamental questions of human life, the familiar logic of every-day language fails us; and our language begins to do unusual things as it is stretched beyond its normal range of meaning. Some of these strange things are represented in symbolic, metaphorical, and other types of non-literal language.[17]

According to the best understanding we have of the Scriptures, both from the history of the church's usage of the bible and from current exegetical studies, the religious meaning of the bible cannot be opened to us with any degree of adequacy unless we are aware of the extensive use of symbolic, metaphorical, and other forms of figurative language in the bible. The religious consciousness of Jews and Christians over the centuries has been shaped by a cluster of great metaphors. To read these as though they merely communicated a collection of historical data or a summa of doctrinal and moral statements would be to resort to a crude form of theological positivism. If the biblical language of the future is understood in relation to our earlier analysis of time, it becomes clear why especially this form of biblical language must be symbolic and metaphorical in nature. Such language evokes a vision of a future without ever being able to describe it specifically. To say that such language is metaphorical is not to imply that it talks about nothing. On the contrary, it is to say that—whatever the object of such language may be—the *mode* of discourse is not literal but figurative.

In summary, the language with which the Scriptures speak of the future is highly figurative in nature. Through its extensive use of symbols, similes, and metaphors the bible evokes a vision of a future fullness of being and meaning which can be found only in a rich network of relations. The meaning of these images takes us back to the very first pages of the Scriptures where the ideal human life is depicted as one of paradisal harmony between humanity and God and among

[17]Cfr. J.M. Soskice, *Metaphor and Religious Language* (Oxford, 1985), and P. Wheelwright, *Metaphor and Reality* (Bloomington, 1962) for helpful presentations on the use of various non-literal forms of language and the truth-claims involved in such discourse. For the use of symbolic discourse in the construction of a theory of revelation, cfr. A. Dulles, *Models of Revelation* (Garden City, N.Y., 1983).

all the creatures of the world. Life in its fullness is God's desire for creation. Impoverishment of life is the result of a false self-understanding on the part of humanity and a misguided use of human freedom. The garden of Paradise is the pre-eminent symbol of the fullness of life which God desires for creation. It is not accidental that the Christian Scriptures will eventually place the promise of Paradise on the lips of the dying Jesus (Lk. 23:43).

c) Limits and Function of Eschatological Language

These reflections on the figurative nature of eschatological language together with our earlier remarks on the nature of language about the future serve to indicate something of the function and the limitations of eschatological language. It becomes clear that "to know" is not the same as "to hope." In as far as "knowing" is commonly taken to mean a perception of reality as it is, the language in which our knowledge is expressed involves definitions, arguments, deductions, inductions, and similar cognitive processes. The purpose of such language is to express reality as it is now perceived to be, and to do that as accurately as possible. "To hope," on the other hand, expresses the conviction that reality is not now in its finished state. The world as we now find it can be changed for the better. Therefore, the language of hope intends not to define reality exactly but to hold our sense of reality open to what can yet come to be.

From a cognitive viewpoint, hoping for a better future is quite different from knowing the reality of the present condition of the world. In a sense, hope points beyond our power of exact knowledge. Therefore, the primal levels of the language of hope are characteristically the language of image, picture, and metaphor rather than the language of precise definition. If this is true of the language of human hope in general, it is even more the case with respect to religious hope in a future offered to the human race by God. If God is ultimately an incomprehensible mystery never to be comprehended by the human mind, then the final relation between humanity and that incomprehensible divine mystery remains fundamentally unknown to us in history. Revelation assures us that God does, indeed, hold such a relation open to us, and that it is in this relation that humanity will ultimately find its salvation and fulfillment. But revelation does not give any precise definition of that relation. On the other hand, it does employ a wide range of images, similes, and metaphors that point toward the fullness of being and meaning that we hope for together with the rest of humanity, a fullness that can be found only in relation to God. This language is suggestive and evocative rather than descriptive in a literal sense. It holds open to us the sense of a future, both personal and collective, that transcends any of the day-to-day futures from which we live in our every-day existence; for it is a future promised by God and can be measured by no norm but that of God's infinitely generous love. If any limit can be placed on that future, that limit is to be found in the human unwillingness to be fully open to the mysterious presence of God in human history.

While the language of eschatology is the language of image, simile, and metaphor, it is not, for that reason, the language of an empty, idle dream. Though the hope for a God-given future may lead some believers to an attitude of passive waiting in history, such an attitude need not be seen as the inevitable outcome of eschatological expectation. It is Rahner's conviction that it is precisely the hope in a transcendent, God-given future which remains always a mystery that liberates humanity from becoming enslaved to any this-worldly program or any ideology of the future. The language that holds such a future before us serves to hold open the space of human freedom in history. And such language is important precisely because it does not clearly define and close reality, for only an open reality can be the place in which human freedom and responsibility can be exercised. Seen in this way, the language about the transcendent future plays an important role in mapping out a sense of human responsibility in and for history. This will be treated more fully in the discussion of the theology of history.

READINGS

Bloch, E., *Man on His Own*, tr. E.B. Ashton (Herder & Herder, New York, 1970).

_____*The Principle of Hope*, tr. N. Plaice, S. Plaice, P. Knight. (MIT Press, Cambridge, Mass., 1986).

Carr, A., *The Theological Method of Karl Rahner* (Scholars Press, Missoula, Montana, 1977).

Macquarrie, J. "Eschatology and Time," in: *The Future of Hope: Theology as Eschatology*, ed. F. Herzog (Herder & Herder, New York, 1970) pp. 110-125.

Marcel, G., *Homo Viator: Introduction to a Metaphysic of Hope*, tr. E. Crauford (New York, Harper & Row: Torchbook edition, 1962), reprinted from original English edition by V. Gollanz, Ltd., London and H. Regnery, Chicago, 1951.

Rahner, K., *Hearers of the Word,* tr. M. Richards (Herder & Herder, New York, 1969).

_____"The Hermeneutics of Eschatological Assertions," in: *Theological Investigations* 4, tr. K. Smith (Helicon Press, Baltimore/ Darton, Longman & Todd, London, 1966) pp. 323-346.

Ricoeur, P., *Time and Narrative*, vol. 1, tr. K. McLaughlin and D. Pellauer (University of Chicago Press, Chicago, 1984).

Schillebeeckx, E., *The Understanding of Faith. Interpretation and Criticism* (Seabury Press, N.Y., 1974).

Soskice, J.M., *Metaphor and Religious Reality* (Clarendon Press, Oxford, 1985).

Von Balthasar, H. Urs, "Eschatology," in: *Theology Today* I, ed. J. Feiner et al. (Bruce Publishing Co., Milwaukee, 1964) pp. 222-244.

4

ESCHATOLOGY AND INDIVIDUAL DESTINY

In Christian eschatology, the destiny of the individual person is intimately related to that of the human race and the world. In the chapters dealing with the Scriptural tradition, we saw that the first kinds of questions that emerged in Jewish history had to do with the future of the nation. Only later in the tradition did the question of individual destiny become an issue to merit particular reflection. In the Christian Scriptures also, the primary symbols and metaphors of the future are those that elicit an awareness of the collective future. It is within the context of the collective that the question of the individual must be situated. This bond between the individual and the collective is deeply rooted in a relational, organic understanding of human nature. Human persons cannot develop their potential and reach their fulfillment in isolation from other human beings and from the world. Each individual pertains to the whole; and the whole is incomplete without all the individuals that make up its fullness.

Even though the present chapter will concentrate on the issue of individual destiny, the questions to be treated cannot be understood in isolation from the next three chapters. The central issue to be treated in this chapter is the theology of death, which—whatever else may be said about it—is certainly the end of the individual's personal history. Inseparably related to this issue is the question of the individual's destiny beyond death and the common, theological concept of an interim-state that fills the gap between the completion of an individual's history and the completion of universal history. The treatment of these questions is related, in turn, to the metaphors surrounding the idea of the "return" of the Lord and the end of the collective history of the human race which will be discussed in the following chapters.

1. The Theology of Death

a) The Biblical Tradition

While the theme of death does not stand at the center of the Christian Gospel, yet the Gospel of hope raises the question of the ultimate limit of human hope. What can we hope for in the face of death? Is it true that death consumes everything that time brings forth? Or can we hope for a fulfillment beyond death?

A study of the bible reveals that the Scriptures offer no uniform understanding of death. At times death is seen as a normal element in the pattern of human life; it is something that is to be expected after a long and full life (cfr. Gn. 25:7-11; 2 Sm. 14:14). Early biblical ideas about the fate of the dead have much in common with the views of the surrounding nations. The dead pass on to the underworld (=sheol), to a state that could hardly be called an existence. It is neither reward nor punishment. So weak a hold do the occupants of the underworld have on existence that they are known simply as "shades." This fact of biblical history should put the lie to the claim that religion has its roots in the desire for an after-life or an eternal reward. In the early biblical religion, the important concern was the quality of life in this world, not the expectation of a better life in another world.

Yet this is hardly the whole picture. Death after a long and full life is not the experience of huge numbers of people, then or now. Many suffer intensely during life with no apparent reason. Many die prematurely. The picture of an aged patriarch preparing for death, surrounded by his family in the comfort of his home is hardly an answer to the problems raised by the more common experience that life seems to be very unfair. How is one to relate the experience of death in its more tragic forms with belief in a God who creates the world and all in it and has entered into covenant-relation with Israel and with the world out of pure goodness?

One of the insights of the Hebrew Scriptures which is carried on into the Christian tradition is the conviction that, in some way, the experience of death is related to the historical reality of sin. The best-known text indicating this connection is found in *Genesis* 2:17. A similar text is found in *Wisdom* 1:12. Neither of these texts provides a sound basis for the idea that the mere fact of biological death for humans is caused by sin. Both citations reflect a religious tradition which understands both life and death in more than biological terms. It is possible to be alive biologically and yet to be as good as dead in terms of other levels of human existence. Life is found in the fuller sense only in community with other people, living together in peace, health, good-fortune, and security. This is what the God of the cove-nant wishes for the covenanted people. The God of the covenant is the God of life. To be alive means to stand in a proper relationship with God and with God's people. To be alienated from the covenant-people and from God is to be dead even though one lives at the biological level.

In such a tradition, it is possible to think of the sinful condition of humanity as itself a form of death. If the fullness of life is the gift of God, then everything that diminishes or threatens life is already part of the reality of death. Sickness, suffering, and poverty are already part of the experience of dying, and in Hebrew theology are closely connected not with personal sinfulness but with the sinful situation of the human race. The actual experience of death for vast numbers of people, just and unjust alike, appears more as a curse than as a peaceful, normal ending to a full existence; for most people die without having reached fulfillment in this life. If this fact is reflected on in the context of the theology of the covenant, it becomes understandable that the Hebrew Scriptures could come to the conviction that there was something "unnatural" about death. As we actually experience death, it cannot be what God wills as human destiny.

A particularly poignant level of reflection on death is found in the Wisdom tradition. The reflection of *Ecclesiastes* (1:12—2:26) borders on the cynical and fatalistic as the author wrestles with the puzzle of human life. Even a life that has been lived fully and richly seems to be nothing but a "striving after wind" (2:26). Nowhere in the Scriptures is the leveling significance of death so starkly expressed as in these chap-ters. If death is the common lot of us all, what final difference is there between sinner and saint, fool and wise person? Finally, it all seems to be an empty game. There seems to be no clear, logical explanation to the mystery of human life. Elsewhere in the Wisdom literature, the idea of retribution appears as part of the argument leading to the affirmation of survival beyond death. Thus, Job moves from the experience of total personal devastation to the moving confession: "For I know that my Redeemer lives . . . and after my skin has been thus destroyed, then from my flesh I shall see God" (Job 19:25-26).

A similar hope for vindication by God was an important element in reflection on the fate of the martyrs of the faith and led to hope in some form of meaningful survival beyond death. The earlier notion of shadowy existence in the underworld for good and bad alike is significantly changed with the expectation that the good will be rewarded and the evil punished. This development eventually led to the concept of resurrection as a form of divine vindication (Ps. 16:10; 73:23-28; Dn. 12:2; 2 Mc. 7:9). The notion of resurrection is part of the larger symbolic framework by which the hope in a divine re-creation of the world was expressed.

These themes and styles of reflection are taken up in the Christian Scriptures. Life and death are not understood in mere biological terms. Jesus' call to conversion is a summons to open oneself to God and to the claim which God's reality makes upon the human person. Only those who undergo the radical conversion from stifling self-affirmation to the generous service of God and fellow human beings will find true life (Mk. 8:34-35).

The relation between sin and death is developed with considerable emphasis especially by Paul. Far from being a purely biological phenomenon, death represents all that is contrary to God in its most radical form; it is a power that has held humanity under subjection. Its power has been broken through the death and resurrection of Jesus (Hebr. 2:14; 2 Tim. 1:10). Paul develops this theme with particular power by contrasting the condition of humanity under the sway of sin and death with the condition of grace and redemption brought by Christ (Rm. 5:12-21; 6:23). The text depicts the solidarity of the human race in the history of sin and the solidarity of all in the mystery of redemption and grace. Sin has become, as it were, an omnipresent power in human history leading to a spiritual death already in this life, and to the possibility of eternal death in the next. It is the power of God's redemptive act in Christ that has broken the strangle-hold of sin and death and opened human history to the possibility of new and richer life. Only when death, the final enemy of God, has been destroyed will Christ deliver the kingdom to the Father (1 Cor. 15:23-26).

In the light of the Christ-mystery, Christian faith comes to recognize that the final word about human destiny is communion, not isolation; life, not death.

The crucial factor here and in all Christian reflection on the reality of death is the mystery of the resurrection of Jesus, for it is in the light of the resurrection that the early community came to see the deeper meaning of the life and the death of the Lord. Both his manner of living and his manner of dying are seen to reveal the deeper, religious meaning of human life and death. In this early Christian reflection, it is not the external form of Christ's death that is central but the internal attitude of obedience to God and radical trust in God's faithfulness that would become crucial not only for Scripture but for later theological reflection on Jesus' death. Without the resurrection, the life and death of Jesus appears to be a paradigm of the absurdity of life. With the resurrection, it can be said that such a life and death in deepest fidelity to the demands of God's presence finds eternal acceptance in the very life of God. In this sense, death has lost its sting (1 Cor. 15:54-55). Death no longer appears to be the final seal on a hopeless and meaningless existence but now can be seen as the decisive moment of re-birth into the fullness of life promised by the God of life.

From this understanding of death, it is possible to look at the experience of life and to see that the ongoing experience of death to oneself for the sake of others is, in effect, a harbinger of the final moment of death and re-birth into the life of God. The little death experienced over and over in the course of life is not a loss but a birth to fuller sharing of life with others. Similarly, the great death that awaits us all at the end of our historical course is—in the Christian understanding—a birth into the fullest sharing of life.

Paul describes this as a dying and rising with Christ. As Paul's theology is worked out in *Romans*, this dynamism constitutes the core of Christian existence from baptism to the end of life (Rm. 6:2ff). In his personal experience, Paul sees the work of his missionary career as a daily dying in the death of Christ (1 Cor. 15:31). The power of death is overcome when, in union with Christ, the believer opens his or her existence to the demands of God's presence by turning away from a self-centered, self-affirming existence to a life that is fundamentally open to the presence of others and to God. In such a life, biological death is not removed but is relativized by a deeper possibility for life. This Pauline vision seems to be confirmed by the Johannine tradition:

"We know that we have passed out of death into life, because we love the brethren. He who does not love abides in death" (1 Jn. 3:14).

These reflections on death in Scripture are sufficient to indicate that, in the world of the bible, the terms "life" and "death" cannot be limited to the biological level. Clearly the most important level is that of the quality of life made possible by entering into a relation of communion with others and with God, for this is truly the life to which the God of the covenant calls us. A biological existence in the absence of this quality is death. The Jewish hope that a communion with God might be stronger than death because of God's fidelity is brought to a more explicit level through the resurrection of Jesus. Trust in the life-giving power of a faithful God places the hope for an eternal destiny with God at the heart of the Christian confession of faith.

b) Death in the Theological Tradition

1) Death and Sin

The theological tradition has long maintained that the human experience of death is intimately related to human sinfulness. On a number of occasions, this has been solemnly affirmed by the hierarchical magisterium without any detailed explanation (DS 222, 372, 1511, 1521). While the Scriptural basis for this teaching is commonly sought in *Genesis* (2:16ff; 3:19) and in *Romans* (5:12), the church has never officially defined a particular exegesis of these texts as binding.

Each of these texts raises numerous questions for the modern exegete and theologian. It is fair to say that the common understanding of hand-book theology read these texts in a straightforward way. They were taken to mean that the first human beings, had they maintained their original state of justice, would have retained the preternatural gift of immortality. In the thought of Augustine the gift of immortality did not mean that it was impossible for human persons to die (=non posse mori), but that—by virtue of the gift of God's grace—it was possible for them not to die (=posse non mori).[1] Thus, the human person is not naturally immortal, but enjoys freedom from death only through a gift

---

[1] *De Genesis ad Litt.* VI, 25, 36 (PL 34 354).

of God that transcends nature. This view of Augustine had an extensive influence on Western theology throughout subsequent centuries. It has commonly led to the theological position that, had there been no sin, humanity would not have experienced death as a biological event.

While this has become a commonly accepted theological position and is one of the presuppositions from which the official statements of the magisterium were formulated, it is not the direct object of any magisterial definition. What is affirmed by the magisterium concerning sin and death is the fact that there is a relation between the reality of sin and the human experience of biological death. The precise nature of that relation is not clarified in any detail.

2) Death as Separation of Soul and Body

The traditional understanding of what happens to a person in death was shaped by either the Platonic or the Aristotelian understanding of human nature. In the first instance, the human soul inhabited the body much as a sailor lives in his boat. In death, the soul is liberated from the restrictions of its material dwelling place. This philosophy, with its negative understanding of the body, exercised considerable influence on the thought of Christian theologians prior to the emergence of Aristotelian thought in the Middle Ages. As the influence of Aristotle was felt by the Christian West, the rather loose relation between body and soul characteristic of Platonism and neo-Platonism was tightened up by the philosophical doctrine of material and formal causality. In the formulation of Aquinas, the soul is the form of the body. As the form that determines matter to be precisely a human body, the soul is seen here as an intrinsic element in the corporal, material existence of the human person.

Whether from the basis of the Platonic tradition or from the Aristotelian tradition, theology commonly thought of death as the separation of the soul from the body. For theologians working in dialogue with the Aristotelian philosophy, it was necessary to modify the strict Aristotelian concept of form in order to conceptualize the possibility of the soul existing in even temporary separation from the body. In the strict philosophical sense, a form exists only in as far as it is actually informing matter to constitute a particular individual being. As an intrinsic cause of a particular being, the formal cause exercises a causality which is fully simultaneous with the material causality of matter. This means that, in the strict Aristotelian sense, if the soul is conceived as the form of the body, the soul ceases to exist when the human being ceases to exist as a human being. From a strictly philosophical perspective, the form that had made this matter to be a human being ceases to exist when the person dies. A corpse is not a human being. And the form that informs the matter of a corpse is not a human soul. Aristotelian philosophy did not include the possibility that the individual human person might survive death in some way.

For this reason it was necessary for Christian theologians who wished to employ the Aristotelian theory of matter and form to transform the notion of form in order to make it possible to express the theological concerns of the Christian tradition. This adaptation led to the notion of the soul as a form which possessed an intrinsic relation to matter but which could exist temporarily without that intrinsic orientation to matter being realized in actuality. In essence, this is the theological notion of the separated soul which exists separated from the body after death but which has an intrinsic orientation to be reunited with the body eventually. Since the soul as a form is intrinsically related to materiality, the thesis that postulates a separated soul fulfills two functions. It provides a basis for conceiving of the fundamental identity of the person beyond death, and it provides a basis for conceptualizing the fundamental incompleteness of the person prior to the resurrection of the body.

3) Death as End of Personal History

It is common teaching in the theological tradition that death is not only the biological event but a personal event of great importance, for it marks the end of a personal history. Whatever may be meant by death in a clinical or medical sense, there is a point, according to the theological understanding of human life, from which there is simply no return. We may not know precisely when this point is reached, and it may not coincide with any clear biological data. But for Christian theology, death is truly the end of a personal history. Whatever existence awaits us, it is not a return to space and time experience, nor is it an endless continuation of our temporal existence in another world. The time for significant decisions about the direction and quality of human life is past with death.

From this we can conclude that the phenomenon of "near death" experiences that have drawn so much interest in recent years are precisely that; they are "near death" experiences. From a theological perspective, they are not the experience of death itself but experiences at the outer limits of life.[2] From the descriptions given by patients who have undergone such experiences, often a clinical death followed by resuscitation, we might place these experiences in the category of altered states of consciousness familiar to us through the study of mystical experiences and chemically induced states of consciousness. That the world of human consciousness is a multi-layered reality is an incontestable datum of modern awareness. In such a context, the fact of "near death" experiences should come as no surprise.

Viewed critically, they are not a proof that there is a life beyond death even though they may have a powerful impact on the person who has had such an experience. These experiences may have a different kind of significance for theology, however; for they seem to provide solid evidence that the human person may be actively engaged in life-experiences even when there are no clinical signs of conscious life. Indeed, there is sufficient empirical evidence to support the claim that a person may well be personally engaged in the process of living and dying right up to the very experience of death itself. The significance of this will appear in the contemporary theological reflections on death.

Related to the idea that death is the end of one's personal historical existence is the church's teaching that after death, the souls of the just in need of no further purification enter immediately into the enjoyment of the beatific vision, while the souls of those who die in the state of mortal sin enter immediately into the suffering of hell (DS 1000ff). The official teaching of the church has been most discreet in making any claims about the eternal destiny of any particular individuals. Because of the basic Christian faith in the resurrection of Christ, Christian doctrine makes a positive statement about the reality of heaven which is restated in the case of the dogma of the Assumption of Mary and in the canonization of saints. There is, however, no parallel statement

---

[2]For a more detailed discussion of this question, cfr. H. Küng, *Eternal Life?*, tr. E. Quinn (Garden City, N.Y., 1984) pp. 1-21; 147-175.

concerning hell. Here, the teaching of the church holds the basic possibility of eternal damnation, but there is no official teaching concerning the actual damnation of any specific human being.

In summary, the traditional teaching of the church concerning death is not extensive. In as far as it is developed at all, it concentrates more on what precedes and what follows death, and not on the reality of death itself except to describe it as the separation of soul and body. What precedes death is the need for contrition and the administration of the last rites. What follows death is expressed in the doctrines of particular judgment, heaven, hell, purgatory, and the intermediate state. Since all these particular doctrines are shaped by the assumption that death is adequately defined as the separation of soul and body, when this understanding of death undergoes a radical revision, the related doctrines will be in need of reinterpretation as well.

c) Death in Contemporary Theology

At the heart of the contemporary reformulations of the themes of individual eschatology is the understanding of death. What is it that happens to the human person in death? Much of the contemporary discussion begins with the conviction that the traditional definition of death as the separation of the soul from the body is not adequate for the needs of theology today. But if the traditional definition is found to be inadequate, where are we to go to gain further insight?

The principal developments in this area are associated with three major names: K. Rahner, R. Troisfontaines, and L. Boros.[3] While Troisfontaines is influenced strongly by the philosophy of Marcel, Rahner and Boros work on the basis of transcendental philosophy. All attempt to provide a convincing argument for the claim that human death is not just a fate that is passively suffered but a profoundly human, personal act in which the person is actively engaged. Since the work of Rahner has been the most influential, we shall concentrate on

[3]Rahner's initial reflections appeared in: *Zeitschrift für katholische Theologie* 79 (1957) pp. 1-44. A revised version appeared in the form of a monograph *Zur Theologie des Todes* in 1958 as the second volume of the ongoing series of *Quaestiones Disputatae* published by Herder. The English translation of this appeared under the title *On the Theology of Death* (N.Y., 1961). Cfr. also R. Troisfontaines, *I Do Not Die* (N.Y., 1963); and L. Boros, *The Mystery of Death* (N.Y., 1965).

his view and the impact it has had on the work of Boros.

At the core of Rahner's argument is the conviction that death is not simply something that happens to a person from outside, a fate that is brought about by causes over which we have no control. It is that, certainly, but it is more besides. Human death is an act in which the person is deeply engaged. Not only does death "happen" to us, but we actively die our death. To understand what Rahner means by this and how he arrives at such a viewpoint, we need to reflect at least briefly on his understanding of human life.

Human existence, for Rahner, is a search for meaning and fulfillment. Human life is, in this view, an ongoing process of interaction between the human person and the wider world of people and things that make up the context of the person's life. The human person is acted on by others and, in turn, reacts to the presence of others. In short, human life is an ongoing dialectic of passivity and activity. We are passive, first, in the sense that we "are given" our very existence without our consultation or choice. But what is given to us we must take up actively and personally in some way. At the other end of our history, our existence will be taken from us by powers over which we have no final control. Death is seen as the most intense form of the dialectic of passivity and activity that runs throughout the whole of life. Death for a human being cannot be simply the biological breakdown of the bodily organism, as it seems to be for sub-human forms of life. It is that, to be sure. But beyond that, death is an act performed by the human person from within. At the moment when a person suffers a total domination by powers not under human control, that person is called to make the final and decisive expression of his or her freedom.

Understood in this way, death is the active consummation of human life which brings to fulfillment all that a person has accomplished during the personal history that comes to its end in death. This active side of death is seen to be the final and decisive act of human freedom, prepared for throughout the whole of a personal history, and made irrevocable in the act of dying. Death is the privileged moment of human freedom in which a human being has the power to decide something that is of irrevocable, eternal significance.

From this, it becomes clear why Rahner finds the traditional definition of death as the separation of soul and body to be inadequate. Death is the end of the personal history for the entire person. It is not only the body that is affected, but the soul as well. For in dying, the soul reaches its own proper consummation. It enters into a new and deeper relation to the world which Rahner calls a "pan-cosmic" relation. By surrendering the limited bodily structure of its history, the soul becomes open to the whole of the universe.[4]

Rahner has provided a strong argument for the thesis that death for a human person is fundamentally different from the termination of sub-human life. Human death is a personal, human act. While Rahner's analysis has been basically philosophical in nature, this thesis is not without significant biblical and theological warrant. Rahner himself points to the Scriptural presentation of the death of Jesus. There we can see a strong polarity of the passive and active dimensions suggested in the philosophical analysis. Jesus' death was clearly something that he did not seek; it was something that was done to him, something that he suffered (Mk. 14:32-41; 15:34). On the other hand, the death of Jesus is interpreted by the Scriptures as a personal act; he gave himself freely into the hands of his loving, merciful God (Lk. 23:46; Jn. 14:2.28; 16:7; 19:30). Following this Scriptural lead, centuries of theological reflection would argue that the death of Jesus was the supreme act of obedience to the will of the Father. It is in this deeply personal dimension of death that the theological tradition sees the salvific significance of the crucifixion. Rahner's analysis brings new levels of insight into this traditional understanding of Jesus' death.

The direction set by Rahner is carried further in the work of L. Boros, who develops Rahner's philosophy of freedom consistently in his own understanding of death. Death is the privileged moment of human freedom which opens the human soul totally to the world. But if the soul is opened to the world, it is simultaneously opened to the ground of the world, namely, God. In the most pointed formulation of his position, Boros writes:

> Death is man's first completely personal act, and is, therefore, by reason of its very being, the place above all others for the awakening of consciousness, for freedom, for the encounter with God, for the final decision about eternal destiny.[5]

---

[4]*On the Theology of Death*, p. 27ff.
[5]Boros, *The Mystery of Death*, p. 84.

It is clear that this orientation places great weight on the one act that determines the individual's destiny for eternity. But it does not follow from this, as critics of the thesis claim, that the moment of death is isolated from the life that has preceded it. On the contrary, as Boros argues, while the decision made in death is not simply the sum total of the decisions that have made up this particular life, it is determined to a certain degree by preparatory decisions that precede death. We might envision the prior history of the person's free acts as a fundamental conditioning for the free decision that occurs in death. But it is important to emphasize that a person's prior history is a conditioning and not a total determination of the future. While the final decision in a sense stands above all the decisions that have preceded it, yet—in another sense—it grows out of those decisions and is unthinkable without them. Viewed in this way, the thesis of final decision cannot be used as an excuse for a life of moral irresponsibility or indifference. As Boros views the thesis, it is in full harmony with the scriptural call for watchfulness throughout life, and with the traditional concern about the uncertainty of our personal salvation.[6]

This line of thought has been very influential for Roman Catholic theological reflection on death. Despite differences in argumentation, those who follow this direction agree that the moment of death for a human being is a unique and privileged moment for human freedom. When viewed from the perspective of the theological tradition, the thesis appears as an attempt to deal with the traditional conviction that death is the irreversible end of each individual, personal history.

The implications of the contemporary theological discussion of death as a human act can be summarized in the following points:

(a) Death is the final point of the dialectic of suffering and action that is characteristic of human life. Empirical observations indicate that this dialectic is present in the process of dying. The theology of final decision carries this dialectic further into the very act of dying itself. Because the act of dying is a personal act, it can be seen as the active fulfillment of a personal history from within. It is the end of a life process.

(b) Death is an act of final self-surrender. This is a statement of what death ought to be, not of what it in fact is in particular cases.

---

[6]Boros, *op. cit.*, p. 97.

Taken in this sense, death ought to be the final act of what is lived throughout life in the attempt to live a life of love and self-giving. Because of the ambiguity of human experience, it is never clear what lies in store for us in or beyond death. Do we finally meet a void of nothingness, or do we meet a mystery of fullness and completion? No one standing on this side of death can claim to know the answer to this. Is the emptiness of death nothing but annihilation? Or is that emptiness the condition for the final fullness of our being in the presence of the God of life? Viewed from the perspective of the death and resurrection of Christ, death can be seen as the final act of self-surrender to that Mystery which one has trusted in life, and which one has believed to be a God of love, forgiveness, and acceptance. Death is the final extension of the risk of love experienced throughout life. In specifically Christian terms, the free act by which we give ourselves into the hands of God's love and mercy is the way in which the believer enters most fully into the mystery of the dying and rising of Christ.

(c) Death marks the end of a personal history. The theology of death as a personal, human act provides a new way of expressing and understanding the traditional view which envisioned death as the end of a personal pilgrimage. Life is lived but once. The decisions made during this life, particularly the final decision made in death, have eternal significance.

2. Related Questions

a) Death and Sin

We have already indicated that the theological tradition, particularly in the teaching of the magisterium, has long held that there is a relation between sin and death, and that there is a basis for this conviction in the texts of Scripture. While the more familiar theological view sees this relation almost in terms of a physical causality, contemporary theology suggests a different way of thinking about the issue. It is not the mere fact of biological death that is caused by sin. It is the way in which human beings experience death that is the result of sin. Contemporary theology, therefore, speaks of the anthropological modification of death. Death appears to us as the great enemy of all that we try to accomplish with our lives, calling into question the ultimate significance of our very existence. Why does death appear to us in this way? Why does the prospect of death cause anxiety in us? Theology associates this way of perceiving death with the reality of sin. It is the fearful andpainful quality of death that is the result of sin, and not the mere fact of biological death as such.

b) Death and Judgment

In the traditional theological understanding, one dimension of the final encounter between the human person and God is called "judgment." Theology has commonly distinguished a "particular judgment" from a "general judgment," the first coming immediately after the death of the individual and the second coming at the end of history. We are here concerned only with the former. The question of the "general judgment" will be treated in chapter six.

The doctrine that there is a particular judgment for the individual person immediately after death is not a defined dogma in the strict sense of the word. But it is presupposed by the church's teaching that death marks the end of the possibility for conversion and for merit or demerit, and that the souls of the departed proceed to heaven, hell, or purgatory immediately after death (DS 801, 856-858, 1000-1001).

Neither is the concept of a particular judgment of each individual at the time of death expressly taught in Scripture. In as far as judgment plays a role in the Hebrew Scriptures, it is related to faith in God's justice. Human beings are answerable before God for the quality of their lives. Personal responsibility cannot be swallowed up in a nameless collectivity. Similarly in the Christian Scriptures, the idea of divine justice and judgment evokes a sense of the importance of what is done in this life. The apocalyptic language of the Scriptures is, in essence, a summons to a serious decision about the quality and direction of human life before God. The words and actions of Jesus are the measuring rod for the meaning of life. And each person is responsible for the quality of his or her life.

The anthropological orientation that characterizes the theology of death leads to new nuances in the understanding of judgment. Instead of thinking of judgment as something that happens to the human person from the outside, this theology is inclined to see it as the full personal realization of the individual's own decisions. The encounter with God has as its intrinsic effect the full illumination of the person's life-history with all the personal decisions that have made the person to be precisely what he or she brings into the encounter with God. In the presence of God, my true reality becomes fully clear to me. The divine judge needs to do nothing. Judgment is the experience of the reality I have made of myself as seen in the presence of God.

In this sense, one can describe judgment as self-judgment. But this designation can easily be misleading, for it can create the impression that humanity itself is the norm of judgment. What is meant here is that all human beings are called to that sort of loving, trusting existence embodied in Jesus Christ. Each individual experiences himself or herself in relation to the quality of life that has been revealed in Christ. Together with all the good that has been accomplished in life, the person sees the painful results of personal failures and sins. In this sense, judgment is not something that is done to the person from outside. It is precisely the full experience of what the person has made of the existence bestowed by God as a gift and as a promise.[7]

While this interpretation of judgment may seem far removed from the metaphors of the Synoptic gospels and the *Book of Revelation*, it can appeal to the *Gospel of John* for Scriptural support. In John's view, the Son of God comes not to condemn the world but to bring salvation and life as the gift of God to the world. Life is God's gift to those who believe in the Son. Those who refuse to believe bring about their own condemnation (Jn. 3:16-18).

c) Death and Purgation

As a specifically Christian teaching, the doctrine of purgatory expresses the conviction that those who die in the state of grace but still burdened with temporal punishment due to sin already forgiven or still having the guilt of venial sin must undergo purgation after death. The doctrine of purgatory implies that those who are fundamentally in the state of grace at the time of death can increase in perfection after death until they have reached a state worthy of union with God.

---

[7] H. Urs von Balthasar, "Gericht," in: *Communio: Internationale katholische Zeitschrift* 9 (1980) pp. 227-235.

While there is no Scriptural evidence that contradicts the doctrine of purgatory, the biblical basis for the doctrine remains unclear. The theological tradition commonly appeals to 2 *Maccabees* 12:38-46 as a basis for the teaching. In the Christian Scriptures, *Matthew* 5:26 and 12:32 and 1 *Corinthians* 3:11-15 are often cited. While none of these texts teach the doctrine of purgatory directly, they do allow for the possibility that some form of purgation may be envisioned after death.

To present a detailed account of the development of the doctrine would take us too far afield. But several historical points may be of help in evaluating the current understanding of the metaphors of purgation. First, it is helpful to recognize that the traditions of the East and the West reflect a significant difference in this area. In very broad terms, it can be said that Western theology, especially in its soteriology, has tended to develop a strongly moral line of thought and to use juridical-legal categories and metaphors to express itself. This has led Western theology to deal with purgatory in terms of its penal character. The Eastern church, on the other hand, has approached the doctrine of soteriology, grace, and fulfillment from the perspective of growth and maturation. This can be seen clearly in the traditional patristic doctrine of deification. Consistent with this understanding of the spiritual life, Eastern thought has tended to think of purgation in terms of growth and maturation rather than in terms of punishment. As E. Fortman has pointed out, the two mediaeval attempts to bring Eastern and Western Christianity into closer union, the Councils of Lyons II (1274) and Florence (1439), were able to come to some agreement on essential elements in the doctrine of purgatory: 1) The souls of the just who have not done sufficient penance for their sins before death are cleansed after death; 2) the prayers and suffrages of the faithful on earth can be of positive significance for the deceased in their condition of purgation. These two points were defined again by the Council of Trent (1563).[8] It is significant that nothing is said about purgatory as a place. Neither is anything said about the nature of the purgative fire or the duration of purgatory.

It seems that it is possible to speak of the essential elements of the traditional dogma without assuming that purgatory is a specific place in a world beyond or that some sort of real fire is involved. J. LeGoff

---

[8]E. Fortman, *Everlasting Life after Death* (N.Y., 1976), p. 132.

has traced the development of the doctrine of purgatory with careful detail. He argues that, while language about purgation is common in the writings of the early Fathers, it is not clear that purgatory was envisioned as a specific place until late in the twelfth century.[9] In late mediaeval theology, the relation between the doctrine of purgatory and the practises of the faithful surrounding death became highly developed and integrated into the juridical structures of the church. Suffrages, penance, and indulgences found a common focus in the doctrine of the power of the Keys. This sort of development was difficult for the Eastern church as well as for the communities of the Protestant Reformation in the sixteenth century. In view of the problems that the mediaeval view raises for even many Roman Catholics today, the history of the doctrine can help theology to sort out the basic theological issue that lies behind the elaborate structure of doctrine, practise, and law.

The anthropological shift that we have been tracing in eschatology in general, and in the theology of death in particular, becomes clear in the contemporary attempts to re-interpret the basic metaphors of purgation. Paraphrasing an ancient text of Augustine, H. Urs von Balthasar writes: "God is the Last Thing of the creature. Gained, He is its paradise; lost, He is its hell; as demanding, He is its judgment; as cleansing, He is its purgatory."[10] There is perhaps no more compact statement of the anthropological-theological reduction of eschatology in Roman Catholic literature of the recent decades. Here all the last "things" are reduced to dimensions or aspects of the final encounter between God and the human person. The text speaks neither of place, nor of time, nor of fire, but solely of the intensity of the encounter in its diverse dimensions.

This anthropological-theological orientation is given a specifically Christological coloration by Cardinal Ratzinger in his exegesis of *1 Corinthians* 3:10-15. Purgation is effected by the transforming power of the Lord who himself is the "fire of judgment." This interpretation echoes the Pauline understanding of conformity to Christ and the Patristic tradition of grace and glory as deiformity. Purgation, in Ratzinger's view, is a process through which the human person is

[9]J. Le Goff, *The Birth of Purgatory* (Chicago, 1984), p. 163.

[10]H. Urs von Balthasar, "Eschatology," in: *Theology Today* I, ed. J. Feiner et al. (Milwaukee, 1964) pp. 222-244.

made conformable with Christ, with God, and with the entire community of the redeemed. This process is focused in the encounter with the Lord who burns away the impediments of the human heart and immerses the individual in the living organism of his body.[11]

It seems inevitable that when the reality of purgation is seen in such terms, it will be drawn somehow into very close association with the experience of death itself. Indeed, this is precisely what is suggested by authors such as Rahner and Boros. For both, the experience of death itself is the crucial moment of purgation. Rahner speaks of the pain involved when the soul experiences itself in its own harmony or lack of harmony with the objectively right order of the world. This pain he sees as an integral element in the experience of death.

Developing the seminal ideas of Rahner in a more explicit way, Boros consciously sets about the process of dismantling the common understanding of purgatory as a torture chamber with fire and other instruments of torture. Appealing to the suggestion of Von Balthasar cited above, Boros argues that the idea of purgatory as a place must be transformed into the idea of a process; and that the understanding of process must be interpreted in terms of a personal encounter. Death means that a person is torn from the familiar context of this world and is handed over to God. In as far as this is a fundamental rupture of our present existence, it is painful. Specifically, in as far as our ontological need to love and to reach out to others is unrealized by less than perfect decisions in human life, walls of self-affirmation have been built up to "protect" the person from the inroads of others. In the presence of the ultimate mystery of love, these layers of resistance must be broken down. The more resistant the encrustations, the more painful the experience of purgation. The integration of human reality into the mystery of God's love will inevitably involve suffering.[12] Interpreting the text of *Revelation* 1:12-17, Boros gives his thought a specifically Christological nuance. The text speaks of one like the son of man whose eyes were "like a flame of fire." Identifying this figure with the person of Christ, Boros speaks of the encounter with God in Christ. To meet God in the flaming eyes of Christ is "the highest fulfillment of

---

[11]J. Cardinal Ratzinger, *Eschatologie: Tod und Ewiges Leben*, (Regensburg, 1977) p. 187.
[12]Boros, *op. cit.*, pp. 135-6.

our capacity for love and also the most fearful suffering our nature ever has to bear."[13]

Assuming the necessity of de-objectifying the common Western understanding of purgatory, these suggested re-interpretations of the basic metaphor of purgation through fire offer helpful insight into the religious meaning of the doctrine. Focusing as they do on the dynamics of personal encounter, these interpretations have more in common with the Eastern tradition and with the mystical-spiritual traditions in general which commonly use the metaphor of fire in the context of deep religious experiences of God even in this life. In the Western Victorine tradition of the twelfth-century, such imagery was used to express the dynamic whereby the soul was moulded into the deepest possible God-likeness in a union of love. Thus, these apparently recent interpretations can be seen to have deep roots in the most venerable religious traditions not only of the Christian world but of the great world-religions in general.

How is the relation between death and purgation to be thought of more specifically? If purgation is seen as an aspect of the experience of death itself, what is to be said about its duration? While the opinions of theologians differ on this question, it seems that once the shift has been made from the concept of purgatory as a place to the concept of personal encounter, the question of any sort of temporal duration may be an inappropriate understanding of the symbol. If there is any measure to purgatory, it can be taken only from the depth of whatever it is in human existence that stands in the way between the person and God. Purgatory is neither long nor short in temporal categories. It is intense in proportion to the need of purgation in the individual person.[14]

In all these positions, whatever particular differences there may be in the theology of death, there is a point of convergence in the current theological reflection on death, judgment, and purgation. The courtroom scene conjured up by the late mediaeval and more recent handbook theology is replaced with an interpretation in which the primary metaphors are derived from the experience of personal encounter. The traditional symbols are not lost but are given a new interpretation

[13]Boros, *op. cit.*, p. 139.
[14]Ratzinger, *op. cit.*, p. 188.

which stands fully within the framework of theological possibilities left open by the church's magisterial teaching.

d) Christian Piety: Suffrages for the Dead

It is not possible to suggest this shift in eschatological thought without raising questions about the status of many aspects of Christian piety with respect to the dead. The magisterial teaching of the church referred to above expresses the conviction that the dead may be helped in some way by the prayers and good works of the living. This traditional concern was reaffirmed by the Congregation for the Doctrine of the Faith in 1979 with the strong caution that the church "excludes every way of thinking or speaking that would render meaningless or unintelligible her prayers, her funeral rites and the religious acts offered for the dead."[15]

With respect to the doctrine of purgatory, the following issues may be singled out. First, the doctrine is firmly situated in the larger theological understanding of the communion of saints. Second, the doctrine of purgatory is unintelligible except in reference to the traditional Christian belief in life beyond death and the hope of resurrection.

The communion of saints as an article of the Christian creed is a reflection of the profound solidarity of the human race. This sense of solidarity has deep roots in the biblical tradition and is the key issue in both the church's doctrine of original sin and the doctrine of redemption. This theological sense of solidarity may be clarified through philosophical anthropology, as we have suggested in chapter three. Philosophically, we are dealing with the essentially relational character of human nature. Theologically, we are confronted with the religious conviction that this relational or social nature of humanity is not left behind when we approach the question of grace and salvation. This is expressed traditionally in the great scriptural and patristic metaphors of the People of God, Temple, and Body of Christ. When this sense of solidarity is brought into association with the belief in eternal life with God, the idea emerges that just as our human destiny transcends history, so does our human solidarity. If as human beings we are

[15]"Letter on Certain Questions concerning Eschatology," (Vatican City, 1979) #4.

bound together by nature and grace within history, those bonds do not cease with death.[16] This, we suggest, is the fundamental issue involved in the relation between the doctrine of death, purgation, and Christian suffrages. From this perspective, we will consider the positions suggested by various authors discussed above.

In the case of Rahner, the theological basis for suffrages is clear. It rests in the idea that even though death involves a final decision, the full impact of that decision may not be worked out fully in a single moment. It is possible to think of a "ripening" of the entire person which is not focused entirely in the moment of death. This notion of maturation bears a certain analogy with the traditional concept of a shorter or longer duration in purgatory. It is difficult to become more specific in explaining how the prayers and good works of the living have any significance for those undergoing such a process of maturation.

Yet Rahner's own philosophy provides resources for developing some further insight. His anthropology has made a strong case for the fundamental unity of the human race, and for the essential relatedness of each individual person to the whole of the race. As we are interdependent during this life, so, it can be argued, we are interdependent in a way that transcends death. Human solidarity reaches even beyond the border of death. What we are with respect to each other makes a difference in the life of the individual. This fact is clear enough in this life. When applied to the notion of after-life and purgatory, it would suggest that the after-life is not a question of individuals standing alone in isolation before God. Rather, it is a question of standing in the context of all the relations that make this particular person to be precisely what he or she is. If purgation is thought of in terms of healing and maturation, it might be suggested that it is the entire network of relations through which others have influenced this person and in which this person has influenced others that is in need of healing.[17]

Cardinal Ratzinger suggests a similar view. The encounter with Christ in death is an encounter with the Body of Christ. It is, therefore, an encounter with all the individual's guilt against the suffering mem-

---

[16]Pope Paul VI echoes this tradition in the final two paragraphs of "The Credo of the People of God" (Vatican City, 1968).

[17]R. Schreiter, "Purgatory: In Quest of an Image," in: *Chicago Studies* 24 (1985) 2, pp. 167-179.

bers of the Body and with the loving forgiveness flowing from Christ, the Head of the Body.[18] The doctrine of purgation and suffrages may be seen as a way of addressing the issue of human solidarity in its widest scope. The doctrine expresses the church's faith in the salvific power of love that transcends the grave. Death places no limit on the imperative to love. Perhaps it is not helpful to become too detailed in our understanding of what happens beyond death. But the argument from human solidarity provides a strong basis for the general claim of the church that the prayers and works of the faithful can be of positive significance for the deceased.

The position of Boros is more difficult in that it situates the entire process of purgation in the moment of death. His argument involves a strange telescoping of time and history into the moment of death. Can the suffrages of the faithful be of help to the deceased? Boros answers in the affirmative. But he goes on to explain:

> For God, all is present: for him our prayer and the death of the person for whom we are praying coincide; for him, the human being whom we love and whose decision we want to make easier by the support of our prayer is dying at the moment when we are praying for him.[19]

This position is given a more problematic formulation by G. Lohfink who argues that the whole of history is with the individual in the moment of death.[20] Lohfink's formulation occurs in his argument concerning the identity of the particular and general judgment which we will discuss in greater detail in chapter six. What is of concern for the present question is his claim that God is equally near and equally distant to every point of time. This provides him with the basis for his argument that the eschatological coming of God is not to be situated at some future end-point of time but should be associated with the death of each and every human person regardless of when they have lived in history. This would mean that any talk of purgation must be

---

[18]Ratzinger, *op. cit.*, p. 189.

[19]"Death, A Theological Reflection," in: *The Mystery of Suffering and Death*, ed. M.J. Taylor (New York, 1973) pp. 147-8.

[20]G. Greshake & G. Lohfink, *Naherwartung, Auferstehung, Unsterblichkeit* (Freiburg, 1975) pp. 61-62.

concentrated in the moment of death. With this, the claim that everything in time is equally present to God is the only possible basis for legitimating the Christian suffrages for the dead. Everything that has occurred or will occur in history is "with" the individual person in death. This includes all the prayers and good works that have been or will be offered on that person's behalf. It makes no difference to God when those prayers or works have been performed.

The chief weakness of this theory lies in its implications about the future, and here it reveals its true vulnerability. If human history is truly a history of freedom, this must mean that the future remains basically open and undetermined. As such, it is not only unknowable but it does not exist in reality. Only when a free, human decision has been made is a future possibility turned into a present reality. As long as we think of history as a history of freedom, the future must remain undetermined. It is difficult, therefore, to give a convincing conceptualization to the claim that what remains as an undetermined potential can somehow "be with" the person who dies before that potential has been determined and made actual. The theory fails on two interrelated points. It implies a weak philosophy of history and freedom. Because of this weakness, it provides no convincing rationale for the practise of Christian suffrages.

In the light of this discussion, we can conclude that the theory of death as final decision can be interpreted in a way that is fully compatible with the traditional doctrine of purgatory and suffrages. In this sense, the theories which interpret purgatory more in terms of maturation than of punishment stand fully within the framework of theological possibilities set out by the official teaching of the church. The major attempts to interpret the theory of final decision in such a way that purgation is concentrated totally in the moment of death have not yet found a convincing line of argument that would make the practise of Christian suffrages theologically intelligible.

e) Limbo

Any discussion of limbo must take into account a number of basic facts. First, the concept of limbo is a theological postulate intended to shed light on a theological question. What can theology say about the eternal destiny of someone who does not seem to measure up to the requirements for being consigned either to heaven or to hell? A specific instance of this would be the case of a child who dies without baptism, but also apparently without the opportunity of making a personal decision for or against God. Second, the hierarchical magisterium has offered no clear, definitive position on the matter of limbo. From these two facts, it becomes clear that, in the event that it should be possible to deal with the theological problem without postulating a place such as limbo, then this place of waiting, between heaven and hell, will be removed from the map of eschatology.

A survey of the current theological literature leads to the following observations:

1) In a number of very recent discussions of eschatology by some greatly respected theologians, the question of limbo is not brought up. This is the case with Schmaus, Ratzinger, Vorgrimler, and Nocke.[21]

2) When the question of limbo is discussed, this may be done in two different ways. In some instances, the matter is discussed as a purely historical question.[22] In this case, the issue is largely a matter of showing the roots of the problem in Patristic theology and the development of a variety of ways of dealing with it throughout the centuries.

On the other hand, there are authors who still discuss the issue as a matter of systematic theology. In this regard, Fortman assesses the situation accurately when he says that some form of the theory of death as final decision is by far the most common orientation for dealing with the issue at the present time.[23]

While it is true to say that, among those who discuss the matter, the theory of final decision is in the ascendency, this is not without its problems. By treating the death of an infant in essentially the same way as it treats the death of an adult, this theory runs the risk of denying any real significance to the human experience of growing to maturity through the experience of history. The point of this argument is not that the theory of death as final decision is fundamentally

---

[21]Cfr. M. Schmaus, *Dogma 6: Justification and the Last Things* (Kansas City, 1977); J. Ratzinger, *Eschatologie—Tod und ewiges Leben* (Regensburg, 1977); H. Vorgrimler, *Hoffnung auf Vollendung. Aufriss der Eschatologie* (Freiburg, 1980); F.J. Nocke, *Eschatologie, Leitfaden Theologie 6* (Düsseldorf, 1985); H. Küng, *Eternal Life?* (Doubleday, 1984); M. Kehl, *Eschatologie* (Würzburg, 1986). None of these studies treats the question of limbo.

[22]Cfr. E. Fortman, *Everlasting Life after Death* (New York, 1976) pp. 143-155. This study presents historical material on the question as well as a survey of more recent theories.

[23]Fortman, *op. cit.*, pp. 154-155.

wrong, but that—while it may shed significant light on the adult experience of death—the extension of such a theory to infant death may be pushing it to the outer limits of its intelligibility.

According to Boros, for example, the theory of death as final decision applies to all human beings without exception. This includes undeveloped infants and the mentally defective. Even such persons "would be able to make their decision in full liberty and knowledge at the moment of death."[24] Like all other human beings, these undeveloped persons "awake in death to their full liberty and complete knowledge."[25] In his most emphatic statement, Boros writes that "no one dies as an infant," for—in death—even the biological infant "enters into the full possession of its spirituality."[26]

We can hardly read such statements without asking: If this is, indeed, the case, what is the point of undergoing a human history with all the ambiguity, pain and agony that is the common lot of human beings? Would not the fate of infant-death be far preferable to a long life? Though it is theoretically possible to extend the theory of final decision in this way, the attempt to do so seems to invalidate what Boros has argued concerning life as a "rehearsal" of death. This becomes clear when Boros himself employs the analogy of the decision of the angels to clarify the death of undeveloped human beings. One cannot escape the feeling that, after all that has been said concerning the relation of life to death, in this extension of the theory we are confronted with a highly Platonized view of human existence. The intrinsic relation of life to death on which the major premise of the theory stands has been relativized in a disastrous way. This is not to say that the theory of final decision is fundamentally wrong. But, clearly the theory is in need of further refinement if it is to be used effectively in the discussion of the destiny of unbaptized infants.

The history of theology over the centuries has offered a variety of theories to deal with the destiny of unbaptized infants. It would not be useful here to suggest yet another theoretical solution. But it would be appropriate to close this discussion by highlighting a number of theo-

[24]Boros, *op. cit.*, p. 109.
[25]*op. cit.*, p. 110.
[26]*ibid.*

logical concerns which must be taken into account in any future development of the question:

1) The entire discussion ought to take more explicit account of the nature of theological language. It may be that by pushing metaphors in a far too literal sense, theologians have forced metaphorical language to say more than it is really capable of saying. We have already mentioned the traditional use of court-room metaphors in eschatology. Such language, as we have argued in chapter three, must be interpreted with all the necessary limitations implied in analogical and metaphorical discourse. To the extent that this is not done, it may be that theology creates a problem that is truly insoluble. The only way around the problem would be to approach it on the basis of other assumptions.

2) One of the central issues in the discussion is the conviction that God does not relate to human beings in a mechanical or automatic way. If the eschatological destiny of humanity is the final, life-giving relation between a personal God and personal creatures, it is impossible to conceptualize such a relationship coherently without seeing it to involve a human act at some level. But such a human act assumes a certain level of personal maturity, and maturity presumes some degree of historical experience. This is where the application of the theory of final decision creates problems, for it seems to claim that a mature, human decision is possible in the absence of any historical experience.

3) Generally not given sufficient treatment in the discussion is the theological principle of the "universal salvific will of God." The New Testament speaks of "God our Savior, who desires all men to be saved and to come to the knowledge of the truth" (1 Tim. 2:3-4). Here and in many other instances the Scriptures praise the loving mercy of God that reaches out to humanity universally (Rm. 11:32).

It is precisely when the mystery of the incalculable love and mercy of God is brought into the picture that we see most clearly the inadequacy of the older court-room metaphors. As Rahner has argued in another context, the only limit to the effectiveness of God's love and grace is a bad conscience.[27] In view of this, we might conclude that no theological theory should place unjustified restrictions on the range and effectiveness of God's grace. Precisely if we are dealing with the deepest levels of relation between a personal God and a personal

---

[27]K. Rahner, *I Remember. An Autobiographical Interview*, tr. Harvey Egan (N.Y., 1985) pp. 77-78.

creature, we may never arrive at an adequate understanding of how a person is brought to respond to the divine presence.

This might be taken to mean that, while theoretical constructs may be important up to a certain point, the mystery of God's love cannot be contained within any theoretical construct. The Christian may not be able to *know* how the love of God works in a particular situation, but there is every reason to *hope* that salvation is possible even when it is impossible to have recourse to the ordinary means of salvation. This Christian hope is grounded not in the human ability to come to an intellectual understanding but in the incalculable mystery of God's grace and love.

4) Whatever the fate of the unbaptized infant might be, there is no reason to assume that it must involve an experience of God that is like that of an adult in every respect. There is a common teaching in Catholic theology operative in the traditional discussion of heaven and hell which states simply that the degree of reward or punishment after death is proportionate to the quality of the life of the particular person. Heaven and hell do not mean precisely the same thing for different individuals.

This common teaching of the theological tradition might steer us away from the tendency to conceive of the destiny of unbaptized infants too much according to an adult model.

5) A final issue that pertains to the question is the Christian doctrine of the communion of saints. As a symbol of faith, this reflects the Christian sense of our human solidarity in grace and salvation. While, at one level, we ourselves are responsible for our decisions before God, yet, at another level, it is important to say that our experience of both sin and grace is interwoven with our relations to one another. The discussion of the fate of unbaptized infants should not envision the infant in complete isolation from the human history and human community into which he or she has been born. However we might try to think of the personal act of the infant, that act is made possible not simply by the spiritual powers of the infant in isolation, but by the entire context of sin and grace in which the infant dies. This context includes the presence of God and that of the community of the redeemed who have preceded this infant in death.

This suggests that even before any question of a personal act is raised, the situation of the infant is not neutral. Rather, it is a situation conditioned by a history of sin and grace. And the Christian may hope that where sin did once abound, "grace abounded all the more" (Rm. 5:20).

•

These remarks are not offered as a solution to the problem. They are intended merely to highlight factors that ought to play some role in discussing the issue. It would be difficult to hazzard a guess as to which direction this discussion might take in the future. A modified form of the final-decision theory would seem to be likely. By this we mean a form of the theory that does not make infant death the moral equivalent of adult death, and yet leaves room for some level of personal decision on the part of the infant. Such a view would allow us to envision how God's salvific will can be effective for those who, for no reason of their own, are excluded from the use of the ordinary means of salvation.

READINGS

Boros, L., *The Mystery of Death* (Herder & Herder, N.Y., 1965).

_____ *Living in Hope* (Herder & Herder, N.Y., 1970).

Cox, D., *The Triumph of Impotence: Job and the Tradition of the Absurd. Analecta Gregoriana*, vol. 212 (Gregorian University, Rome, 1978).

Dyer, G.J., *Limbo: Unsettled Question* (Sheed & Ward, N.Y., 1964).

Kübler-Ross, E., *On Death and Dying* (Macmillan, N.Y., 1969).

Le Goff, J., *The Birth of Purgatory*, tr. A. Goldhammer (University of Chicago Press, Chicago, 1984).

Léon-Dufour, X., *Life and Death in the New Testament: The Teaching of Jesus and Paul*, tr. T. Prendergast (Harper & Row, San Francisco, 1986).

Moody, R.A. *Life after Life* (Bantam Books, N.Y., 1975).

Rahner, K., *On The Theology of Death* (Herder & Herder, N.Y., 1973).

_____"The Life of the Dead" in: *Theological Investigations* IV (Helicon, Baltimore, 1966), p. 347-354.

Troisfontaines, R., *I Do Not Die* (Desclee Co., N.Y., 1963).

5

HISTORY AND ESCHATOLOGY

1. Theology of History

a) The Roman Catholic Debate

In the period between Vatican I and Vatican II, Roman Catholic scholarship was engaged extensively in the study of the theological tradition. The "return to the sources" meant not only a deeper penetration of the Scriptures but the study of the Fathers and the Scholastics as well. Two important insights that emerged from this period bear directly on the questions under discussion in this study. The first was the awareness that the theology of the Scriptures and of the Fathers was cast in a mold very different from that of the Scholastics and the neo-Scholastics. The general framework for developing theology until well into the twelfth-century was an historical framework. God had communicated revelation and salvation through a history which could be called salvation-history. Theology was, by and large, a reflection on the events of that history and the meaning of that history for the present. The second insight was the rediscovery of the eschatological nature of Christianity itself. The history of salvation is, by its very nature, open to an eschatological fulfillment. Christianity is thoroughly eschatological in nature.

These two insights help to locate the basis for an important controversy carried out among Roman Catholics in the 1940's and 1950's: the debate between the Incarnationalists and the Eschatologists. While these historical studies represent influences internal to the church, it would be naive to think that there were no external influences. Many of the fundamental impulses of the modern world going back at least to the philosophical revolution of the seventeenth and eighteenth centuries and the political, social, and economic revolutions of the eighteenth and nineteenth centuries stood in a very strong tension with the Christian understanding of reality. The traditional manner of communicating the Gospel seemed totally alien to the concerns of the emerging "modern" mentality. What was the Christian to do with historical consciousness, with the development of science and technology, with the revolutionary philosophy of Marxism and the atheistic forms of humanistic philosophies which saw a hopeless chasm between the search for human authenticity and Christian faith in God? Feuerbach had argued that the very notion of God is a human projection that lies at the root of human alienation. Marx had seen religion as the "opium of the people," a power that alienates human beings from their necessary engagement in the social, political, economic order. Freud would argue that religion is a childish illusion that must be outgrown for the sake of psychological maturity. Is it true that religious faith in God is the root cause of human alienation? If Christianity, at its core, is concerned about a transcendent, eschatological future for humanity, does faith in the God of that future by its very nature isolate the believer from any humanistic concern for the condition of the world in which even the believer must live? The convergence of these factors both within and outside the church gave rise to serious questions about the nature of Christian faith and Christian identity in the modern world.

Does hope in the biblical promise have anything to do with the human search for a better future? Is there any relation between human cares about the future and the eschatological hope expressed in symbols such as the return of Christ, judgment, and the Kingdom of God? Can Christian faith direct the believer to a serious concern for the movement of history? Or does Christian hope ultimately turn the attention of the believer totally away from the world and its plans for the future? These are the questions that lead to theological reflection on history. The recent development of theology reveals a diversity of viewpoints on these questions. We shall sketch the major stages of this development first within Roman Catholic thought itself, and then in the interaction between Roman Catholic, Protestant, and Marxist thought.

1) Incarnationalists

The debate between the Incarnationalists and the Eschatologists revolves largely around the question about Christian identity and

Christian concern for the process of building the world. Among the Incarnationalists, we include H. De Lubac, P. Teilhard de Chardin, G. Thils, and A. Dondeyne. While there is considerable variation in the details of their thought, the Incarnationalists as a group tended to center their position around the theological concept of the incarnation, seeing in it the central model for conceiving of God's involvement with the world and its history. In their theological efforts, they took a positive interest in the questions raised by science and technology, by Marxism, and by evolutionary thought patterns.

Seeing the church as in some way a prolongation of the incarnation of the Word in history, they tended to emphasize the values of earthly reality and human culture. If God has so loved the world as to send his only Son, can the Christian be unconcerned about the world? If God has taken on human flesh in its materiality, does this not mean that in some way material reality has been sanctified? If an Augustine could take up the values of pagan antiquity into a Christian context to create the foundation of a long-standing tradition of Christian humanism, can the Christian today be less concerned about the values and concerns of contemporary culture? Incarnationalism, therefore, tended to place a strong emphasis on the necessity of Christian engagement in the human task of building the world together with others who do not share the Christian faith. Building a world more amenable to human life is a task which the Christian shares with all human beings. Faith, if properly understood, need not lead to alienation but to engagement in the great human tasks. The Incarnationalists were convinced that such worldly-looking activity was a necessary human contribution to the realization of God's Kingdom.

But what of the eschatological nature of Christianity? It must be admitted that in some instances the incarnational model was so strongly emphasized that it was difficult to recognize any sense of a transcendent Kingdom which cannot be created by human projects within the world. The theology of the Incarnationalists offered an understanding of Christianity which was decidedly more this-worldly in orientation than the familiar theology of the hand-books.

2) Eschatologists

This more worldly form of Christianity was objectionable to another group of Roman Catholic theologians known as Eschatologists. Among them are included L. Bouyer, J. Daniélou, R. Guardini, and J. Pieper. Their thought centered more strongly around the Kingdom of

God in its radical otherness as a pure gift from God, the catastrophic end of history, and on the Second Coming of Christ. If the Kingdom is purely a gift of God, it cannot be made even partially by human endeavor. These theologians were also aware of the incarnation of the Word, but they did not hesitate to point out that the agony of the cross stands between Jesus' historical life and the glory of the resurrection. This points to a discontinuity between history and the Kingdom. And if the eschaton is the goal which is important above all else, the discontinuity between history and the Kingdom makes history fundamentally unimportant. We have here "no lasting city" (Hebr. 13:14). The final goal of human history is not the city of humanity but the city of God. These authors emphasized the triviality of earthly concerns and turned with enthusiasm to the things of the spiritual realm.

A strong apocalyptic sense was reflected especially in Pieper and Guardini. As a Christian philosopher living in the difficult time of Germany between the two World Wars, Pieper recognized the need for some devotion to worldly concerns, but the convergence of his cultural situation and the apocalyptic tradition of the Scriptures led him to hold that the end of time is to come in an explicitly apocalyptic manner. It is in the light of the final apocalypse that the Christian must interpret the meaning of history. Sharing the same tragic cultural experience, Guardini thought he was witnessing the collapse of classical culture in Europe. In what must have appeared as a drastic cultural situation, Guardini argued that the Christian living in such a context must face it with responsibility and decision. The only authentic Christian decision would have to be the decision to have faith in God alone. The collapse of culture may be a summons to purify one's faith. A purified faith would be a faith in God and not in culture.

3) The Need for a Dialectical Understanding

The fact that both sides of this debate can claim a strong basis in Scripture points out the need for dialectical sensitivity in Christian eschatology. From a position that is well grounded in the Scriptures, the Eschatologists warn us not to become too hopeful about our cultural situation. We can ill afford to resurrect the naive optimism of nineteenth-century Liberalism. Only the hopelessly naive can look at the last decades of European and North American history and not see the immensity of evil in our world. It would clearly be wrong to let our culture write our theological and spiritual agenda. A Christianity that is incapable of standing against its cultural context, at least in crucial instances, is not worthy of the name of Christianity. If it is necessary for theologians to demythologize the texts of the Scriptures, it is just as important for modern humanity to demythologize itself. Not only must we as human beings interpret the Scriptures, but we must be ready to allow the Scriptures to interpret us. In the mystery of Jesus Christ, the Scriptures offer a self-understanding for humanity that has the power to radically transform the self-understanding communicated by our culture. Each of these concerns, so strongly represented by the Eschatologists, is an important and valid concern for Christian identity.

On the other hand, the Incarnationalists, speaking from a similarly well-grounded position, can point out that the Eschatologists' interpretation of the Scriptures sounds ominously similar to the modern philosophies of the absurd. Have the Eschatologists allowed the prevailing cultural emphasis on the tragic character of human life to determine too much of their reading of the Scriptures? If modern experience is itself ambiguous, reflecting both humanistic optimism and existential pessimism, have the Eschatologists been too much influenced by the sense of pessimism? Is it possible to see the progress of scientific technology as a real and positive development without falling necessarily into a false optimism?

The tension between these two schools of thought is not just of historical interest. On the contrary, the polarities that are here drawn out into two conflicting styles of theology are present as dialectically related poles within the heart of the Christian faith. Christianity does, without doubt, believe that we find God in the midst of our earthly experience and work. There is no place else available for us to find God but in the context of our earthly experience. Even the most exalted mystical experience is an experience that is mediated through objects and persons in the world. On the other hand, Christianity holds out to us the prospect of a future that transcends the world of historical experience. God is not to be identified with the world. And the future which God offers the world cannot be identified with any human, inner-worldly program or project. Historic Christianity is emphatically committed to faith in a transcendent future for the human race. The Kingdom of God is not merely an empty symbol whose function is to stimulate us to live and act "as though" we had a future. On the contrary, the metaphor of the Kingdom symbolizes a *real future* with God.

In the tension reflected in these differing viewpoints and in the unresolved state of the debate we see the significance of the question raised by Feuerbach, Marx, and Freud, and more recently by Bloch. It is true that historic Christianity holds firmly to the concept of a transcendent God and a transcendent future. Does it follow inevitably that these convictions lead with logical necessity to the alienation of the believer from the great human issues and projects of the modern world? Does the belief in a transcendent future inevitably function as a spiritual placebo to keep the poor and the suffering in their miserable situation within history by holding out the hope that—even though they have to put up with misery in this world—they will be rewarded for thus "accepting the will of God" in the next world?

b) Christian-Marxist Dialogue

It was precisely this sort of question that played a central role in the Christian-Marxist dialogue of the 1960's.[1] Does the very nature of Christian faith of necessity distance the believer from any significant role in human history? In the context of his philosophy of hope, E. Bloch had restated the Marxist critique in a new way. The problem, as he sees it, is the impact that the concept of a transcendent future has on the believer. The same problem surfaces in the writings of R. Garaudy, a French Marxist who was a participant in the discussions of the dialogue. By preventing the believer from arriving at a mature level of self-awareness, Christian faith—so it is argued—places a barrier in the way of historical progress.

This intellectual encounter between Christians and Marxists provided the occasion for many Christian theologians to develop their eschatological insights more explicitly. As early as 1960, K. Rahner had published his widely-influential essay on the interpretation of eschatological statements. J. Moltmann had taken up the provocative thesis of Bloch in his *Theology of Hope*, first published in 1965. J.B. Metz and W. Pannenberg, each in his own way, had studied the question of the public and social dimensions of the Christian faith. All of these would develop their thought further as a result of the Christian-Marxist dialogues. The basic issues at the heart of these discussions

---

[1] The dialogue took place in the atmosphere created by Schema 13 of the Second Vatican Council. Three symposia were organized by the Society of St. Paul: Salzburg in 1965, Herrenchiemsee in 1966, and Marienbad in 1967. Each of the symposia involved an exchange between Christian theologians and Marxist theoreticians.

would be the nature of the future and the relation of Christian hope to the processes of world-building in history.

In this context, this Christian understanding of the future found an apt expression in Rahner's formulation: Christians believe in and hope for an *absolute future*. This term expresses the conviction that the human race is open to a future that transcends all the futures that can be conjured up, planned and brought about by human, scientific, technological, and political means. Beyond all human programs, the absolute future is a future that cannot be programmed; for it is pre-eminently the self-gift of God, in which the creature finds its ultimate fulfillment. The Marxist, on the other hand, looks to a future which is the product of human activity alone. The Marxist future can be only a future which is brought about through human planning and activity by means of the resources present in the world, and by nothing else. From a Marxist viewpoint, what Christians call belief in God must be translated without remainder into belief in humanity and its inner-worldly future.

When the problem of the future is formulated in this way as the difference between an absolute future and a categorical future, the question of the historical engagement of humanity in worldly processes is clearly highlighted. As long as we are dealing with a categorical future, it is relatively easy to understand that such historical futures lie in the hands of human beings, at least in part. Clearly there are natural processes that place limits on human cleverness and ingenuity, but human freedom is capable of transcending such processes at least to a limited degree. If the world has been made into a place that is ugly and painful for many human beings to live in through human decisions and human structures, then the world can be remade and transformed by tearing down the structures and building new ones more congenial to human life on a broader scale. This pertains to the level of categorical futures. It is such a future that the Marxist has in mind when he or she speaks of a classless society.

The situation is quite different for the Christian. As long as the Christian maintains faith in an absolute future, it remains unclear how we can see an intelligible relationship between this absolute future and any categorical futures with which we are engaged during our historical existence. Is this time of historical existence merely a period of moral testing? Or does that which we accomplish for the good in history in some way enter into the absolute future of God? There can be no doubt that throughout the centuries, Christians have been deeply engaged in activities that have built human culture, science, and society. What remains unclear is whether that activity proceeds from religious motivation and has a clear religious significance, or whether it is simply something that Christians engage in for purely natural, humanistic motives. And regardless of what the motivation might be, does it make any difference in the end when Christian faith holds out to us an absolute future which we do not create but which we finally receive?

c) Vatican II on the Christian in the World

This question, which moved so clearly into the center of eschatological reflection in the Christian-Marxist discussions, has long been a vexing problem for Christian theology. As we can see in the discussion between the Incarnationalists and the Eschatologists, there is no unanimity of viewpoints among Roman Catholics, to say nothing of Protestant theologians. Even prior to the Christian-Marxist discussion, Vatican Council II addressed the question in the *Pastoral Constitution on the Church in the Modern World* (nn. 33-39). The language of this document clearly reflects the theological ambiguity surrounding the question. On the one hand, the Council calls Christians to work with others in the effort to make the world a place more congenial to human life. The Council indicates that this task flows from the very nature of Christian faith. Christians should "allow their eschatological faith to leave its imprint on the structures of earthly life." One recognizes immediately the difficulty involved in trying to translate such a statement into a practical mode of activity. In a most telling text, the Council writes: "While we are warned that it profits a man nothing if he gain the whole world and lose himself, the expectation of a new earth must not weaken but rather stimulate our concern for cultivating this one. For here grows the body of a new human family, a body which even now is able to give some kind of foreshadowing of the new age" (n. 39). The message of the Council was developed strongly by Pope Paul VI in his encyclical letter, *Populorum progressio* (1967). The Pope summons believers to active engagement in the process of creating a better world so that the hope of freedom and fullness of life will not be but an empty dream (#47, 79).

The Incarnationalists of an earlier era could take heart from this statement. It seems to affirm all that Incarnationalism stood for in the debate with the Eschatologists. The call to engagement in the process of remaking the world is seen as a religious obligation. The text reflects a strong sense of some positive connection between the present and the eschatological future. The human concern about the future of the world is placed emphatically within the context of eschatological hope for a "new heaven and a new earth." Earthly service for the cause of humanity provides the "material of the Kingdom of God." No Incarnationalist could have said it more clearly. The "new heaven and the new earth" is not the replacement of this world but its radical transformation. It is not only love itself that remains, as St. Paul intimates, but the works of love as well.

But, Incarnationalists beware! For the Council makes it emphatically clear that the other-worldly vocation of humanity must be clearly distinguished from any merely humanistic, worldly task. As we have already heard from the Eschatologists, human progress in history cannot be identified with the "growth of the Kingdom of God." There are two types of language being used here in a way that points to the central issue for a Christian theology of history. No Christian theology of history is possible that does not bear the clear marks of belief in an absolute, transcendent future. But does such a belief in a transcendent future unavoidably deny any ultimate significance to human efforts to improve the world and make it more amenable to human existence? This question is highlighted by Rahner when he asks whether the world of human meaning and values created through the cultural history of the human race is only the 'material' for the moral testing of humanity. Will this 'world' simply be done away with? Or will it pass into the *eschaton*, even though inconceivably transformed?[2]

d) Further Discussion Among Contemporary Theologians

The problem of history and human engagement in the historical process is one that flows from necessity out of the heart of the Christian faith. While it may seem, at first, to be a very abstract question, the way in which it is approached reflects and reinforces important aspects

---

[2] *Theological Investigations*, 10, p. 266.

of Christian self-understanding. Is concern about the created world and human history a peripheral concern for the Christian? Or is it a concern that springs from the depths of Christian faith itself?

As we have seen, the teaching of Vatican II does not resolve this question but simply highlights the tension between concern for this world and hope for the absolute future. Neither is there unanimity of viewpoint among theologians in the aftermath of the Christian-Marxist discussion. Among Protestants, Moltmann and Pannenberg stand out as theologians who have attempted to shed some light on the issue. Among Catholics, the problem is currently highlighted in the work of liberation theologians.

Moltmann approaches the question of history and eschatology in the context of a theology of hope characterized by a strongly negative form of dialectic. Dialectic always involves contrasting realities or ideas. But contrast may be of several sorts. Some contrasting realities are complementary and mutually affirming. Other contrasts are contradictory and mutually negating. Moltmann's basic dialectical structure seems to be of the latter sort. Present and future, experience and hope stand not only in contrast with each other but in contradiction with each other. Christian eschatology, as Moltmann sees it, is not focused on present reality as Bultmann would have it, nor on a past mid-point of history as Cullman would have it, but on a real future; namely, the future of God. That future, which lies at the heart of the church's preaching, stands in stark contradiction to our present experience of reality. When the Gospel is preached authentically, and the Christian hears the word of the Gospel appropriately, the Christian becomes conscious of the immense disproportion between the future of God and the present condition of humanity in the world. Christian reaction to the Gospel, therefore, cannot lead to harmony with the present but only to conflict with it. Hope stands in conflict with experience. It is not a sense of harmony between nature and grace, or history and eschatology that leads the Christian to action in the world. On the contrary, it is the sense of disproportion and disharmony evoked by the proclamation of the promise of God in the Gospel that leads to Christian concern and action.

What form is such action to take? In sharp contrast with the view of the Incarnationalists, Moltmann envisions Christians as entering into the world by contradicting its present state, by upsetting it, and thus bringing the world beyond its present condition. Eschatological preaching, as Moltmann sees it, is a summons to enter into the pain of the suffering Messiah in the attempt to bring humanity to a new level of consciousness and eventually to bring about a new reality for the world.

This may sound like another form of harmless religious rhetoric until it is understood as a summons to political involvement. It seems clear that, at least in Moltmann's earlier writings, the negative dialectical structure was meant to be taken quite strictly. The relation between the present and future is one of contradiction. We can move into the future only through the upheaval of the present. When such a dialectic is translated into political terms, it is the basic recipe for revolution of the most radical sort.

If this is to be taken seriously, Moltmann offers an understanding of Christian hope that would lead believers beyond the narrow world of excessively existential and personalist theologies such as that of Bultmann. But at what cost? Moltmann's theology is intended to be explosive. But how consistent is it? If the future is truly the future offered by the divine promise, then it cannot be identified with the future brought about by a political revolution. And if these two futures are not identical or even positively related, then it is not clear how the attempt to create a new political situation really has anything to do with the future of the divine promise. In fact, Moltmann seems to take the Kingdom of God as a metaphor with direct political relevance. The Scriptural basis for doing so is highly questionable as we might conclude from our earlier chapter on the Christian scriptures.

Cardinal Ratzinger has taken sharp exception to this approach. Against Moltmann, Ratzinger points out that the entire project runs the risk of transforming the Gospel into yet another ideology of the future. Thus, in the name of the God of the promise, such a theological position would falsify the Gospel in which the promise is enshrined for Christians. Viewing the issue from another perspective, Ratzinger argues that such a procedure would falsify not only the Gospel, but political reality as well. If the future can be brought about only by the complete destruction of the present, then the proclamation of the Gospel of the Kingdom becomes the basis for political irrationality. Does this not amount to the denial of human responsibility in the final analysis?[3]

---

[3]Ratzinger, *op.cit.*, pp. 19-20.

Approaching Moltmann's dialectical structure from a different perspective, L. Gilkey sees it as inconsistent with the very program Moltmann suggests. As Gilkey evaluates Moltmann's position, it flows from the desire to move away from any position that would hold a universal and immediate presence of God to humanity in history as the source of faith. By reserving the presence of God for the future alone, Moltmann removes the basic condition for making any talk about God even minimally intelligible. If we were to take Moltmann's suggestion seriously, it would not only be a radical critique of the familiar classical theological style, but it would make any theological program fundamentally impossible by removing any point of departure in human experience for faith and theology.[4]

Moltmann intended to overcome the divorce between Christian faith and worldly involvement. It is not clear that he has succeeded in doing this in a way that is intellectually intelligible. While Ratzinger and Gilkey have critiqued the position largely in terms of its unfortunate results, it is possible to critique it in terms of its relation to the biblical tradition as well. If it has a basis anywhere in the biblical material, that basis would be most clearly found in the area of apocalyptic with its emphasis on the transcendence of God as the source of the final power to overcome the tragedy of historical existence. But certainly the prophetic tradition and the Christological tradition would suggest a different sort of theological model. To choose the apocalyptic as normative for the construction of a theological program seems motivated more by personal, subjective factors than by concern for an adequate representation of the biblical tradition. In the end, Moltmann's style of dialectic sounds very much like a new version of the classical grace-works controversy now formulated in language about the future.

Pannenberg offers a theological style that seems more satisfying on a number of scores. At the most basic level, Pannenberg attempts to deal with the centrality of eschatology by working out the ontological implications of an eschatological view of history. If eschatology implies that a primacy must be give to the future, this may mean that we must give up our common understanding of the relation between present and future. In ordinary terms, we think of what we do today as the

[4]L. Gilkey, "The Universal and Immediate Presence of God," in: *The Future of Hope: Theology as Eschatology*, ed. F. Herzog (Herder & Herder, 1970) pp. 81-109.

cause of that which happens tomorrow. This notion of causality ought to be reversed, according to Pannenberg. It is the magnetic power of the future that causes the present. It is the God of the future that draws us beyond our present reality.

Pannenberg's approach places a great emphasis on the meaning of the apocalyptic consciousness in Scripture. As perceived through the eye of apocalyptic, human existence reveals a "proleptic structure." By this Pannenberg means that in the human search for meaning, the dynamic of human experience tends to anticipate the future. Put in other terms, the future acts on the present like a magnet drawing the present beyond itself to something basically new. This proleptic structure of human experience is not simply a subjective reality. On the contrary, it is grounded in the proleptic structure of reality as described above. Reality is stamped by the future to which it is directed. The human person as a conscious being lives out and enacts this proleptic future orientation in his or her quest for meaning.

Pannenberg's thought takes an emphatically historical orientation with the conviction that the question of meaning in which the proleptic structure is revealed is intrinsically tied into history in its most universal terms. At this point we can discern the influence both of apocalyptic theology and of the great nineteenth-century philosophies of history. Both the apocalyptic theology of history and the philosophies of history imply a vision of history as a process whose true meaning is located at the end. As the meaning of each part of a literary text is related to the meaning of the whole text, so the meaning of each moment or event of history is related to the whole of history. This means that the question of meaning is intrinsically related to the question of the whole of history. Since it is impossible to speak of the whole of history until history has run its course, it follows that the meaning of history can be seen fully only from the end-point of history. As long as history has not reached its end, the meaning of its parts is possible only in the light of the end. But if the end has not yet been reached, how is it possible to know, even in a limited sense, the meaning of the parts? No one is capable of standing at the end of history. Yet we must have some knowledge of the end if we are to have any understanding of the meaning of the present.

It is at this point that Pannenberg introduces the mystery of Christ into the picture. Interpreting the resurrection of Christ in terms of the apocalyptic context of the Christian Scriptures, Pannenberg argues that the end of history has been realized proleptically in Jesus. What apocalyptic theology had seen as an element in the future Kingdom of God—the resurrection of the dead—Christians affirm as the destiny of Jesus Christ. While Jesus is clearly an individual human being, what is claimed about him is far more than his individual destiny. Indeed, it is that. But by affirming his resurrection, the Christian community employs an apocalyptic metaphor which implies that what has happened between God and Jesus as an individual is in fact the anticipation of the universal destiny of the human race and of the world. In this sense, the end of history has been realized in Jesus. Because of this, it can be said that Jesus, in his resurrection, reveals and constitutes the meaning of history by actualizing its future, final end. It follows from this that Jesus Christ becomes the indispensable key to interpret the whole of the historical process in all its parts.

From this basis, Pannenberg can see the true vocation of the church to consist in its mission to anticipate and to represent the destiny of all humanity, the goal of universal history. "Whatever significance the church has for the world depends upon the degree of the church's devotion to this universal and humanizing vocation."[5] Such a theological framework leads us to expect that we might find a more positive relation between present and future. God is not absent from the present; rather God is in the present precisely as its futurity. The present is somehow stamped by the future to which it is drawn. Using the Scriptural metaphor of the Kingdom as the metaphor for that future, Pannenberg can see positive signs of the kingdom already in the present as the future makes its power felt in history. "Creative love, unloosed by faith and hope, has the power to pierce this fragile and mortal life with flashes of eternal meaning and joy. Thus we can know the peace of wholeness and integrity."[6]

If this is followed consistently, it must lead to the conclusion that the dialectical relation between present and future in Pannenberg is not one of total contradiction as it seems to be in Moltmann. The task of the Christian in the world is related to the universal destiny of the human race in its quest for meaning. More specifically, the life of the church as a faith community must become ever more an anticipation of the reality of the kingdom of God. It thereby becomes a living

[5]W. Pannenberg, *Theology and the Kingdom of God* (Philadelphia, 1969) p. 74.
[6]*op. cit.* p. 89.

expression of the destiny of the human community as a whole. The proclamation of the Gospel has the power of judgment. But that judgment is against all that stands in opposition to the kingdom, and against every tendency to be satisfied with any limited anticipation of the kingdom wherever that may be found in history.

The most recent stage in the development of the issues under discussion is found in the work of the liberation theologians. Recent developments in the Roman Catholic church have made it clear that the term *liberation theology* should not be understood to represent a unified, consistent body of doctrine. Even a superficial reading of authors such as Leonardo Boff, Gustavo Gutiérrez, and Juan Luis Segundo would be sufficient to make it clear that they do not represent a common body of doctrine. While most recent interest has centered on Latin American authors, it must be said that liberation theology is not limited to Latin America but may be found in a variety of forms in North America as well. If liberation theologians have anything in common, it may be the common search for an appropriate method for engaging in theological reflection from the experience of some level of participation in the process of liberation.

Major differences are found in liberation authors depending on what experience of oppression forms the point of departure for the praxis of liberation and theological reflection. In theory, any experience of oppression may provide the point of departure. Thus, the experience of oppression of the Black people may lead to a style of Black liberation theology. The sexist oppression of women may lead to a feminist style of liberation reflection. The social, economic oppression of the poor in Latin America has led to that style of liberation theology that has been most recently discussed in two Vatican documents.[7]

In whatever form we look at liberation theology, we are confronted with theologizing in the context of massive social suffering and the great social movements of the twentieth-century. Liberation theologians will not be satisfied with a style of theology or Christian life that

---

[7]The Congregation for the Doctrine of the Faith has issued two important statements on Liberation theology: "Instruction on Certain Aspects of the 'Theology of Liberation'," in: *Origins* 14 (1984) 13, pp. 193-204; and "Instruction on Christian Freedom and Liberation," in: *Origins* 15 (1986) 44, pp. 714-728. The official Latin text of the first instruction is found in *Acta Apostolicae Sedis* 76 (1984) 10, pp. 876-909. As of the present, no official text of the second instruction has appeared in the *Acta*.

remains within a Christian or Catholic ghetto. In as far as liberation theology is consciously involved in movements of social transformation, it cannot by-pass the question of the relation between social, historical advances and the Christian understanding of eternal life in a transcendent future. Liberation theologians are inclined to see a far closer relationship here than is possible in the familiar hand-book tradition. Disturbing as this may be to many Christians, it can make its appeal to the biblical theology of creation and to the apocalyptic hope that God would, in the end, vindicate the very act of creation. And, as we have seen in the case of the Christian Scriptures, the kingdom of God in Jesus' preaching and activity takes seriously the earthly side of salvation (healing of the sick, religious liberation from the slavery of legalism, etc.). Jesus' preaching is not focused on earthly forms of salvation in any exclusive way. But neither does it exclude the earthly dimensions of human life. It takes these dimensions with it as it pushes to greater religious depth. Thus, in the Lord's Prayer, the Scriptures include both earthly and eternal salvation. Our ultimate salvation lies in the power and love of God, and as such is beyond our grasp: it will come to us. On the other hand, salvation must announce itself in the real symbols of human action. The message of Jesus is not an escape from human responsibility. On the contrary, it is the opening up of human powers in this world on the basis of the hope and the promise of eternal life given by God in biblical history.

Perhaps even more unclear and disturbing in liberation theology is the question of the relation between truth and praxis, for each form of liberation thought involves an appeal to praxis as, in some way, a source and criterion of truth. Liberation theology looks for a consistent harmony between life and doctrine. The value of a theology is determined by a praxis in which the Christian faith in Jesus Christ is enacted and made visible. In such a context, the essential questions for theologians are not questions about the relation between faith and knowledge, but questions about the relation between faith and justice. This means, eventually, that reflective theology must be accorded a secondary role. The reality of liberation itself is more important than reflection on it or speech about it. In this sense, liberation theologians emphasize the priority of praxis over theory.

This does not have to imply a denial of divinely revealed truth, but it is often understood in that way by those who find liberation theology problematic. And it must be admitted that a good deal of the blame for this difficulty lies with the liberation theologians themselves. Not only have they been vague and unclear on this issue, but their theological writings are often very ideological in tone. On the other hand, it must be admitted that the Word of God opens itself to us always anew through history. It ought to be admitted also that the deepest meaning of God's Word is opened to us at least in part through praxis. This was the case with Jesus himself, who embodied his message in a praxis that eventually led him to the cross. The grace of salvation must be enacted in human life. But the truth of God is prior to human action and is not limited by human weakness and limitations. If the truth is of God, it has the power to draw us beyond the limitation of any particular human experience, whether individual or social. It is this prior reality of the divine truth that remains unclear in much of the literature of liberation theology.

In the development of liberation theology, Christian consciousness reaches an unprecedented level of awareness concerning the social implication of the Scriptures. Since the summons of these theologians is not only to a new consciousness but to the creation of a new reality in the political and social order, it is not surprising that the event of the Exodus should become an important point of departure for theological reflection; for this event can be seen readily as a primal act of divine liberation on behalf of an oppressed people. Among the various biblical metaphor of eschatological significance, that of the Kingdom of God plays a crucial role. It is this metaphor, above all others, that provides the possibility of linking faith and social-political reality. While the Kingdom in the Christian Scriptures elicits the awareness of a future beyond history, that future—for liberation theologians—is emphatically related to the process of history and to the structures of society.

2. The Absolute Future and the Eschatological Reserve

This discussion makes it clear that Christian thought is far from a unanimously accepted understanding. If we wish to deal responsibly with the modern critique of Christianity raised by all projection – theories, then we must try to give an intelligible and coherent account of the relation between the notion of a transcendent future and the conviction that Christians must, by reason of their faith, be involved in the historical process with other human beings. Keeping the critique of religion in mind, we offer the following reflections as a conclusion from the above discussion.

We have spoken of hope at two levels: every-day hope and radical hope. Corresponding to these two levels of hope, we may distinguish two levels of meaning for the word *future*: categorical futures and the absolute future. Every-day hope is directed to specific objects and projects in the world. It is these that make up our categorical futures. Such futures are the proper concern of futurology as we see it in the many volumes that fill the shelves of our book-stores. Radical hope, as we have argued above, is not directed to any specific object or project. It is rather a hope about the possibility of life as such. It is not grounded in a specific experience of hopefulness. In fact, it corresponds to the final question about the possibility of meaning even though most of the signs of our experience may point to the opposite. It is in relation to radical hope that we place the term *absolute future*.

Granted that there is hope in human life, it has been argued by some that the meaning of hope is to be found in the reality of hoping itself and not in any fulfillment of hope. Hope is seen as a mechanism needed to create the illusion that life is worth living. The mistake would be to think that hope will find fulfillment. Meaning lies in hope itself and not in its fulfillment. The Christian understanding, by way of contrast, is that hope in its most radical sense is destined for fulfillment. It is in that fulfillment that the meaning of hope ultimately lies. In view of the fact that radical hope seems never to be fulfilled within the experience of history, such hope can be seen as meaningful only in relation to a transcendent or absolute future.

Different as these two positions are, from an epistemological viewpoint it must be said that both of these represent a form of faith. One is a sort of nihilistic faith; the other is a faith in ultimate meaning and fullness. Neither of these can be demonstrated as true on the basis of empirical data or irrefutably convincing logic. What is the task of theology with respect to this? Reflective theology can endeavor to show in what sense the Christian faith and hope in fulfillment can be a responsible approach to the mystery of human life. It can, we believe, show that Christian faith may be seen as a more coherent vision of life than any nihilistic philosophy of the absurd. But it cannot deliver the definitive proof that what the Christian believes is true. On the other hand, neither can the nihilist offer such a proof for his or her philosophy. We are here confronted with irreducible convictions about the nature of reality. We can affirm them, analyze them, draw out their implications. But in the end, the mystery of reality is such that neither view can be definitively demonstrated as true.

This being the case, we can ask about the humanistic significance of an absolute future. What difference does it make for our understanding of human life? Here we are asking not about the actual practise of theistic believers in contrast with the practise of atheists. As we indicated above, praxis may be one element among many in the discovery of truth, but it is not the only source of truth. In some instances, the praxis of Christians may reflect little if any empirical difference from that of non-believers. In other instances, the praxis may appear very different. At times, that of the atheist may appear better than that of the Christian. At other times, the reverse may be true. To argue practise against practise would be fruitless in the end. It is possible, however, to approach the question in terms of the need to construct an adequate theoretical framework for practise. At this level, it may make a significant difference for our understanding of human reality whether we accept an absolute future or not.

As we have seen, the rejection of an absolute future leaves humanity only with its categorical futures. A categorical future, by definition, is a future within history. Such futures may correspond to individual, personal projects or to communal, social projects. At the individual level, we must ask what sort of categorical project can really sustain the weight of ultimate questions about human life? Is there anything within this world of our experience that is really worth spending all our energy for, or perhaps even dying for? Is there any project or profession that will not, in the end, betray us? Human experience raises this question in many ways. And it is dealt with not only by religion but by literature, drama, and the other arts as well. It is raised in one of its most eloquent contemporary forms in Arthur Miller's play, *The Death of a Salesman.*

At the communal, social level we must ask similar sorts of questions. But in this instance, the relation of the individual to the community becomes a specific problem. If all the community has is its own categorical projects to keep it moving, how does the individual fit into the picture? With the denial of God, the human community has nothing but itself to fall back on to determine what its values and projects will be. By what process is this accomplished? What is the role of the individual in that process? What is to be done about the individual who does not agree with the communal goals? What is to be done with those who are physically or psychologically incapable of fulfilling the roles assigned to them, or any creative roles in the community projects?

In the absence of a transcendent ground of meaning, how can we avoid a totalitarianism of the community? If the meaning of each present moment is finally determined by what it can contribute to the creation of a better earthly future, how is it possible to avoid an ideology of the future in which the future becomes the idol to which each generation must be sacrificed? If the meaning of reality lies in the future, and if the future can only be an earthly future, there seems to be no way to develop a humanism that respects both the present and the future, both the individual and the human community.

Again, from a purely theoretical viewpoint, if we move from the affirmation of an absolute future our vision of human reality differs in a number of significant ways. The absolute future is not future simply with respect to particular projects within history. Rather, it is the total, all-embracing, transcendent fulfillment of the world and its history as a whole. It is a future, therefore, both with respect to the individual and to the whole that embraces the individual within history. Such a future is, by definition, a future that transcends the futures of any individual or group including the human race as a whole. It is a future both for the individual and for the whole of the human race. In as far as it is seen to be a real future, it holds history open in a more radical way than any categorical future can do. In the light of the absolute future, no historical condition, program, or plan can be absolutized. Thus, hope in an absolute future must express itself in the form of judgment on any attempt to define the ultimate meaning of human life in terms of any categorical futures. It will not allow human life, individually or collectively, to close in upon itself. The absolute future relativizes all categorical futures. They may be important, but they are not ultimate. Since they are not ultimate, they are not the ground for affirming the dignity and importance of the individual person. If the dignity of the individual is grounded ultimately in the absolute future, then even the person who can no longer make any concrete contribution to the accomplishment of the inner-worldly future still retains his or her dignity in the light of the absolute future. Thus, it can be argued at least theoretically, that the affirmation of an absolute future provides the basis for a more consistent humanism than does any philosophy of the absurd, of nihilism, or of atheism in whatever form.

It remains to be seen, however, what relation exists between the categorical and the absolute future. Here again the importance of a dialectical understanding becomes central. If the question is formulated as an either/or issue there seems to be no way around it: hope in an absolute future isolates the believer from the historical process. All talk to the contrary will do little to change that. This is the problem that first surfaced in our discussion of the Incarnationalists and Eschatologists. But there is solid theological reason for arguing that this is not an either/or question but a both/and question.

This can be clarified by appealing to the principle of the analogy of faith. As a theological principle, the analogy of faith implies that in theology we are dealing not with isolated symbols whose meaning can be adequately expressed with no reference to the other symbols of faith. On the contrary, the symbols of faith ought to be seen as a relatively coherent system of inter-related symbols. The meaning of each individual symbol must then be interpreted in relation to the other symbols to which it is related within the total symbolic structure of faith. It is through the whole of the symbolic structure that the relation of the believer to reality is articulated. If we approach eschatology from this perspective, it can be shown that there is a genuine theological reason for affirming the internal relationship between the categorical futures of human experience and the absolute future of eschatological faith.

What are the particular elements of the Christian symbolic structure that pertain most clearly to this question? The most basic elements are the eschatological symbols that stand at the center of the controversy: the symbols of the Kingdom of God and the resurrection of Jesus Christ. The symbol of the Kingdom is a symbol of that collective state of salvation in which the final relation between God and the world will be realized. The resurrection is a symbolic affirmation that the Kingdom has been realized in Jesus, and that what has been realized in him is the anticipation of what God intends for the whole of the human race and the world. The Christian use of resurrection-language indicates, already in Scripture, that the Kingdom in which we are to find our future lies beyond historical experience and beyond death. This is what is meant by the absolute future.

But these eschatological symbols are situated within a structure that includes the symbols of God and creation, of incarnation and sin, of resurrection and the cross. In each instance, these paired symbols reflect a way of defining the believer's relation to the world that oscillates between two poles. In the first pair, creation-theology is the basis for the Christian affirmation of the fundamental goodness and redeemability of the world. Creation-theology is a strong affirmation of the world as good. But, placed in juxtaposition with the symbol of God, that affirmation of the goodness of the world is qualified as a shared or participated goodness. The world is good, but it is not the absolute good.

With the second pair, the symbol of incarnation intensifies what has already been said about the nature of the world. Not only is the world good, but it is a place of divine presence in history. The symbol of incarnation speaks not only about the presence of God in Jesus, but also about the presence of God throughout the world and its history. But here the limitation of the first pair which saw the world as a participated goodness is intensified with the awareness that the world in which the Word of God becomes incarnate is not simply the good world as it comes from the hand of the Creator. It is a world that has been worked on by human beings over the centuries of history. As such, it is a world that embodies not only the goodness of humanity but the sin and treachery of human history as well. In this sense, there is a profound ambiguity about the world. It is not only limited ontologically, it is sinful historically. This world of humanity cannot be affirmed in the same clear positive sense as the world of creation.

In the case of the third pair, the resurrection is the affirmation of the decisive acceptance of the world into the life of God. It symbolizes the completion of what God began in the act of creation. But the cross, which stands between Jesus' experience in the world and the reality of the resurrection, emerges as a symbol of God's judgment on the sinful world which has been made such as it is through human decisions. The cross points to the disproportion between God's Kingdom and the ways of humanity in history. That chasm can be bridged only by God's grace and by the profound human conversion and radical transformation brought forth by grace.

From these reflections on other elements of the Christian symbol system, we can argue that the Christian relation to the world is always conditioned by the reality of the transcendent God and the absolute future. But this is not to be interpreted as a theology of world-denial. On the contrary, as long as these paired symbols are held together as they ought to be, we find a religious affirmation of the world deeply rooted in the biblical tradition and not found in many other religions. But this is always a qualified affirmation. It is a *yes, but....* The world is good, but it is not the ultimate good. If we attempt to make it the ultimate good, we will inevitably find that it cannot carry the weight of ultimacy. It will betray us. On the other hand, if we place our ultimate concern in a transcendent God and in the future promised us by that God, then the world and all in it can be found in a new way. "But seek first his kingdom and his righteousness, and all these things shall be yours as well" (Mt. 6:33). Christian faith is not a choice between God and the world. It is a question of finding God in and through the world, and of finding the world in terms of its relation to God.

Granted, then, that a solid case can be made for worldly concern on the basis of Christian faith and not simply because of a desire to be relevant to today's cultural mood, how is the historical task of Christians to be understood? In what does it primarily consist? Again, many of the symbols of Scripture and Christian tradition can be brought together to argue that the core of the historical task for humanity, as perceived in the light of Christian faith, is to transform the human race as universally as possible into a community of loving persons. It is in love that God enters most deeply into the world and exercises the divine rule among human beings. An excessively privatized Christian consciousness tends to forget the tradition going back at least to the epistles of St. John which sees a most intimate relation between love of God and love of our fellow human beings. "If we love one another, God abides in us and his love is perfected in us" (1 Jn. 4:12). This Johannine tradition can be seen as a reflection on the even earlier tradition in which Jesus summarizes the Law in the two-fold command: love of God and love of neighbor. In the post-Scriptural period of the Fathers, this tradition is developed in a powerful manner by Augustine.[8]

There can be no serious question that, in the sources of Christian theology, the question of God and question of humanity are intimately related. But this tradition can easily be interpreted in such a way that faith seems to have meaning only on the personal and inter-personal

---

[8] *Homilies on the First Epistle of St. John.* in: *Augustine: Later Works. The Library of Christian Classics,* ed. John Burnaby. (Westminster Press 1955).

level, and has no significance for our understanding of the public order of social and political reality. How one deals with this problem will depend largely on what philosophical understanding of relations is brought to bear on the question. We have argued in chapter three that human existence is intrinsically relational. Each human person becomes what it eventually is through a continuous interchange with the world of people and things around it. Relationship, therefore, is not something superficial and extrinsic to human history, but is the material from which the fabric of history is woven. Political and social structures are elements of the world which condition the quality of human relations. If the Christian and human task is to create a community of loving persons, this must involve dealing with those conditions which limit the possibility of such a community. The world needs to be humanized in order to create the conditions in which the rule of God's love can become a living reality. The quality and depth of the final relationship between God and the world, which is our absolute future, is conditioned by the degree to which human beings have carried out their historical task. Our future is constituted not only by God's readiness to give but also by our readiness to receive and respond to the gift of the divine self-communication.

This position involves yet another dialectical relation: that between the primacy of God's grace from which alone our future becomes possible, and the necessity of human response which, even as a free response, is made possible by the fact that God has first loved us. "In this is love, not that we loved God but that he loved us..." (1 Jn. 4:10). This suggests that the final relation between God and the world ought to be expressed through metaphors drawn from personal relations. A true mutuality of relationship among human beings is far more than mere juxtaposition in space and time. It involves much give and take. It means a readiness to give of self and to receive the self-revelation of the other. No person can enter into such a relatonship alone. Each is dependent on the other. A person may be "in love" with another and truly desire a depth of relationship with the other. But if the other refuses to let that person into his or her life, no true mutuality can result. The offer of love does not "come home" unless it is received and responded to. Taking into account the limitations of any metaphor when it is used theologically, this may provide a more helpful way of expressing the relation between God and world, and between the absolute future and our historical task.

As a metaphor, it would suggest that the outcome of history (i.e. the Kingdom) will be the result of the interaction of two freedoms, that of God and that of human beings. The future, while ultimately conferred by God, just as existence is conferred in the act of creation, is radically *conditioned* by the quality of human, historical response to God. That future will be conditioned by the response of individuals in changing themselves and creating the possibility for others to change within history. The future of the individual is related to the future of the community so deeply that no individual is saved in isolation from the destiny of the human race. In no sense does this do violence to the primacy of God's grace, nor does it turn God and humanity into equal partners in a sort of team effort. What humanity does, it can do only as a response to God's grace. The human response is made possible only because human nature is enabled to perform it through grace. But God never does what humanity is called to do. Only in as far as grace succeeds in evoking a positive response in the heart of the human person can it be said that God's offer of love "comes home." Without this, grace remains inefficacious.

The point of this argument has been to show that there is solid theological reason for the claim that active involvement in the social, political processes of the human community may be seen as flowing from the heart of Christian faith and hope. It does not have to be seen merely as an optional adjunct to Christian hope. Such a view implies that hope is not a mere waiting for a future that purely and simply "happens to us." On the contrary, hope becomes active as a co-creative power in the coming of the Kingdom. But Christian activism must always proceed from the interior renewal of the heart, and it must be directed to interior conversion; for without the reality of moral and religious conversion, activism is cut off from the depth of its religious grounding.

This argument should not be taken to mean that all Christians must become active in the social and political movements of the world. It is meant simply to open the possibility that such activism may be seen as a genuine component of Christian history. This does not provide the Christian with any particular blueprint or program. The need for discernment becomes crucial, for it is never fully clear what specific form of action is an appropriate Christian response to a situation. As Rahner has argued, while eschatology is not identical with utopianism, yet faith in the absolute future should generate historical utopias. But historical utopianism can take numerous forms. The monastic tendency, for example, with its emphasis on interiority, contemplation, and mystical union, can be seen as a form of utopianism which emphasizes the "eschatological reserve." Political and liberation theology, on the other hand, can be seen as a form of utopianism that emphasizes the values of commitment and secular planning. We should not allow ourselves to be forced to decide between them as though only one of these could be the appropriate Christian response to the world. May it not be that the Christian community needs both, and that only the living presence of both will keep the fuller dimensions of the Christian Gospel alive in the church?

Christian eschatology, as Cardinal Ratzinger has argued, does not have to be a form of escape from the tasks of the world, nor need it be a concentration on individual salvation to the exclusion of all else. It is fundamentally a vision of reality that sees ultimate meaning to be grounded in the God of truth, justice, and love. Therefore, it gives believers the courage to place themselves with radical seriousness at the service of truth, justice and love. Christianity is a resounding Yes to life in as far as life is seen to be a gift from God and a reflection of the God of life. Historical experience is scarred with pain and suffering. But without suffering, life does not come to its fullness and fruition.[9]

The theology of history, if conceived along these lines, should not be confused with philosophies of inevitable progress, nor with purely immanentistic philosophies of evolution. From a theological viewpoint, it is the interaction between divine freedom and human freedom that lies at the core of history. Since God has freely created the world with a purpose or goal in mind, theology must view history in terms of a general teleology; there is a direction in which human history ought to move. But because human freedom is involved, the actual course of history and its future remains always unpredictable and incalculable. Because we are confronted with a fallen and sinful world, the interaction between good and evil must always be a part of the theology of history. In view of this, history will not be conceived as an inevitable improvement of the human condition in a development that follows an uninterrupted straight line. On the contrary, one must envision massive experiences of the power of evil in contrast with the experience of the good.

---

[9] *Ratzinger, op. cit.*, p. 89.

Two symbols have been used to express the experience of history. One is the circle; the other is the line. The symbol of the circle emphasizes the experience of recurrence and consistency. There are regular seasons of the year. There are the cycles of birth, growth, maturity, decline, and death. There seem to be patterns of predictability at all levels of our experience in the world. Pushed too far, however, this symbol becomes the expression of fatalism. Nothing new really occurs. Reality is the way it is, and there is nothing that can be done to change it fundamentally. The ancient myth of Sysiphus expresses this well in the figure of the man who is forever doomed to push the rock up the hill only to see it roll back down again.

The other symbol is that of the straight line. As a symbol, this highlights the experience of the unique and unrepeatable. What has happened in one time and place can never be exactly reproduced in another time and place. Historical events are unique and unrepeatable. The line expresses the sense of a clear direction and openness to something new. When pushed too far, this orientation tends to become overly optimistic and to minimize the power of evil in human history.

Each of these symbols expresses important dimensions of historical experience. If we combine them, we could take as a more satisfactory symbol an ascending spiral. The circular dimension of the spiral recurring at different levels may be taken to express recurrent patterns present in history. The linearity of the ascending spiral expresses the fact that the recurrence takes place on constantly new levels and with some degree of new content. Something new emerges out of the old. The spiral itself would indicate that history is not a direct, one-dimensional movement, but a multi-dimensional process including the power of evil and the power of good. In its linearity, the symbol indicates that history is going somewhere. The fact that it is a spiral symbolizes that the dynamic of the movement includes freedom. History is not a mechanistic process.

Such a symbol would allow us to hold together the various dimensions of the theological understanding of history. The sense of direction corresponds to the theological conviction that history is moving toward one God-intended end which has been anticipated in Christ. The polarities expressed in the oscillation of the spiral reflect the struggle between good and evil. It is possible, in this symbolic model, to envision a radicalization of the powers of evil. It does not express a naive, romantic optimism since it does not envision the inevitable defeat of evil within history. It leaves room open for the Christian hope that humanity will be successful in carrying out its historical task, but it does not know with certainty that this will be the case. This remains an object of hope. This is a radical hope since it is grounded in God's final word to the world in the mystery of Jesus Christ. This word remains alive despite the darkness and threatening character of human history as we now know it. Finally, it would envision an end to the history of humankind. This is not identical with the end of the universe nor with the fiery cataclysm of apocalyptic thought. The history of humankind is essentially that sector of cosmic history in which human freedom is enacted. As this comes to a terminal point for the individual person in death, so the theology of history envisions a terminal point in the collective history of the human race. By this we would understand that there will be a point at which our present historical experience of space-time reality will be transcended in a decisive way, either for good or for evil.

READINGS

Casserly, J., *Towards a Theology of History* (Holt, Rinehart & Winston, N.Y., 1965).

Connolly, J., *Human History and the Word of God* (Macmillan, N.Y., 1965).

Cullmann, O., *Christ and Time* (Westminster Press, Philadelphia, 1962).

Danielou, J., *The Lord of History* (H. Regnery, Chicago, 1958).

Girardi, G., *Marxism and Christianity* (Macmillan, N.Y., 1968).

Lash, N., *A Matter of Hope. A Theologian's Reflections on the Thought of Karl Marx.* (Notre Dame Press, Notre Dame, 1982).

Lubac, H. de, *Catholicism* (Sheed & Ward, N.Y., 1958).

_____*The Drama of Atheistic Humanism* (Sheed & Ward, N.Y., 1950).

Rahner, K., "Christianity in an Evolutionary Framework," in: *Theological Investigations* 5 (Helicon Press, Baltimore/ Darton, Longman & Todd, London, 1966) pp. 157-192.

Von Balthasar, H. Urs, *A Theology of History* (Sheed & Ward, N.Y., 1963).

6

THE END OF HISTORY

With the final remarks of the previous chapter we have touched on the question of the temporal end of history. This, in turn, is related to the cosmic dimensions of the Christian understanding of salvation. Important themes which occur in the history of Christian reflection on these issues are: the return of the Lord (=parousia), apocalyptic signs of the end, and the thousand-year reign of the just with Christ on earth prior to the end of history (=millennium). The latter idea is known either as Millenarianism (from the Latin for a *thousand*) or as Chiliasm (from the Greek for a *thousand*).

1. The Delay of the Parousia

From the beginning of its existence, Christianity has found history to be problematic. The reason for this lies in the eschatological nature of the Christian faith. As the first two chapters of this presentation have shown, the Hebrew Scriptures had looked forward to a future eschatological event. Christians, on the other hand, have claimed that the eschatological event has been realized in the life, death, and resurrection of Jesus Christ. But if the Christian claim is to be taken seriously, then Christians must somehow deal with the fact that history continues much as it had been prior to the existence of Jesus, at least if history is viewed from an empirical perspective. If the eschatological event is understood to be the goal of history, would it not be reasonable to expect either that history would come to an end when this goal had been reached, or at least that it would be radically altered? If, as

Christians claim, the eschatological event has taken place in Jesus, why does history continue, and much in the same way that it was before? This question confronts theology with the problem of interpreting a cluster of symbols with which Christianity has surrounded the mystery of the universal destiny of the human race and the cosmos.

The question about the end of history is practically unavoidable for the thinking person. It is hard to imagine looking at the course of events, both in one's personal life and in the social life of the human race, without asking at some time whether it all has some meaning beyond what can be discerned at the empirical level. And if so, how can that be known? If we can speak of history at all—and the Western mind has been strongly inclined to do so—this must mean that the objects of our experience are more than individual objects that stand next to one another in temporal juxtaposition. But how are they related more deeply? And if there is truly an historical process, to what is it leading? Does it have an end in the sense of a unifying meaning? And does such a unifying meaning imply that it must also have a temporal end? These are questions of the philosophy of history. But even more so, they are questions for Christian theology because of its fundamental vision of reality, which sees created beings to be bounded by the mystery of an absolute origin (=creation) and an absolute end (=eschatology). Christian theology cannot omit the question about the end of history.

2. Apocalyptic in the Theological Tradition

In treating the material of the Christian Scriptures in chapter two, we have pointed out the apocalyptic background of Christianity as well as the presence of apocalyptic material in the Christian Scriptures themselves. In numerous instances we have seen examples of texts that look with expectation to the end of history and to the return of the Lord in judgment. The most sustained instance of such apocalyptic reflection is found in the *Book of Revelation*. Once Christians identified Jesus' resurrection as the eschatological event and as the beginning of the new age, they left themselves open to the problem caused by the fact that the return of the Lord seemed to be delayed. The Scriptures reflect the transformations instigated by this. The shift of emphasis from a future return to a present activity of the Lord in the community is symptomatic of this development.

But the fact that the return of the Lord was delayed did not mean that Christians gave up all interest in apocalyptic matters. The later levels of the Scriptures are clear evidence that this was not the case. The literature of the patristic period shows considerable interest in apocalyptic questions, even though the use of the specifically apocalyptic literary genre faded with time. Questions about the end of history and other apocalyptic issues were incorporated into commentaries on the Scriptures and in other forms of theological writing. That there was such a transformation is clearly attested to by abundant textual evidence. It should not, however, be assumed that this transformation involved some sort of catastrophic sense that the message of the Lord had been shown to be mistaken. As J. Pelikan has argued, the textual evidence points to a shift within the relation of the *already* and the *not yet* of biblical eschatology. The problems involved in such a shift led to a variety of solutions.[1]

Of special concern were themes and issues raised by the *Book of Revelation* such as the duration of history, the figure of the Antichrist, and the meaning of the millennial kingdom in *Revelation* 20. Reflections on these themes took the form of millenarianism or chiliasm. These two terms refer to the doctrine, based on *Revelation* 20:1-10, that Christ would reign on earth with his elect for a thousand years following the general resurrection and prior to the end of history. Justin the Martyr gives evidence of a variety of views in the early second century. Some, he says, depicted the final reign of Christ in great detail, while others did not attribute much importance to such detailed descriptions.[2] In the Eastern church, Origen led the battle against the literal and materialistic interpretations of *Revelation*, which he saw to be unworthy of the divine promises. In the West, Jerome pointed out two approaches to the *Book of Revelation*. Some of his contemporaries took the book quite literally while others read it in a very spiritual fashion. In Jerome's view, the literal reading amounted to a Judaizing of the text and was therefore unacceptable.

While Augustine, in his early years as a Christian, seemed to have no problems with a moderate form of chiliasm, he would later reject it

[1] J. Pelikan, *The Emergence of the Catholic Tradition (100-600)* (Chicago, 1971) p. 124.

[2] Justin, *Dialogue with Trypho* 80.2.

vigorously. In the *City of God,* Augustine seems to be convinced that he is living in the final age of history. Yet he sees no need to look for specific signs of the end nor for any detailed information about how the end will happen. Did not the Lord himself tell his overly eager disciples: "It is not for you to know times or seasons which the Father has fixed by his own authority"(Acts 1:7). The thousand-year reign of *Revelation* 20 is here identified with the time of the church, and all millenarian speculations are rejected (*City* 20:7-10).

B. McGinn concludes that by the end of the fourth century, Jerome and Augustine had succeeded in consolidating the anti-millenarian position in the West. In their view, the whole of the book of *Revelation* was to be given a spiritual interpretation. The result of this was that the mainline of Western theology came to see the book principally as a message about the present life of the church rather than a prediction of the future. A spiritual, moral, ecclesiological interpretation dominated over the literalist tendency to historicize the figures and symbols of the text.[3]

Yet, the tendency to read the book in a very literal sense and to identify the symbolic elements with historical persons and events never died out completely. In the twelfth century, Rupert of Deutz attempted to interpret many elements of *Revelation* in relation to events of his own historical period even though the spiritual tradition still reigned supreme. The same can be said of the Abbot Joachim of Fiore of the same century. Joachim did not succeed in escaping the influence of the Augustinian, spiritual tradition. But he integrated this tradition in the framework of his own more personal concern which saw *Revelation* principally as a detailed message concerning God's plan for history. Joachim's work, which was largely concerned with a broadly-conceived theology of history, became an influential source for interpreting the book of *Revelation* and for speculation about the end of history that reached far beyond his own time.

Joachim's work was not without an impact even on the period of High Scholasticism, a period usually thought to be far more rationalistic in its orientation. Much as Augustine had reacted against the millenarianism of his time, Aquinas reacted against the too fervent eschatological awareness of Joachim's disciples, rejecting both the basic

[3]B. McGinn, *The Calabrian Abbot: Joachim of Fiore in the History of Western Thought* (New York/London, 1985) p. 74ff.

interpretive principles of Joachim and specific points of Joachim's doctrine.[4] On the other hand, Aquinas' great contemporary, Bonaventure, attempted to undertake a critical appropriation of Joachim's thought, rejecting what seemed to be objectionable and incorporating Joachim's positive insights into his own theology of history. Scholastic though he was, and trained in all the intellectual techniques of the university of his time, Bonaventure was, nonetheless, apocalyptic in outlook. He was convinced that he lived near the end of the final age of history. He could see in his own times clear signs of the final crisis of history. Yet he looked forward—much as Joachim had done—to a final period within history that would be a time of the fullness of peace, grace, and revelation.[5]

The history of interpretations of *Revelation* and of speculations concerning the course of history and its end continues throughout the centuries. Millenarian views are associated with the Moravians and the Anabaptists, and more recently with the Adventists and the Jehovah's Witnesses. Aside from these communities with a venerable history behind them, millenarianism is associated today with many lesser sectarian movements claiming to have a secret knowledge of things to come. For them, the Great Tribulation, the Rapture, the Battle of Armageddon, and similar events are seen to be infallibly predicted in the Scriptures. Such views are based on a literal, materialistic interpretation of sources such as *Ezekiel, Daniel*, and *Revelation*. Often prophetic symbols are identified with the potential for nuclear warfare. This feeds a desire to escape the great holocaust and to be taken up in the Rapture. For some Fundamentalists, the notion of the Rapture is drawn from 1 *Thessalonians* 4:13—5:10. It is associated with the notion of the double coming of the Lord. Jesus will come before the nuclear holocaust to take up (=rapture) the saved. He will come another time accompanied by the saints to reign a thousand years on the earth.

Popularized in Hal Lindsey's *The Late Great Planet Earth*, a viewpoint known as Dispensationalism sees history to be divided into seven great ages or dispensations. Beginning with the age of innocence in *Genesis*, history moves through stages until it arrives at the age of the millennium predicted in *Revelation* 20. God's promises to Israel will be fulfilled literally when Israel lives in the land of Palestine under

[4]McGinn, *The Calabrian Abbot*, p. 210ff.
[5]McGinn, *The Calabrian Abbot*, p. 213ff.

the rule of a king from the Davidic line in Jerusalem. In the millennium, Jesus Christ will rule on David's throne over an earthly kingdom.

Only the spiritual, allegorical style of exegesis could help Christians escape the pitfalls of making too direct a connection between apocalyptic symbols and concrete historical realities in the classical period of theology. Today, the historical-critical reading of the Scriptures would have the same function. Yet, the tendency remains as a basic human tendency; one wants to know the future. When appropriate critical tools are not available or not employed even though available, it is almost inevitable that Christians will read the text of *Revelation* as a sort of eyewitness account of the course of history and especially of its end phase.

It is significant also that the latter part of the so-called secularized twentieth century has given rise not only to such fundamentalist apocalyptic speculations but to a wealth of secularized apocalyptic as well. Novels, movies, television programs and a variety of extended treatises deal with the future of the earth and of the human race. This literature commonly expresses the fear that humanity has within its power the possibility of annihilating itself and the world which is its habitat. Explicitly apocalyptic language and imagery is used, though it is now separated from the religious context which gave to this sort of speculation its original meaning. In this context, apocalypticism becomes almost identical with bleak, negative forecasts of the self-destruction of the human race. Shorn of its religious base, apocalyptic of this sort can become nothing but a philosophy of pessimism quite different from the original, biblical apocalyptic hope that, despite the overpowering experience of evil in history, the creative power of God would overcome the forces of evil in the end.

3. The Parousia as a Symbol of the End of History

Christianity, from its earliest years, has stood in expectation of the "coming of the Lord" in glory to judge the living and the dead. Reaching to the Son of Man tradition of *Daniel*, the Gospel accounts speak of Christ's coming on the clouds of heaven in the great drama that will bring history to its conclusion. Liturgical prayer and Christian creedal formulas (DS 6, 10, 13-19, 125, 150) express the ancient Christian expectation of the return of the Lord and the coming of God's kingdom. Christian art and iconography over the centuries offers a wealth of pictorial representations of the Last Judgment with the glorified Christ exercising the role of divine judge. Without doubt, the hope in the final, glorious coming of Christ at the end of history has been a fundamental element of Christian consciousness over the centuries. The central Christian metaphor for the end of history is the second coming of Christ, or the parousia. Around this center stands a cluster of related themes such as: the signs of the end, general judgment, resurrection of the dead, heaven and hell, the kingdom, the new heaven and the new earth.

As an article of the Christian creed, the idea of the return of the Lord seems to be inseparable from the concept of the end of history, at least at the level of popular understanding. Is it, then, an article of Christian faith that history will have an end? And if it is argued that it is not an article of faith in the strict sense, is it nonetheless a necessary condition for something that is an article of faith: namely, the future coming of Christ?

As we have already seen, the word *end* can be understood in a number of ways. When we speak of the end of history, the meaning that most clearly comes to mind is that of a temporal ending. As creation is thought to involve a first moment of time in an ongoing temporal sequence, so eschatology is thought to imply a final moment in that sequence. In this sense, for example, O. Cullmann argues that with each moment we come closer to the end of history. This, however, is not the only meaning of the term. Another important meaning can be seen when we ask a person about to embark on a perilous journey: "What end do you have in mind in making this journey?" Here, the question is not one of time but one of purpose and finality or one of meaning.

Obviously these are two quite distinct usages of the same word. Both of these usages can be involved when we ask about the end of history. In the first case, we are asking whether there will be a final, temporal point in the movement of history. In the second case, we are asking whether there is a unifying goal or purpose that invests the whole of the historical process with meaning. Normally, we think of both of these together. But it is possible to see them as two distinct questions and to ask whether there can be a unifying goal that invests history with meaning even though we may be able to say nothing about a temporal end. On the other hand, from scientific research, it may appear easier to speak of a temporal end and admit to agnosticism concerning a unifying goal. The question concerning a unifying goal is more directly theological in nature. It is rooted in the eschatological, apocalyptic background of the Christian faith and is brought into center-stage by the proclamation of the resurrection of Jesus. How and to what extent this theological sense of *telos* or end is to be seen in relation to the temporal extension of human and cosmic history is not clear.

Theologians such as Rahner, Pannenberg, and Ratzinger stand under the influence of nineteenth-century philosophies of history at least to the extent that they share the conviction that history is a process which is radically unified by its end. Only when the dialectic of history has been brought to a resolution is the question of the meaning of the historical process decided. This philosophical conviction is brought together with the theological conviction that salvation is the fulfillment of God's world. If we are to speak of the meaning of universal history at all, we must envision a situation in which our present experience of spatial-temporal realities will be transcended. At least in this sense, history will have an end.

To speak of an end to history in this way is not to speak of the annihilation of the world. But it does reflect the conviction that this universe, and humanity in it, unfolds as a unified process which moves as a whole to its consummation. The theological point can be expressed by drawing an explicit analogy between the notion of individual history and universal history. As the history of an individual moves to an end, so the history of the human race is envisioned as moving to an end. And as the history of the individual points to a future for the individual, so the history of the human race points to the future for the entire body of humanity. This self-transcendence of history into eternity is the future of the historical process as a whole.

From this perspective, the tendency to re-interpret the symbol of the parousia of the Lord becomes understandable. The parousia is not a return of a Lord who has been absent from the world since the resurrection, but the final breaking through of the victorious presence of divine grace that has been present continuously throughout history, and in a special way since the death and resurrection of Christ. The parousia is not so much a question of Christ coming back to the world, but of the world arriving at its goal with God in Christ. It may be unfortunate to use the term "second" coming at all, since the usage seems to distinguish it from a "first" coming in the incarnation and to set these two "comings" over against each other as two distinct and mysterious events.

In reality, the word *parousia* can mean either "presence" or "arrival." When the emphasis is placed on "arrival," and eschatology is cast clearly in a chronological mode, then the parousia turns out to be a future event that brings history to an end. But when the emphasis is placed on "presence," then the whole of history after the death of Jesus is the mystery of his abiding presence or parousia. What remains is for the fullness of that mystery of grace to work itself out in the human race and the world. In this sense, the parousia symbolizes the saving presence of Christ to history, and the completion on a cosmic scale of the process begun in his life, death, and resurrection. In brief, parousia is the symbol of the consummation of history in God.

4. Resurrection and the Interim-State

What is the fate of those who die before the end of history? This question has been the object of much debate especially among Roman Catholic theologians in recent years. The Catholic debate was preceded by an earlier discussion in Protestantism that found a clear and influential statement in O. Cullmann's Ingersoll Lecture written in 1955 and entitled "Immortality of the Soul or Resurrection of the Dead."

Cullmann sets up a sharp contrast between two different ways of conceiving human salvation. The notion of the immortality of the soul he presents as a pre-eminently Greek concept; the notion of the resurrection of the dead he sees as properly biblical. It is one of the great misunderstandings of Christian history that has led to a situation where most Christians simply assume that the concept of the immortality of the soul is the self-evident Christian concept of salvation. It is more in harmony with the bible, so the argument runs, to see death not as the separation of body and soul but as the end of the human person in all that makes it a human person. Christian hope, then, is properly expressed as a hope in the resurrection of the entire human being.

With this, the distinction between two ways of conceiving of salvation enters into the stream of contemporary theology, setting the stage for the Roman Catholic discussion concerning the fate of those who have died before the end of history. In his doctoral dissertation, G. Greshake argued that it is possible to deal with the theological question without having recourse to the Scholastic theory of the separated soul.[6] His argument builds on the earlier work of Rahner and Boros, and presents the thesis that it is the entire person that dies and encounters God in death, and not just a disembodied soul. This thesis is expressed most pointedly in the claim that resurrection takes place in death and not at some future time at the end of history. Greshake's thesis has found a considerable following among German theologians, many of whom think that such a view makes the meaning of the traditional symbol of resurrection of the flesh more understandable in the context of contemporary understandings of human nature. Even Rahner states that the position, though strange to the ears of those accustomed to the Scholastic formulation, is a theologically defensible position.[7]

Greshake's position was vigorously attacked by Cardinal Ratzinger on the grounds that it fails to take serious account of the corporal dimension of the Christian hope for salvation, and that it does not allow for a true openness of history since, according to at least one formulation, the whole of history is present with each person at the moment of death.[8]

The question re-opens issues on the nature of material reality and its relation to spirit, as well as the issue of time and its relation to eternity. As it pertains to the question of the end of history, Greshake's thesis leaves the distinct impression of human persons encountering God in death and thus arriving at eschatological fulfillment while the material cosmos is turned over to endless time, much as it was in the philosophy of Aristotle. As Ratzinger assesses the situation, in such a viewpoint the ultimate meaning of history can never be resolved. Rahner also senses this problem when he asserts that the theory of resurrection in death is possible always provided that the theologian who holds such a thesis "does not mean that the time-scheme of world history itself can also be eliminated from his theological statement."[9]

[6]G. Greshake, *Auferstehung der Toten* (Essen, 1969).

[7]*Theological Investigations*, 17, p. 115.

[8]Ratzinger, *Eschatologie* ..., p. 92ff.

[9]*Theological Investigations*, 17, p. 115.

W. Kasper writes to the point: "The perfection of the individual and that of all of mankind cannot be complete until the cosmos, too, is included in that completion."[10] In very pointed terms, Kasper relates the question of the end of history to the problem of the antagonistic and tragic character of history as it is found in apocalyptic theology and concludes: "The whole mess has got to stop sometime. The fulfillment of this primordial hope is what Scripture expresses in apocalyptic terminology. . . . God has accepted the world finally, in Jesus Christ, and God is faithful, so the world and history will not simply vanish into nothingness, rather God will be its 'all in all' at the end (1 Cor. 15:28)."[11]

In 1979, the Sacred Congregation for the Doctrine of the Faith issued a "Letter on Certain Questions concerning Eschatology" (May 11, 1979). In its attempt to clarify this and a number of related issues, the Congregation expresses its understanding of the destiny of humanity after death. It affirms the church's belief in resurrection, understanding that term to refer to the whole human person. Concerning the issue of the immortality of the soul, the Congregation affirms that a "spiritual element" survives and subsists after death. This spiritual element it understands to be the "human self" endowed with consciousness and will. Aware that the use of the term "soul" to designate this spiritual element may be technically problematic, the Congregation does not see the problems involved as a valid reason for rejecting the term. The most pointed statement bearing on the theory of resurrection in death is found in the affirmation that the church looks for the glorious manifestation of the Lord, which it believes "to be distinct and deferred with respect to the situation of people immediately after death."

Recognizing that it is impossible to give any clear and unambiguous account of life after death, the letter highlights two principal concerns of the church: 1) The fundamental continuity between the present experience of grace and the future consummation of grace; 2) the radical break between the present life and the future one. For the most part, this is a restatement of previous magisterial teaching made with obvious concern for this new formulation.

---

[10]W. Kasper, "Hope in the Final Coming of Jesus Christ in Glory," in: *Communio: An International Catholic Review* 12 (Winter, 1985) p. 378.

[11]Kasper, *op. cit.*, p. 379-80.

In as far as the theory of resurrection in death can be distinguished from the question of the end of history, the incompleteness of each individual prior to the full actualization of the Body of Christ can be treated by giving a strong emphasis to the organic nature of humanity. It is also possible to render a convincing account of the Christian concern with suffrages for the dead on the basis of this relational understanding of human nature. In as far as all the members of the Body are interdependent, perfect fulfillment can be envisioned in this model only when all have attained their place within the whole of the Body. At least in this sense, the theory of resurrection in death comes under no censure in this document. However, when the theory is joined with the denial of an end of history, the matter is not so clear. For in this form, the theory envisions individual resurrection and universal resurrection to coincide. If such is the case, there is no longer any basis for speaking of the incompleteness of the individual. Nor does there appear to be any significant basis for the practises of Christian piety.

With the cautions of the Sacred Congregation in mind, we conclude that the question of the interim-state remains an issue open for theological speculation and discussion. For Catholic theology, the teaching of the magisterium sees a state of incompleteness for all between individual death and the universal resurrection. In this condition, the deceased exist in a state of consciousness, but in a manner different from earthly existence. It is the task of speculative theology to place this conviction in a coherent and relatively intelligible context. No theological explanation will be completely adequate. If the more traditional understanding is felt to be problematic on a number of scores, the more recent theory of resurrection in death is not without its own problems.

5. The Coming of Christ, Judgment, and Signs of the End in Contemporary Theology

The understanding of the parousia given above is strongly related to the modern sense of history. The parousia has been described as the world arriving at Christ rather than as Christ returning to the world after a long absence. It would be a mistake, however, to see the fulfillment of history symbolized by the parousia simply as the result of a dynamism that is purely immanent to the world. Christianity offers, first of all, a religious view of the future. It sees a future that is opened to the world by God. With its roots in apocalyptic theology, Christianity sees the meaning of history to be ultimately grounded in the creative act whereby God vindicates the initial act of creation itself. In the face of the experience of evil, pain, and tragedy, the basic hope of Christianity is that, in the end, love will be more powerful than hatred, justice will prevail over injustice, truth will emerge triumphant over all deception, and life will be victorious over death.

The outer limits of created existence are expressed in the claim that creation has its ultimate origin and end in God. But these outer limits are connected by history. And the concrete course of history between creation and the eschaton is a matter of the interplay between God's freedom and human freedom. With freedom as a major factor in history, it becomes impossible to speak of an inevitable progress, for freedom involves the possibility that human beings might attempt to create their history in contradiction to God's eternal purpose. If we look more closely into the reality of past history, it is impossible to see the final future simply as the immanent ripening of history itself. The element of evil is too pervasive for that. History, viewed from the perspective of the Kingdom of God, seems like an ongoing battle between the ultimate divine aim and the ways of humanity. The presence of evil in history seems to be more than the notion of evolutionary immaturity can account for. This is part of the insight of the apocalyptic vision, which was inclined to see history not as a smooth, evolutionary process but as an ongoing confrontation between opposing powers of good and evil. It is this perception of history as antagonistic which gives rise to two further eschatological concerns. Not only must history end, as we have argued above, but the end must come as a creative act of God and as an act of judgment.

a) Parousia and Judgment

With this the theme of human responsibility emerges in the context of eschatology. The conviction that human history is the fruit of free, human decisions leads to the conviction of the Judaeo-Christian tradition that both collectively and individually, human beings are responsible for their actions in history. The ancient Jewish prophets had proclaimed a coming Day of the Lord when the sinful would be called to judgment (Jer. 25:30-31). For early Christianity, this Day of the Lord was associated with the parousia of Christ. In the imagery of apocalyptic, the Lord would come to judge the living and the dead as Lord of history. The suddenness of his appearance calls for constant readiness (Mk. 13). The coming of the Lord was eagerly awaited as the day of salvation.

As Christian theology developed, especially in the Middle Ages, the focus shifted to the coming of Christ as a judge who would examine each life in minute detail. To say that there was a shift of emphasis is not to say that early Christianity knew nothing of individual responsibility. But, very likely because of the expectation that the end of history was near, the early community would have looked more directly to the collective dimension of judgment. As the centuries passed and the intensity of near-expectation weakened, the focus on individual judgment grew apace with the development of a stronger emphasis on the individual spiritual journey. The sense of eager anticipation in the early Christian literature gave way to the mediaeval fear and trembling before the "day of wrath." The mediaeval *Dies Irae* of the Requiem Mass, particularly in its great musical settings, embodies this sense of terror before the final Judge in a way that underscores the contrast between the early Christian sense of confidence and the mediaeval attitude of fear. The drama of the momentous conflict between good and evil which apocalyptic envisioned at the cosmic level now appears at the level of individual history and destiny.

The concept of judgment is troublesome for many modern people. At one level, problems arise simply from the use of language derived from juridical categories to describe the relation between humanity and God. Too often such language communicates the idea of vindictive anger. But how can we associate this with the God of the Christian Scriptures who is seen as a mystery of unlimited and unmerited forgiveness, mercy, and love? At another level, problems of a different sort emerge from the modern tendency to wash out any strong sense of personal responsibility for the decisions we make in human life. It is easy to explain away the evil done by human beings as signs of psychological immaturity or emotional instability. In such a context, it is difficult for many to be convinced that moral choices are far more important than certain psychological categories would seem to indicate. A moral choice is an exercise of human freedom, and the quality of our choice has far-reaching consequences. Only if we have a human sense of responsibility for our actions can we find a meaningful basis in our experience for speaking of the religious reality of judgment. If we take the human awareness of responsibility to one another as the starting point for reflection on judgment, then it is possible to move to significant reflections on our responsibility in the presence of that Other whom we name God. With that, the theme of judgment can take on importance as an eschatological theme.

Our earlier discussion about history and eschatology, and especially the contemporary discussion on death and resurrection, have shown an understanding of history that is basically dialogical. That is, we are dealing with an ongoing interaction between a personal and free God and the free reactions of personal creatures. History is the reality of that which is brought into being through this interaction. This model of dialogue appears not only in the interpretation of history, but in the understanding of the final, or eschatological, relation between God and creation. The eschatological condition has the structure of a dialogue which is profoundly personal in nature. Within this model, the theme of judgment takes on a much more anthropological interpretation.

This can best be seen by recalling that in theology generally, and in eschatology particularly, we are dealing not with isolated symbols or concepts, but with a circle of symbols which provide a context for interpreting the meaning of human life in terms of its ultimate meaning. We may take hold of that circle at different places, and we may thereby give different kinds of emphasis or different colorations to our understanding of Christian faith. There is no single, all-embracing definition of the mystery of God or of our relation to the divine. In our more recent past, Christian theology and preaching has tended to grasp the circle of Christian symbolism at the point that emphasizes the disproportion between the creature and God, and therefore to emphasize the themes of purgation and judgment. Often this took the form of reflection on the divine wrath with a corresponding sense of fear and terror before such a God. This is not to say that the divine mercy was forgotten, but any concern for that divine attribute had to be placed under the controlling metaphor of wrath and judgment. Unfortunately, in this context the categories of law and vindictive punishment tend to become the dominant symbols for expressing the relation between God and humanity. Every set of symbols has its limits. Here the appropriateness of envisioning the relation between a personal God and personal creatures too emphatically in categories of law is an obvious problem. And if this orientation is allowed to develop without any correction from other elements of the Christian symbol-system, the theological view of judgment will be dangerously misleading. What suffers most in such an orientation is the biblical sense of God as mercy, love, and forgiveness.

If we look at the biblical tradition, the theme of divine judgment is as real as is the theme of divine mercy. The two are not mutually exclusive. The *Epistle to the Hebrews* argues that it is precisely the sign of a father's love that the father disciplines the child (Hebr. 12:3-11). Today, in popular parlance, we speak of "tough love" in the context of parent-child relations. By that we mean a love that lets the child know exactly what the parent thinks and expects, and clearly makes known what the child is responsible for. This might provide a point of departure for understanding the relation between divine mercy and divine judgment.

Scripture offers abundant evidence that God offers forgiveness, mercy, and love indiscriminately. We are capable of love because we have first been loved by God (1 Jn. 4:10). We find salvation not by doing something to appease an angry God, but by accepting and responding to the salvific grace which God offers us out of pure love. "But God shows his love for us in that while we were yet sinners Christ died for us" (Rm. 5:8).

God's love is free and unconditional. We need do nothing to earn it. We can only receive it and respond to it appropriately. But if grace is the free offer of a personal presence on the part of God, it can be freely refused on the part of the human person. The presence of God in human life is not simply a static condition. On the contrary, the whole of the spiritual tradition indicates that the divine presence is always a call to transformation and growth to deeper levels of being. The refusal of that presence on the part of the human person, therefore, is a refusal to become that fuller being that God calls one to become. What is meant by an appropriate response to God's offer is clearly stated in the preaching of Jesus in the form of the twofold command of love of God and neighbor (Mt. 22:34-40; Mk. 12:28-34; Lk. 10:25-28).

This ethical imperative is radicalized when Jesus extends the command to love one's neighbor to include even one's enemy. Jesus describes the indiscriminate love of God as the model for the perfection of his disciples. "You, therefore, must be perfect as your heavenly Father is perfect" (Mt. 5:43-48). The nature of God as love is here translated into a moral imperative of far-reaching significance for human life. It is in full harmony with this Gospel-tradition going back to the teaching of Jesus when the first Epistle of John pin-points the deepest identity of the Christian in terms of agapistic love.

A genuine faith-response to the God revealed by Jesus can never be a neutral, purely intellectualized affirmation of a doctrine about God. It must take the form of the personal acceptance of grace and personal response to grace in the form of self-giving love. The Christian appeal to a God of love is by no means a justification of moral lassitude. Quite the contrary. The imperative contained in the affirmation of God's love is so radical that no human being can honestly claim to have lived it out fully and to the end throughout his or her life.

From this perspective, we can gain insight into the current attempts to interpret the symbol of judgment as an eschatological symbol. We may say, first of all, that even now in our every-day life, when we hear the proclamation of the Gospel imperative, we are called to judgment. Christians have, for twenty centuries, argued around the imperative of Jesus and rationalized it in so many ways as to render it practically harmless. Yet it remains. God is indiscriminate love, forgiveness, and acceptance. If I live and move and have my being in the power of such love, and if the same is true of all my fellow human beings, what else can be an appropriate response to this but to love others as God loves both me and the others?

Even though this sort of response to God's offer of grace is possible only because of grace, it remains true that grace makes possible a free human response. Cardinal Ratzinger writes directly to the point: "There is a freedom which is not cancelled out even by grace and which, indeed, is brought face to face with itself precisely by grace: our final fate is not forced upon us without regard for the decisions we have made throughout our life."[12] Such a view will prevent us from falling into two one-sided views on the relation between grace and human endeavor. On the one side, while it is grace that enables us to respond to God, our response is, nonetheless, a free response. Our personal

---

[12]J. Cardinal Ratzinger, *Einführung in das Christentum* (Munich, 1968) p. 268. An English translation is available under the title *Introduction to Christianity* (N.Y., 1971). The text, which I have given in my own translation, will be found there on page 247.

responsibility is never removed. We cannot appeal to God's love and grace as a justification for a sort of Quietism or extreme passivity before God. And because the response is free, it can be refused. We can freely attempt to keep God out of our lives. The appeal to God's love is no justification for a naive, uncritical confidence that overlooks the power which human freedom has to finally fail in our life project.

On the other hand, since grace makes freedom possible and sustains our freedom, we need not be overcome by the obvious destructive power of human beings. For if we can trust in a creative power that is even stronger and more persistent than the destructive power of humanity, then we need not expect that humanity must save itself totally by means of its own resources. If this were the case, our history thus far would have to make the thoughtful person sceptical of the eventual outcome. If God is as Jesus has revealed God to be, then it is possible for us to take ourselves and our world seriously without expecting them finally to provide salvation. For to be able to do that is to be God.

Thus, the theological insistence on human freedom and responsibility provides an understanding of humanity that moves between uncritical fideism and equally naive, naturalistic humanism. Salvation is possible, in the final analysis, only because God offers it to us as pure grace. But the offer of grace is efficacious only if and to the extent that we accept and respond to it. God does not do what only we can do: decide in freedom the kind of life we will live.

Therefore, when we interpret the parousia of Christ, as we have discussed it above, it becomes clear that the coming of Christ is not only salvation; it is simultaneously judgment. Contemporary theology has tended to move away from the familiar court-room metaphors and to develop this theme in terms of dialogue and insight into oneself. Historically, this model can be associated with the thought of Origen, who, because of his neo-Platonic tendency, was inclined to think of salvation in terms of authentic knowledge. "Know thyself" was a dictum going far back into the Socratic and Platonic tradition of philosophy. Drawn out in the context of Christian theology, it is reflected in the enduring mystical tradition which emphasizes the intimate relationship between the depths of self-knowledge and the human knowledge of God. Such knowledge was not simply a conceptual knowledge about something, but a living, salvific contact with the divine reality. In such a context, the categories of the *Gospel of John* had a particular significance. Its dominant image of Jesus is that of the divine Pedagogue; he is the one who opens the possibility of the deeper, salvific knowledge of the self and of God.

In contemporary thought, the model can be associated with such theologians as Ratzinger, Von Balthasar, Rahner, Schmaus, and Breuning.[13] Judgment is seen as the symbol of the confrontation between the truth of humanity and the truth of God. In contemporary authors, a stronger sense of the organic or relational nature of humanity provides a basis for understanding individual and collective judgment not as two distinct and separable actions, but as two interrelated dimensions of one, unified mystery: the manifestation of the truth of history, individual and collective, in the light of the truth of God.

b) Signs of the End

Scripture speaks of certain signs of the end-time. A familiar instance is found in *Mark* 13 which speaks of the appearance of false messiahs, wars, hunger, earthquakes, persecution of Christians, the desecration of holy places, and the proclamation of the Gospel to all the nations. Similar material can be found in the other Gospels (Mt. 24; Lk. 18:8; 21:5-7). The second *Epistle to the Thessalonians* speaks of a son of perdition thereby providing the basis for the notion of an Antichrist (2:3; cfr. also 1 Jn. 2:22; 4:3; 2 Jn. 7). Paul looks forward to the final salvation of the Jews (Rm. 9-11). An exegetical tradition would develop this into the expectation of the historical conversion of the Jews to Christ as a sign of the end. This sort of material has often been interpreted as providing clues that would enable people to know when the end was approaching.

Over the centuries, the interpretations of this material have differed greatly. For many now and in the past, the calculation of the time of the end on the basis of these signs has been a significant preoccupation.

---

[13]Ratzinger, *Eschatologie*, p. 168ff.; H. Urs Von Balthasar "Gericht," in: *Communio: Internationale katholische Zeitschrift* 9 (1980) pp. 227-235; K. Rahner, "Letztes Gericht," in: *Lexikon für Theologie und Kirche* (Freiburg, 1957-65) IV, col. 734-736; M. Schmaus, *Dogma 6: Justification and the Last Things* (Mission, Ks., 1977) p. 200ff; W. Breuning, "Gericht und Auferweckung von den Toten als Kennzeichnung des Vollendungshandelns Gottes durch Jesus Christus," in: *Mysterium Salutis* (Zurich/Cologne, 1976) V, p. 844ff.

The history of such concerns is a part of the history of millenialism discussed above. What one expects to find in these texts and in similar texts in the *Book of Revelation* will be determined by one's basic understanding of the nature of the bible as revelation.

We have already discussed the kind of assumptions that would lead to the conviction that proper biblical understanding must be concerned with interpreting the "signs of the times" by searching history to identify either the persons or the events that correspond to the "predictions" of Scripture. It is important, however, to emphasize that these are precisely *assumptions* about the nature of the bible. Such a set of assumptions may no more be identified with the true meaning of the word of God than any other set of assumptions. The fact that we always approach the bible with some operating assumptions, however implicit they may be, should make us very careful in accepting particular interpretations of what the true meaning of such texts must be. This becomes particularly important when religious interpretations are directly related to current politics, and a personal prophetic sense becomes the platform for urging particular political choices as the inevitable will of God.

At the present time in North America this is the concern of many militant evangelists who draw direct connections between certain Scriptural texts and current personalities and events of international politics. Apocalyptic images are related to a nuclear holocaust which is seen as a necessary step in the preparation for the coming of Christ to lead the armed forces of the elect in the battle of Armageddon. The grisly details of this vision are chilling. In this interpretation the authentic Christian looks forward to the nuclear holocaust since it is seen as a necessary and inevitable step in the movement to the Millennium. Instead of campaigning for nuclear disarmament, the militant believer encourages the build-up of arms, for this policy can more readily be seen as a contribution to the necessary holocaust.

We may take this as an influential instance of what Rahner meant when he referred to "false apocalyptic." This particular brand of self-styled "orthodoxy" is no more than one-hundred and fifty years old, taking its origins from the idiosyncratic belief-system which C.I. Scofield superimposed on the bible in the late nineteenth-century. In this approach, the bible is taken to be a sort of almanac predicting future events in sometimes minute detail. Revelation comes in the form of a sort of jig-saw puzzle to be deciphered by a clever, modern prophet who gains the privileged insight into historical events by his clever manipulation of Scriptural texts. Known as Dispensationalism, this style of interpretation has been propagated on a regular basis by militant preachers on television and radio, and popularized in books such as Hal Lindsey's *The Late Great Planet Earth.*

The work of main-line Christian theologians stands in dramatic contrast with this viewpoint. In general, it is guided by the principle that the basis for any significant biblical interpretation must be the original meaning of the text as that can be determined by historical, critical studies. The attempt to follow such a principle helps the interpreter to avoid the excesses of willful subjectivity. In line with this principle, the so-called signs of the biblical texts are to be understood in terms of apocalyptic symbolism and not as a detailed reportage of the final, empirical events of history. The "signs" are not presented as a chronology of events. They offer no possibility of establishing when the end of history will come, nor do they offer any answers to our questions about the concrete course of future history. The important issue is what we do with the time allotted to us. At all times, the Christian is called to a radical trust in the absolute future which God holds open to us. For the rest, the so-called signs of the end simply point to the ongoing conflict in history between those who are concerned with the Kingdom of God on the one hand, and everything that stands opposed to God on the other hand.[14]

If we read the Scriptures in their entirety instead of isolating a number of texts as the Dispensationalists are inclined to do, then it appears that there are two distinct strands in the Scriptures themselves. On the one hand, there are the texts that speak in vivid terms of cosmic signs that will precede the parousia of Christ (Mt. 24:29; Mk. 13:24; Lk. 21:25-27). But in the very texts which seem to present clear signs of the end we find a strong emphasis on the fact that no one can know the time of the end (Mk. 13:32-37). The great apocalyptic text of *Mark* 13 ends with the emphatic exhortation to watchfulness precisely in view of the incalculable nature of the end. As an exegete, H. Schlier summarizes the Scriptural matter in the following words: "There are indeed signs of the coming end, but they are always ambiguous. One cannot note the presence of God's time and substantiate it as he can other events. Nor is it your business to know the time or the hour

---

[14]Schmaus, *op. cit.,* pp. 184-186.

which the Father in his power has set." (Acts 1:7)[15]

A closer look at the signs might lead us to believe that they point not to events in a final generation of history but to factors that are a part of the dynamic of history in all ages. What they point to is that the end of history may not be an age of historical maturity but an inner collapse of history itself. History will come to an end, as Ratzinger argues, for otherwise the basic question of history's meaning will be left unresolved. But no specifics can be given. The only meaningful answer to the question raised by the signs is found in the other strand of the tradition: Watch. Every age is in need of vigilance.

This applies even to the figure of the Antichrist. Much ink has been spilled in attempts to unravel the meaning of this figure in the history of Christianity. The Scriptural material is ambiguous at best. He is seen at times as an individual person and at times as a collectivity. It would be in harmony with the symbolic nature of apocalyptic texts to interpret this figure as a personification. As Ratzinger has argued, since every period of church history experiences historical powers opposed to the rule of God, the figure of the Antichrist may be seen as a principle of church history as a whole. Believers are always dealing with the conflict between the rule of God and those things or persons that stand in the way of that rule.[16]

All these suggestions may be summarized in Rahner's fundamental principle that Christian eschatology is basically talk about a real future made from the basis of the present experience of faith and grace. The experience of grace in the limitations of the present together with the never-ending experience of evil, the ongoing need for ever-deeper conversion to God, the freedom and responsibility of human persons in taking up their historical task, the eschatological significance of history, the fulfillment of history in God: all this is called to mind by the dramatic symbols with which Scripture surrounds the mystery of the final end. Beyond this, we must humbly say: "But of that day or that hour no one knows, not even the angels in heaven nor the Son, but only the Father" (Mk. 13:32).

[15]"The End of Time," in: *Theology Digest*, Fall, 1969, p. 203.
[16]Ratzinger, *Eschatologie...*, p. 160ff.

READINGS

Davies, P., *God and the New Physics* (Simon & Schuster, New York, 1983).

Efrid, J.M., *End-Times: Rapture, Antichrist, Millennium* (Abingdon Press, Nashville, 1986).

Halsell, G., *Prophecy and Politics: Militant Evangelists on the Road to Nuclear War* (Lawrence Hill Co., Westport, Connecticut, 1986).

Küng, H., *Eternal Life? Life after Death as a Medical, Philosophical, and Theological Problem* (Doubleday, N.Y., 1984).

McGinn, B., *The Calabrian Abbot: Joachim of Fiore in the History of Western Thought* (Macmillan, N.Y., 1985).

Pendergast, R.J., *Cosmos* (Fordham University Press, New York, 1973).

Robinson, J.A.T., *Jesus and His Coming* (Westminster, Philadelphia, 1979²).

Weber, T.P., *Living in the Shadow of the Second Coming* (University of Chicago Press, Chicago, 1987).

7

THE FINAL CONDITION

1. Definitive Failure:
Hell and the Problem of Universal Salvation

It is common today to hear of the inability of the modern mind to accept or to understand the concept of hell. To many it seems to be a miserable remnant of a mediaeval system which is best left behind. To others, it is an affront to the modern consciousness of humanity. From a theological perspective, it is often seen as incompatible with the biblical concept of a God of love. What are the real religious and theological issues involved here?

a) Official Teaching of the Church

The official teaching of the magisterium on the topic of hell is quite limited. In the sixth century, the Synod of Constantinople condemned the views of certain followers of Origen who held that there would be a final restoration and reintegration of all creation (=apocatastasis), including the demons and any human beings condemned to hell. Against this position, the Synod affirmed that anyone condemned to hell remains there for all eternity (DS 411). This position of the Synod is often understood as a condemnation of the possibility of universal salvation. But such a reading misses the point of the condemnation. The real concern of the Synod was not the possibility of universal salvation but the way in which universal salvation was thought to come about, namely, through some form of radical transformation on the part of those already condemned.

Several Councils addressed the topic of hell during the late Middle Ages. These include IV Lateran in 1215 (DS 801), II Lyons in 1274 (DS 856-58), Florence in 1439 (DS 1306), and Trent in 1547 (DS 1539, 1543, 1575). From all of these we can conclude that the magisterium holds a punishment to begin immediately after death for all those who die in the state of mortal sin. This punishment will be in conformity with the sins of the particular persons involved. The most significant single mediaeval document is the constitution *Benedictus Deus* of Pope Benedict XII in which the pope corrects the erroneous teaching of his predecessor, John XXII (DS 1000ff). Pope John had preached the opinion that the souls of the elect would enjoy the beatific vision only after the final judgment and general resurrection. In the period between individual death and general resurrection, the elect would enjoy only an imperfect sort of happiness. A similar temporary condition was postulated for the damned as well. Pope Benedict rejected this view and affirmed the teaching that the souls of those who were in no need of purgation enjoy the beatific vision immediately after death. The condemned likewise enter into their eternal condition immediately after death. Most recently, in 1979, the Sacred Congregation of the Doctrine of the Faith reaffirmed the traditional teaching of the Councils that there is an eternal punishment for sinners, "who will be deprived of the sight of God." The Congregation makes it explicit that this punishment will have an effect on the whole being of the sinner.[1]

The official teaching may be summarized in the following points. It recognizes a punishment for the lost to follow immediately after death. This punishment is to be everlasting. The idea that those already condemned may have a sort of second chance is rejected. The essence of hell consists in the loss of the vision of God. Beyond this, the magisterium offers virtually no details concerning the condition of eternal punishment. It is significant that in these official teachings, the condition for being condemned is that a person die in the state of mortal sin. Nowhere does the magisterium make the judgment that any particular person has died in this state and that consequently he or she is condemned to hell. The church has canonized individual saints.

---

[1]"Letter on Certain Questions concerning Eschatology," (May, 1979), par. 7.

But it has never judged that a particular individual is, in fact, in a state of eternal condemnation.

b) Scriptural Basis

Limited as it is, this official teaching of the church can claim a strong basis in the Scriptures. Certainly, the early stages in the development of the Hebrew notion of *sheol* are quite unclear. There seems to be no distinction between the fate of the good and that of the evil. All alike enter into the underworld to a shadowy state of being hardly worth calling a form of existence. It was in the two centuries before the beginning of the Christian church that Jewish thought began to envision a distinction between the fate of the good and that of the evil. For the good, the underworld was a place of rest and peace; for the evil, it was a place of suffering and punishment (Cfr. Is. 24:21ff; 15:11; 66:24; Dn. 12:2; 2 Mc. 6:26; Wis. 4:19). The preaching of Jesus and the writings of the early Christian community assume this tradition and make it a part of their own understanding. (Cfr. Mt. 3:10ff; 25:41; 13:42; Mk. 3:28; Lk. 16:19-31). The texts could be multiplied easily. It is clear that the idea of an eternal punishment has a firm place in the Christian Scriptures. It is likewise clear that the early Christian writers, and even Jesus himself, expressed this idea with images drawn from the apocalyptic tradition. In the case of Jesus, the teaching on hell reflects great restraint with regard to descriptive details whereas in later Scriptural texts, the authors frequently present the idea of eternal punishment with the graphic particulars of worms, fire, gnashing of teeth, etc.

c) Early Christian Developments

It is not difficult to understand that the idea of an eternal damnation would, over the centuries, appear to many to stand in conflict with the biblical understanding of God. Early in the Patristic period, Origen developed the hypothesis of a universal reconciliation, presenting this as a position that seemed more in harmony with the logic of God's love and mercy. Other Church Fathers—including Gregory of Nyssa, Diodor of Tarsus, and at least for a time, Jerome—were similarly inclined. But, as we have indicated above, the main-line teaching of the church, as reflected in the magisterial statement of the Synod of Constantinople, moved in another direction. As Ratzinger suggests, the problem with the Origenist thesis is that it has a weak understanding of evil. In this sense, it may reflect an excessive influence of Platonic philosophy. A universal restoration might be the logical conclusion of a neo-Platonist system, but it is not the logical conclusion to be drawn from Scripture.[2] Yet, the appeal to the mercy of God has led over and over again to theories of universal redemption. Any theory of universal redemption will inevitably involve the denial of eternal punishment. At best, a punishment after death would be temporary. The doctrine of hell would then be, at most, a variation on the doctrine of purgation.

What is at issue in the discussion is not any privileged insight into specific details of what awaits us in death. In harmony with our basic hermeneutic principle that eschatological statements are statements about the future made on the basis of our present experience of faith and grace, it would follow that the mystery of hell has its basis somewhere in our present experience. It is not an attempt to describe a future world. This may shed light on the pervasive theological conviction that what is really at stake here is an understanding of human freedom and responsibility.

Christian tradition has long held that the quality and character of human actions has a profound significance for ourselves, for the world, and for history. We have the fundamental power to determine what destiny will be ours despite the many concrete factors which make up the context in which our freedom operates. We are conditioned but not determined in any mechanical way. Basically, what we make of ourselves is rooted in our freedom. This means that any talk of fulfillment or of failure should not be interpreted to mean that reward and punishment are totally extrinsic to the way in which we live. On the contrary, the "reward" for accepting God and living in a loving manner is first the experience of love itself, and then the ability to love more deeply. Similarly, the "punishment" for rejecting God is the self-chosen isolation and separation which the act of rejection inevitably involves. We are blessed or damned not by an extrinsic, divine *fiat*, but by the inner working-out of our own decisions. This we can see already in our experience in the world. A life lived fully in a rich network of

[2]Ratzinger, *Eschatologie*, p. 177.

relations is, in a sense, its own reward; and the impoverishment of a life lived in self-chosen isolation and loneliness is its own punishment.

The possibility of hell may be seen in the historical experience of self-chosen isolation. The symbol of hell is the symbol of the possibility that we may fail utterly and finally in the task of our life-project. In this sense, the possibility of hell is the most radical theological statement about the nature of human freedom. We have the power to decide something of eternal significance. And that decision may turn out to be a disaster. Thus, Rahner declares that it is totally inappropriate to think of hell as a sort of vindictive punishment brought by an angry and jealous God who is appeased by the pain inflicted on the sinner. Hell is not something that God imposes on us from outside as punishment for our misdeeds. Rather it is the intrinsic effect of our own free decisions. Free, human decisions carry within themselves the possibility of hell. Thus, hell is not something into which we are cast by God but a reality which we ourselves create. God is active in the punishment of hell only insofar as God does not reverse the free acts of human beings and does not release the human person from that which has been freely chosen, even though that person's condition stands in contradiction to God's intent.

This understanding may help us to see that there is something of basic importance involved in the Christian language about hell, and to distinguish the fundamental issue from the vivid, apocalyptic imagery with which it is commonly expressed. Hell is seen as a symbol of isolation and lack of communication with the impoverishment of existence which that involves. Hell is the result of choosing to live for and by oneself alone. It is a deliberate choice to live in a manner contrary to our nature as created persons. As Ratzinger suggests, hell is the symbol of a human zone of untouchable loneliness and rejected love. Hell is what happens when a person deliberately chooses to barricade his or her existence from all others and to live for the self alone.[3] If sin is fundamentally the failure to love, then hell can be seen as the final fixation in that state. That people have the power to choose an isolated existence seems clear enough from empirical experience. Whether they have the power to persist in this decision in the naked presence of God is the question about the eternity of hell.

[3]Ratzinger, *Introduction*, p. 228.

d) Universal Salvation in Contemporary Thought

The question of the eternity of hell is related to the problem of the universalism of salvation. In what is definitely the minority report among theologians over the centuries, there are those even today who are inclined to something akin to Origen's view. For them, the concept of an eternal hell contradicts the nature of God as love. Taking the understanding of divine love and mercy as their point of departure, they argue that ultimately all human beings must find salvation. Among current authors, variations of this view are found in J.A.T. Robinson, and J. Hick.[4]

For Robinson, the traditional view which holds the eternity of hell is caught in an insoluble and perhaps unnecessary dilemma. Those who hold the traditional position are forced to choose between human freedom and divine coercion. If we are truly free, we must reckon with the possibility of hell. But if God's salvific will must necessarily be realized, then we must reckon with coercion on the part of God. The problem, then, is rooted in an unfortunate notion of God's manner of acting in relation to human freedom. In a manner reminiscent of Process theology, Robinson suggests that we ought to think of God more in terms of mercy and persuasive love and less in terms of coercive power. Robinson works from analogies derived from the human experience of love. We know human experiences of love so deep that a person is led to freely acknowledge its drawing power and is brought to the moment of total, personal surrender to the beloved. This is not a question of coercion, but one of freely giving oneself over to the other. Such a surrender is not a loss of freedom but the true discovery of our freedom.

If we think of the relation between humanity and God in similar terms, then—in Robinson's view—we will find it intolerable to say that even one person might be lost forever. For saying that means to admit that divine love has "failed and failed infinitely." But the Scriptures, in numerous places, speak in terms that sound like a universal victory of God's love over death and the powers of evil. In the end, all things must be summed up in Christ because, in principle, they already are. Here, Robinson appeals to the notion of corporate personality.

---

[4]J.A.T. Robinson, *In the End God* (London, 1968); and J. Hick, *Death and Eternal Life* (N.Y., 1976).

What has happened in Christ has happened already for all. Therefore, *already* there is no one outside of Christ. If this is the case, then ultimately hell is an impossibility. As human beings, we make decisions that seem to us to be final and irrevocable. But that is only because of the perspective from which we see such decisions. The truth remains that "love must win."[5]

Robinson singles out an important point by calling our attention to the God-image involved not only in this question but in the whole of our theology. Without doubt, there are problems with the ordinary theological understanding of the nature of God. Yet, there are a number of obvious problems in Robinson's argument. Perhaps the argument gets lost in a flow of rhetoric that may appeal to the affectivity but is logically weak. Precisely when we begin with the emphasis on divine love and mercy, it becomes questionable to use language such as "must." "Must" implies necessity. But what sort of necessity can we be dealing with when the fundamental principles at issue are freedom and persuasion? The appeal to Christology, likewise, is ineffective since it leaves little space for the "not yet" of the Christ-mystery. The disproportion between the "already" of Christ's personal destiny and the "not yet" of the Body of Christ raises again the problem of human freedom in response to God. Christian faith believes that Jesus has been raised to a life with God which anticipates the destiny that God wills for all human beings. But faith does not know to what extent that destiny will be realized in the rest of humanity. Christian theology, therefore, cannot claim to "know" that divine love "must" be victorious in the form of a universal salvation. It can only hope that such will be the case.

The argument of Hick takes a similar point of departure. Hick prefers to think of God as a divine therapist who acts in history to remove the blockages that impede the human movement to God. God has created us for fellowship with the divinity itself; and God's action in human life enables us to reach that goal. Unlike human therapists, God works in unlimited time and with perfect knowledge, ultimately controlling and not being controlled by the concrete environmental factors involved in human life. Obviously, the time available in any individual human history is limited. What does Hick have in mind? Without espousing the familiar notions of reincarnation, he does argue

[5] *In the End God*, p. 132.

for stages in this life and beyond this life whereby the divine therapist works to enable the human person to complete his or her journey successfully. Thus, the future vision of faith, for Hick, is a faith in the universal triumph of divine love.

One has to ask whether such a view takes human history seriously enough. In Hick's view, the outcome of history is infallibly predetermined. What significance, then, can be attributed to human struggle within history? In what sense can it be said that God controls environmental factors? The concept of stages of life after death in which God can bring the work of sanctification to completion sounds very much like the intent of the traditional theory of purgatory even though Hick shapes his theory in a very different way. In essence, these "stages" of maturation after death represent precisely what the theology of purgatory attempted to deal with: the disproportion between God and the human being at death in a system that rejected any form of reincarnation into historical forms of existence. Finally, would I really be free if it could be said to me: You may choose for or against love, but in the end you will become a lover? Would this not make one suspect that what really determines my destiny is not my freedom or my love, but something over which I have nothing to say?

With Hick's argument, the question of reincarnation surfaces. This is not to say that Hick espouses reincarnation in its familiar forms. But he does argue in favor of ongoing stages of maturation between the death of the individual in this historical phase and any final, definitive condition if, indeed, such a thing is possible in his theory. It would go beyond the scope of this study to present a detailed account of the various forms of reincarnationalism. But some general observations would be in order.

e) Reincarnationalism

Theories of reincarnation are postulated to deal with a number of issues. First, there is the sense of the distance between the human person and the divine reality. If this distance seems to be immense when the human person approaches death, the idea of another cycle of life suggests itself as a way of closing that gap. If after a second round, the gap has not yet been closed, then another, and so on. Second, there is the persistent problem of innocent suffering. How can we hope to give any explanation for the fact that people are born into the most pitiful situations and have to cope with immense limitations and suffering even though they are apparently totally innocent of sin, at least at birth? Might it be that they are not innocent at all, and that the pain of their situation is to be seen in relation to a previous existence for which they now must pay? Thirdly, there is the so-called scandal of the theological concept of hell. Reincarnation theories in general tend to be forms of universal salvation. It has been suggested that the concept of reincarnation is the "lost chord" of Christianity, which brings the Christian vision of reality to a harmonious resolution by solving the persistent paradoxes of faith in a coherent way.[6]

A study of the major variations of reincarnation reveals that, far from being the "lost chord" of Christianity, reincarnation really represents a different vision of life. While Christianity is a profoundly personalist vision of reality in which the key to reality is love and communion, reincarnationalism is a rationalistic system dominated by the concept of justice. Christianity is a vision of salvation for the whole of the human person, body and soul, individually and collectively. Reincarnationalism, on the contrary, is a doctrine of the salvation of the immortal soul in which the body is merely an instrument for gaining experiences in the world. At the inner core of the various theories of reincarnation is a logical system rather than a vision of freedom, contingency, and love. It is the logical power of the system that requires a theory of universal salvation whenever the system is brought into the context of Christian thought. The concept of reincarnation, therefore, is not just a means of tidying up the house of Christianity where it has some embarrassing problems that it does not seem able to solve. It is, in fact, a fundamentally different vision of humanity and of history which the church has rightly resisted over the centuries.

f) The Majority Report

The universalist argument helps us understand the heart of the majority-report as it is represented in such authors as Rahner and

[6] J. Head & S.L. Cranston, *Reincarnation: The Phoenix Fire Mystery* (N.Y., 1977); S. Cranston, "Reincarnation: The Lost Chord of Christianity," in: *Immortality and Human Destiny*, ed. G. MacGregor (N.Y., 1985) pp. 143-160.

Ratzinger. To understand their argument, it is important to recall that in the official teaching of the church, there has never been a judgment made that any particular individual is, in fact, in hell. The church has taught that anyone who dies in the state of mortal sin goes directly to hell. It has not, however, taught that any particular person has ever died in such a condition. Nor has the church ever canonized the Augustinian theory of double-predestination whereby some people are predestined to hell by an eternal, divine decree. From this we may conclude that hell is not the content of the church's faith in the same way that heaven is, for the positive affirmation of heaven is rooted in the proclamation of the resurrection of Jesus.

What is at stake here is the theological affirmation of the *possibility* of hell. And this possibility is seen to be a necessary implication of the affirmation of human freedom. If the possibility of heaven is rooted in a free act of love whereby the human person accepts and responds to the grace of God, the possibility of hell is rooted in the very same freedom. If we are not free to reject, then neither are we free to accept. Here, for example in Rahner, we find a more metaphysical understanding of freedom. "Freedom is the will and the possibility of positing the definitive."[7] For good or for ill, we have the power of making a decision that has eternal and irrevocable significance for ourselves and for the Body of Christ as well. If we view this in terms of our earlier reflections on the theology of death, we can better understand Rahner's thesis that in the moment of death, the human person either ratifies or reverses the fundamental choice that has been operative throughout his or her life. The result of this decision is either final salvation or final damnation. God never by-passes human freedom in order to release people from the results of their free decisions. The affirmation of the possibility of hell is, therefore, a necessary conclusion from this understanding of human freedom. This is not only a question of the meaning of freedom in the moment of death. It draws our attention to the moral seriousness of all the free decisions of human life as well. Thus, as Ratzinger argues, the real intent of the doctrine of hell is to underscore the seriousness of human existence and human action. If we view our lives as an opportunity for endless revisions and changes of mind, we will be far less serious about the moral character of our decisions

[7] *Encyclopedia of Theology*, p. 604.

than we would be if we lived in the light of the real possibility of final failure.

Without doubt this call for moral seriousness can be misunderstood. The argument is not intended to resurrect the kind of religion of fear conjured up by popular preaching in the not too distant past. For the call to seriousness must be placed within the total context of faith. If we were alone in our attempt to take life seriously, then we might find reason for fear or even for despair; for the record of human history shows over and over the incapacity of humanity to carry out its task well. It is important to place the summons to moral seriousness in the context of the God's promise. While we must make free decisions, it is the offer of God's grace that makes such decisions possible and enables us to carry them through to the end. As Hans Küng has put it: "Anyone who is inclined to despair in the face of the possibility of such a failure can gain hope from the New Testament statements about God's universal mercy."[8]

No modern theologian has argued for this understanding of freedom more convincingly than Rahner. So deeply is history conditioned by freedom that Rahner concludes it would be presumptuous to claim to know theologically that the outcome of history *must* be universal salvation. On the other hand, he points out that it is appropriate for Christians to *hope* that such might be the outcome of history. Christian faith proclaims the victory of God's love in the person of Jesus, and it hopes that the divine love may be victorious in the rest of humanity. But it cannot claim to know that such will inevitably be the case. In the light of freedom, both divine and human, the language of "necessity" seems inappropriate. C.S. Lewis summarizes the matter succinctly: "I would pay any price to be able to say truthfully 'All will be saved.' But my reason retorts, 'without their will, or with it?' If I say 'Without their will' I at once perceive a contradiction; how can the supreme voluntary act of self-surrender be involuntary? If I say 'With their will,' my reason replies 'How if they *will not* give in?' "[9]

The affirmation of the possibility of an eternal hell seems to be the inevitable implication of taking human freedom with radical seriousness. The universalist position seems incapable of accepting the possibility that in creating the kind of world which God has created, the

[8]H. Küng, *Eternal Life?* (N.Y., 1984) p. 142.
[9]C.S. Lewis, *The Problem of Pain* (N.Y., 1969) p. 106ff.

divinity has made itself really dependent on the historical response of free creatures in working out the divine intention. Neither Robinson nor Hick have presented a convincing solution to the questions raised by human freedom. The appeal to the mercy of God does not resolve the problems, but simply pushes them to another level. Freedom involves a degree of contingency which makes it impossible to see the "necessary, universal victory" of divine love as little more than a form of religious rhetoric. How is it possible to speak meaningfully of human freedom if the final result of all human ethical decisions is already determined in advance? But to say that God's love *must* be universally victorious is to determine the outcome of human history in advance. By far, the more convincing position is that which holds such a universal salvation as an object of hope while recognizing our inability to come to any clear and specific knowledge as to the eventual outcome of history. Such a position holds the two elements of the question in an appropriate tension. On the one hand, there is the hope for the salvation of all human beings which is based on the love and mercy of God. On the other hand, there is the real possibility of ultimate disaster which is based on human resistance to God's grace. In the dialectic between these two statements we discover the seriousness of human freedom and responsibility even as we experience the limitations of any eschatological statement.

2. The Kingdom of Eternal Life

Christian hope is ultimately directed to the fulfillment of human life in all its dimensions in a union with God that transcends death. In the earlier chapters of this study, we have seen something of the historical development of this type of religious expectation. We have attempted to see the relation between the religious consciousness developed through the biblical history and the fundamentally incomplete reality of human nature in its history. Viewed from this perspective, the biblical vision expresses a dream for the future of humanity and its world. It is not information about a world foreign to human aspirations, but the dream of a fulfillment of those aspirations which leads us far beyond our fondest human dreams. The story of the Scriptures is the story of the stages in the development of this dream, a development which presents new and provocative images and metaphors at each new level.

a) Biblical Symbols

The dream does not begin with hope for life beyond death. In the early stages, it is centered on a homeland, security, and peace. It is a living hope in God's protective, forgiving, life-giving presence. At a later stage, in the apocalyptic development, it is hope for a fundamental change in reality: liberation from suffering, pain, and injustice. The Christian Scriptures bring this dream to a new, decisive level in the vision of a world ruled by the love of God; a world in which human beings live in peace with one another, enjoying a wholeness of being, both interiorly and exteriorly, which is made possible by the powerful and indestructible presence of God in the risen Christ. The kaleidoscopic flood of images of the future in both the Hebrew and the Christian Scriptures makes it clear that it is impossible to give a final definition or description of that fulfillment which God holds open to us. Kingdom of God, wedding feast, banquet, paradise, the new city, reconciliation, fullness of life: these are but a few of the intimations found in Scripture. Without ever defining the future clearly in a conceptual way, the Scriptural metaphors evoke a vision of a fullness of being and meaning to be found in a rich network of relations with human beings, with the world, and with God. The biblical vision of our future is a vision of the final fulfillment of human existence through love.

It would, however, be a mistake to think that this vision is exclusively a matter of the future. As Rahner has argued in the form of a general principle, eschatology is not special knowledge about the future but a projection to a future completion of the varied dimensions of our present experience of grace and salvation in Christ. This applies in particular to the symbols of human fulfillment. If the Kingdom of God is a symbol of the final rule of a loving and forgiving God, the Scriptures point out that God loves, forgives, and cares for us already now as we seek God in the darkness and ambiguity of historical experience. The Kingdom begins even now in the offer of God's grace and in the loving human response to that grace. But the Kingdom cannot be said to be fully realized until God's grace has penetrated to all levels of human reality. Christian tradition has used the word "heaven" to designate this final fulfillment of human life with God. Here the natural, symbolic power of the physical vault of heaven above us is used to elicit an awareness of the exalted future which God offers us as human beings.

This biblical dream of the fullness of eternal life with God is not based on the fact that humanity has a longing for such a life, and that such a longing must be fulfilled. Neither is it based on the assumption that there is an element in human nature that is naturally immortal. These ideas may well contain an element of truth. But the biblical dream of eternal life is based on faith in an indestructible God of life who has entered into a life-giving covenant with humanity. This God, who has been with the people in their history and who has renewed their life over and over after tragedy, is faithful to the divine promise. Such experience led to the conviction that the fullest form of life is a life in intimate union with God, and that such union with God is not destroyed even by death. In biblical terms, the hope for eternal life with God is a trust in the future which comes as the unmerited, free consequence of the absolute reliability of God.[10] The parables of the lost sheep, the lost coin, and the lost son in the Gospels (Lk. 15) express God's concern to lead humanity back to communion with God. This God is concerned not only with the collective, but with each individual (Lk. 15:1-10; 1 Cor. 8:11; Rm. 14:15).

Thus, there arises in Scripture the hope that—because God is as God has been revealed in Jesus Christ—the living bond between God and humanity will not be lost even in death. The biblical hope is based not on any concept of natural immortality but on trust in the God "who gives life to the dead" (Rm. 4:17). This phrase of Paul is deeply rooted in the Hebrew Scriptures which highlight many times the creative, life-giving power of God (1 Sm. 2:6; Dt. 32:39; Job 19:25ff). Christian hope for indestructible life beyond death is rooted essentially in trust in the creative power and fidelity of God. Heaven, then, is not another world; it is the future of this world of God's creation, transformed by the creative power of God. Going to heaven is not going to another world, but entering into a new relation with God and with this world. Being in heaven is being with God in an indestructible communion of life.

---

[10]Ratzinger, *Eschatologie*, p. 74ff; E. Schillebeeckx, *Das Evangelium erzählen* (Düsseldorf, 1983) p. 167.

b) Dimensions of Life with God

1) Communion

The rich and diverse imagery of the Scriptures suggests that heaven is more a quality of life than a place that could be located somewhere. Heaven is the symbol for the full maturity and perfection of human life in the presence of God. Perhaps the most suggestive biblical word to express this is the Hebrew word *shalom*. The implications of this word become clear when it is seen in relation to its opposite, namely, the effects of sin depicted in the opening chapters of the book of *Genesis*. In that powerful prologue to the biblical account of Israel's history there is a dramatic contrast between a world of harmonious relations and a world in which all the important relations that should make up human life are broken and distorted. This is the contrast between the world as God would have it and the world as we find it because of human failure and sin. Human beings find themselves alienated from each other and from a healthy relation to the world around them. They are profoundly divided within themselves, and they experience the approach of a loving God with fear. The richness which God wills in human life through healthy relations with God and with all of created reality is wasted, and human life is impoverished. The garden of paradise is a concrete symbol of the meaning of *shalom*. For this image conjures up the vision of the fullness of life which will be possible in a perfectly covenanted world. In such a world, all broken relations will be restored. With the restoration of a living relationship to God, humanity will rediscover healthy relations with all created reality. The fullness of life for the individual is inconceivable without taking into account all the relations which make the individual to be precisely this person.

The Christian Scriptures use symbols that evoke the awareness of a similar communion and sharing of life. The Kingdom is like a wedding feast (Mt. 22:1-10; 25:1-13). In the *Gospel of John*, the first "sign" at the beginning of Jesus' ministry takes place at a wedding feast (Jn. 2:1-11). The *Book of Revelation* speaks of the wedding of the Lamb (19:7ff), and the *Epistle to the Ephesians* suggests that earthly love is an anticipation of the reality of heaven (5:25-32). The metaphor of a wedding feast suggests the loving concern of God and the joy to be found in the living relation between God and human beings. Similarly, the image of the banquet (Mt. 8:11; Ex. 24:11; Is. 25:6ff; Lk. 7:36; 19:1-10) suggests a richness of life in the sharing of the goods of the earth as well as reconciliation and friendship among table companions, and the joy of being with one another. No one is excluded by God, who invites especially the poor, the cripples, and the blind to the banquet (Lk. 14:13ff). The Last Supper is the most all-embracing use of the banquet-image in which Jesus makes it clear how those in the Kingdom will relate to each other, the greatest seeing themselves as the least and willingly serving the others.

In less concrete terms, the *Gospel of John* singles out the metaphor of life as the central metaphor for salvation. Life in biblical terms is far more than biological life, and far more than the mere fact of existence. Mere existence is not yet life. In biblical terms, and especially in the fourth Gospel, the concept of life includes a quantitative and qualitative fullness. Life means light, peace, happiness. Life as John sees it is above all an existence in faith and love. Jesus has embodied life in its fullest, and he offers a fullness of life to all who turn to him in faith. Even though such life relativizes mere biological existence and transcends physical death, it is not simply life after death but a quality of life already in our present experience (Jn. 11:25ff). If we read the *Gospel of John* with any degree of accuracy, eternal life is about love. And love is about freedom. We are free to accept or to reject the life-giving presence of God. If we reject that offer, we remain closed in ourselves and our life is impoverished. If we accept the offer, we enter into ever deeper relations with God and with the world. And this is life.

2) Christological and Trinitarian Dimensions of Heavenly Life

What we have suggested above indicates that the Christian vision of heaven is not that of isolated human souls standing alone before the throne of God, but a vision of a fullness of life in which the essentially relational nature of humanity is brought to fulfillment. In this respect, the biblical vision differs from many of the great mystical systems. There is another aspect in which the Christian vision is distinct; it envisions heaven as being deeply conditioned by the person of Christ.

The Christological dimension is expressed by Paul, whose hope is to "be with the Lord always" (1 Thess. 4:17; 2 Thess. 2:1; Rm. 2:23; Phil. 4:19; Col. 13:2ff). Paul sees heavenly life as conformity with Christ

(Phil. 3:21; Rm. 8:29), and speaks of sharing in the resurrection and the reign of Christ (2 Tim. 17:24; Eph. 4:12). Similarly in the *Gospel of John*, Jesus is the way, the truth and the life (Jn. 14:6), and heaven is simply being with Christ (Jn. 14:3). The person who is united with Christ in this life is already a child of God, but it has not yet been revealed what the future fulfillment of this relationship will be (1 Jn. 3:2).

This Christological element in the doctrine of heaven is emphasized strongly by Von Balthasar, Schmaus, Rahner, Breuning, and Ratzinger.[11] The final destiny of creation with God is not some unhistorical place, but precisely that "place" which has been created in the God-world relationship through the history of Jesus Christ. Since the Christian experience of grace is centered on the experience of God as this is mediated to us through the person and history of Jesus Christ, and since eschatological statements are projections from the present experience of Christian grace, it is consistent with this when contemporary theologians argue that the doctrine of heaven, which is a doctrine about the fullness of grace, must take explicit account of the person of Christ. In its primary Christian sense, heaven is not a pre-existing place to which human persons go after death. Rather, it is precisely that relation between God and the world that has been brought about through the life, death, and glorification of Jesus as the Christ. In this sense, heaven is established as a reality when the humanity of Jesus is assumed into the presence of God in the mystery which Christians celebrate as the resurrection and ascension of the Lord. Viewed from this perspective, heaven is the final and decisive self-communication of God to creation, and the full transformation of the creature as it accepts God's self-gift within itself.

This orientation gives a strong emphasis to heaven as a personal relationship, or as a dialogue between God and creation rather than as a place. As a personal relationship, heaven is always marked by its historical source in the Paschal Mystery of Christ. In reflection on this Christological orientation, the trinitarian dimension of the Christian future begins to emerge. This is developed particularly by Rahner,

---

[11]Ratzinger, *Eschatologie*, p. 190ff; Rahner, *Theological Investigations*, 4, p. 77ff; Schmaus, *Dogma* 6, p. 261ff; W. Breuning, "Inkarnatorisch-trinitätstheologische Struktur des vollendenden Handelns Jesu Christi," in: *Mysterium Salutis*, 5, p. 789ff; Von Balthasar, "Mysterium Paschale," in: *Mysterium Salutis*, 3, 2 pp. 133-319.

Von Balthasar, and Ratzinger. Their view has strong historical roots in the theology of the great Fathers of Eastern Christianity and in the thought of Richard of St. Victor and St. Bonaventure in the West. It involves a style of trinitarian reflection referred to by contemporary theologians as "economic trinitarianism." In this style of reflection, the symbol of the trinity is seen as the central expression of the historical experience of God's self-communication.

If the mystery of grace is understood to be the mystery of God's self-communication to creation, then the primary issue in the doctrine of grace is not what the hand-book theology discussed as "created grace," but the mystery of "Uncreated Grace," that is, the gift of the divinity itself as a living presence that brings about that transformation of the human person which is referred to with the term "created grace." It is the conviction of Christian faith that this divine self-communication takes place through history. It is, in fact, the deepest mystery involved in human history. The history of grace has its center and high-point in the history of Jesus Christ. It is from the mystery of Christ's life that Christians come to believe in God as a trinitarian mystery, for the self-communication of God which is centered in Christ reveals a trinitarian structure. It is through Jesus that Christians come to know who the Son of God is in the specifically Christian sense. And it is in the fuller awareness of the mystery of sonship that the specifically Christian sense of God as Father and Spirit comes to Christian consciousness. The trinitarian symbol is, in essence, a symbol of the historical, Christian experience of grace.

Grace, then, is an entrance into the mystery of filiation through our relation to Jesus Christ. But what does filiation mean? This is made known through the historical life of Jesus where we are confronted with a life of total dedication to God for the sake of others. When we say that in the resurrection, God has accepted Jesus and Jesus' cause into the stream of divine life, we mean, as the *Epistle to the Hebrews* expresses it, that the glorified Lord stands forever in that gesture of self-offering to God for the others. Taking its inspiration from *Hebrews*, theology uses cultic metaphors when it calls Jesus the eternal high-priest, who stands before God always making intercession for us (Hebr. 9:24ff). Jesus responds to the love of God with the fullest openness and self-offering to God. His personal mystery is inconceivable without the mystery of the Father and the Spirit. The union of the human person with Christ to which Paul and John refer is, at its inner core, the personal entrance into that gesture of openness and self-giving to God and others which lies at the heart of the mystery of Christ.

Thus, conformity to Christ means that through our relation to Christ, we are drawn into his relation to the Father and the Spirit. Grace is a process of deification whereby created human beings are drawn into personal communion with God as God has been revealed in the history of Jesus, and in this communion of life, are transformed into graced, God-like beings. Union with Christ during this life is already a trinitarian mystery; Christ invites his disciples to share in his relationship with God. The perfection of that union in the future which we call heaven is likewise a mystery of communion in the trinitarian life of God.

Placing this sort of emphasis on the Christological dimension of heavenly life brings with it an unavoidable concern with the social or collective destiny of humanity, for the individual Jesus Christ stands in indissoluble solidarity with the whole of his Body. The creedal symbol of the "communion of saints" finds its final referent here. Heaven is a sharing of life with all those who have lived and died in Christ. If we are fundamentally social, relational beings in our historical life, we do not leave this behind in the experience of grace and fulfillment. The social nature of humanity finds its historical fulfillment in the mystery of the church, and its final fulfillment in the sharing of life with all others who together share the life of God.

3) Beatific Vision

This Christological-trinitarian understanding of the heavenly life seems, at first, to be in conflict with the church's traditional teaching on the beatific vision. In a number of important texts, Scripture describes the final destiny of humanity as "seeing God" (Mt. 5:8; Mt. 18:10; 1 Jn. 3:2; 1 Cor. 13:11ff). These texts intimate that our destiny with God will involve a very intimate, direct knowledge of the divine reality. "For now we see in a mirror dimly, but then face to face" (1 Cor. 13, 12). This sort of Scriptural material has provided the basis for the traditional theological view that the essential joy of heaven consists in an immediate, face-to-face experience of God in which the human person finds ultimate fulfillment. In the papal constitution, *Benedictus*

Deus, Pope Benedict XII describes this as "an intuitive vision and face-to-face" experience of the divine essence which is not mediated by any created reality. In this experience, the divine essence will manifest itself "plainly, clearly, and openly" (DS 1000-1001). The principal conciliar text, coming from the Council of Florence, speaks in similar terms (DS 1305); and the most recent instruction of the Sacred Congregation of the Doctrine of the Faith reaffirms this teaching.[12]

The Scholastic elaboration of this doctrine can easily create the impression that heaven is to be understood in terms of intellectual enjoyment. It is important to keep in mind that any attempt to clarify the doctrine moves from a particular understanding of human nature. For example, the Mediaeval debate between the Thomists, who emphasized the element of knowledge, and the Scotists, who emphasized the element of love, is a debate concerning the unifying center of the human person. However the notion of beatific vision may be clarified in particular, it is basic to keep in mind that the ultimate fulfillment of the human person does not reside in the fulfillment of one faculty in isolation but in the full actualization of all the spiritual powers of the person. Heavenly beatitude may be described in terms of a plurality of acts such as knowledge, love, and joy. The issue that divided the Thomists and the Scotists was the question of the basic, unifying act of the human person in the context of the plurality of acts involved. The anthropology of the Thomists was such that the most reasonable answer to the question was to locate the unifying act in the intellect. For the Scotists, on the other hand, the basic unifying act was to be located in the will.

However one may resolve this issue, the more basic point is the recognition that the doctrine of beatific vision is a specific theological attempt to speak of the total penetration of the human person by the loving presence of God. It is an attempt to deal with the impact which the most intimate and immediate presence of God would have on the human person. Seen in terms of its most basic theological concern, the doctrine of beatific vision is not in conflict with the Christological-trinitarian view suggested above, which also is concerned with the immediacy of God's presence to the creature. But the emphasis on the Christological dimension has the decided advantage of diminishing the

---

[12]"Letter on Certain Questions concerning Eschatology", May, 1979.

excessive individualism that seems to be implicit in the Scholastic notion, for the Christological aspect means that the destiny of the individual must be situated in the context of the entire Body of Christ. Heaven is not simply a question of individual salvation. The relational and corporate nature of humanity remains even here where all human relations are brought to a new depth of fulfillment in the final relation with God.

c) Cosmic Dimension of the Final Condition

In discussing the resurrection of Christ, we referred to the study of P. Perkins who pointed out that the resurrection is part of the scenario of a vision that is cosmic in scope. The resurrection must be seen as the high-point of the history of God's dealing with the world. In treating the mystery of the resurrection of Christ and again in dealing with the notion of resurrection in the moment of death, we have raised the question of the relation of salvation to cosmic reality. What was implied in those discussions must be brought explicitly into this context. To speak of heaven is not to speak of going to another, better world. Rather, it is to speak of entering into a new and fulfilling relation to the only world of God's creation. Christian hope is not a hope in the destruction of the world but a hope for its eventual transformation and renewal.

Both Rahner and Ratzinger have stated the Christological base for this cosmic concern.[13] In the case of Rahner, the issue is treated in the context of his understanding of the death of Christ. In Rahner's view, Jesus' death did not mean that he left this world but rather that he entered into a more all-embracing relationship to the world as he entered into the deepest union with the Ground of the world. This relationship is described as pancosmic by Rahner. This view is in harmony with the Aristotelian-Scholastic concept of the human soul which is traditionally described as "quodammodo omnia." The soul is, as it were, everything; it has the power of taking everything real to itself as an object of knowledge and love; it is potentially related to everything that exists. To this we must add the Scholastic transformation of the Aristotelian philosophy of form in the theological defini-

---

[13]Rahner, *On the Theology of Death*, p. 27ff; Ratzinger, *Eschatologie*, p. 192.

tion of the soul. As a formal cause, the soul has an intrinsic relation to the material cause of the human being. Even though it may be temporarily separated from the body in death, the soul does not lose its intrinsic relation to matter. The echoes of these two Scholastic notions can be heard in Rahner's idea of a pancosmic relation to the world.

Cardinal Ratzinger, while viewing the theology of death from a different perspective, expresses a similar understanding of the presence of Christ to the world on a number of occasions. The glorification of Christ in the resurrection and ascension does not mean that Christ left this world. On the contrary, since the glorification means that the human reality enters into the trinitarian life of God to participate in God's kingly rule over history, the glorified Lord is present to the world in a new manner. It is this manner of presence that is expressed in the traditional symbolic language which describes the risen Lord "sitting at the right hand of the Father." In Ratzinger's terms, the risen Lord is not removed from the world but becomes transcendent to the world and therefore related to the world in a new way. Since heaven is precisely that mode of being and that mode of relationship—a transcendent mode of relationship freed from the restrictions of the temporal-spatial world—it becomes clear that heaven cannot be any sort of geographical place. It is, above all, a question of the final relation between the world and the Ground of the world.

The common understanding of the concept of beatific vision easily creates the impression that, at least in the Scholastic understanding and in that of the Magisterium, the joy of heaven is totally unrelated to the world. A more careful reading of the Scholastic theology on this point, however, indicates that this is not accurate. It is true that Scholastic theology located the essential joy of heaven in the vision of God. The divinity is referred to technically as the primary object of the beatific vision. To speak of a primary object is to imply that there is a secondary object. And in this case, that is the reality of all created things as they are known in God, their creative source. This is an oblique way of saying something of considerable importance in the theology of heaven. For it implies that the presence of God does not exclude the presence of other objects in the ultimate fulfillment of humanity. Salvation, in Christian terms, is not a salvation "from out of the world," but is precisely the salvation "of the world." Salvation is not the eternal existence of disembodied souls with no relation to the world of creation. On the contrary, even this Scholastic understanding of heaven includes the essential relatedness of the soul to the whole of created reality.

It is when theology attempts to fill out this conviction more precisely that we experience the poverty of theological imagination and discourse. The questions and problems that appeared in our discussion of resurrection at the moment of death become inescapable here. The biblical and Christian vision of salvation is that of the salvation of the world. Just as the world is created by God, so it is brought to fulfillment by God. We have become familiar with the kind of problems that centered around the doctrine of creation in relation to the development of modern science. We have learned to distinguish the various levels of questions about the origin of the world, and to allow for some sort of interaction between the positive sciences and theology, for the world which theology describes as the object of God's creative power is the same world which the sciences study through their empirical methodology. A totally existential style of theology was willing to recognize science and theology as two completely unrelated disciplines. This meant, however, that theology would eventually be isolated from the major images through which modern people identify who they are in the world since the images and metaphors of the sciences are dominant at least in Western culture. Uncomfortable with the sort of isolationism that seemed to be the eventual outcome of such an approach, other theologians have sought for some sort of living interaction between the scientific metaphors and theories of the modern world and the religious concerns of the Judaeo-Christian tradition.

The same sort of problematic arises at the other end of the theological spectrum. Does theological eschatology have any relation to the theories of modern physics and astro-physics? In no sense is this a question of looking for scientific insights to prove the truth of Christianity. But, if Christianity has a religious vision of the world and of its future, does this have any relationship to scientific visions of the structure of the world, its physical dynamic, and its future? What are we to think of the Christian vision of an absolute future in a world-view that includes quantum-physics, relativity, black-holes, anti-matter, and the Big Bang? What does the theological notion of the Kingdom of God mean in a world in which human beings have the capacity to destroy the human race either through genetic manipulation or through nuclear holocaust? What has all this to do with the Christian understanding of an indestructible future with God? If the world that scientists study is the same world that theologians believe to be the creation of God, there must be some relation. But precisely what that relation might be is difficult to discern.

It is clear that the scientific level of questioning is distinct from that of theology. The scientist, precisely as scientist, is concerned with tracing the chain of cause and effect at the level of what traditional theology calls secondary causality. The theologians, on the other hand, is concerned primarily with questions of ultimate meaning or primary causality, to use a Scholastic term. The scientist, by virtue of his or her method and discipline, can deal only with matters of empirical observation. The theologian, by way of contrast, is concerned with why there is anything to be observed empirically. Theology is concerned with the questions of the ultimate ground and purpose of existence. Both the scientist and the theologian are looking at the same world, but each looks from a different perspective and with distinct kinds of questions.

Whether the scientist predicts an end to the cosmos, or an end to its present form, or an endless cycle of expansion and contraction, none of these is simply identical with the end of history which we have seen to be the concern of theology. Theology, as we have seen, has no specific information about the physical course of events that lie ahead in cosmic history. Whatever the world may look like to the eyes of the scientist, however puzzling its deepest secrets seem to be, however hostile the vastness of the cosmos may seem to be for human survival, it is the conviction of faith and of theology that this world and its history has an ultimate meaning which cannot be determined or controlled by humanity.

There is no evident contradiction between the theological question of ultimate meaning and the scientific questions about the physical dynamics of the cosmos unless we insist on interpreting the apocalyptic imagery as real, objective accounts of future events. Similarly, there is no evident contradiction between the Christian hope for indestructible life for a transformed humanity in a transformed world and contemporary notions concerning the nature of material reality. One of the tasks of theology is to give a responsible account of faith in terms of the significant modern insights into the mystery of the world.

As an example of this, we can cite the attempt of J. Macquarrie to express the possibility of an eternal life with God in terms that are compatible with modern relativity theories. Similar reflections are suggested by C. Meyer in relation to modern theories concerning the multi-dimensional nature of the created universe. A more detailed presentation of a model for understanding space, time, and matter is offered by R. Pendergast.[14] The point of such speculations is not to prove the truth of faith but to show, within whatever limits it is possible to do so, that the hope of Christians is not necessarily an illusion. It is not a bit of intellectual nonsense to talk of a transformed universe or of indestructible life with God. Indeed, the modern theories and insights of science itself have opened up the mysterious character of the created universe in an unprecedented way. This is not to say that science may eventually prove the truth of faith. But it is not insignificant that the process of scientific study and reflection seems to push to a level of awe and mystery that is not far removed from the concern of religion. In the face of the ambiguity of our experience and the overwhelming mystery of the universe, the question is inescapable: Does it all have any meaning in the final analysis? Or is it all, ultimately, a cosmic charade "signifying nothing"?

The claim of Christian faith is that created existence and history is ultimately grounded in a mystery of creative love in which it finds its perfecting fulfillment. "I am the Alpha and the Omega, the first and the last, the beginning and the end" (Rev. 22:13). The beginning and the end with which theology is principally concerned is the mystery of God. Beyond that, theology has no specific information about the concrete beginning of the world nor about its concrete end. In the beginning, is God. In the end, is God and the fruit of history. Unless we say that, we deny any meaning to the whole of creation and its history.

Theology can give no precise definition of what it means to speak of a transformed humanity existing in a transformed world. Neither can science give a clear description of the future of the physical cosmos. Neither the scientist nor the theologian has an adequate knowledge about the nature and dynamics of the universe to give definitive definitions concerning the nature of matter, of life, or of personal existence. If we do not understand created reality in its present condition, even less can we expect to gain any precise understanding of what its final,

---

[14]J. Macquarrie, *Christian Hope* (N.Y., 1978) p. 117ff; C.R. Meyer, "The Life of the World to Come," in: *Chicago Studies* 24 (August, 1985) n.1, pp. 115-130; R.J. Pendergast, *Cosmos* (N.Y., 1973) pp. 61-82.

perfected condition will be. Yet, this world is the world created by God; and this world is the object of God's redemptive love. Only unmitigated pride and conceit would allow us to say that God is concerned only with the human race and that questions about the rest of creation are of no religious or theological relevance. Rahner can write with good reason that if our fulfillment does not include both the spiritual and material dimensions of our existence, then it is not *our* fulfillment but the fulfillment of part of our nature. Materiality and world are the necessary context for our existence as "incarnate spirit." Should this cease to be the case, then our nature will have been fundamentally changed. We would no longer be human beings.

The glorification and transformation of created reality may be seen as a condition in which the material creation is brought to "participation in the perfection of the spirit."[15] God's victory in Christ will take the form of a perfect society of fully human members living with the glorified Christ in a transformed world. For those who believe that the world is directed to an eternal destiny together with humanity, and that human decisions in and about the world are of crucial importance in bringing about that destiny with God, the world becomes a sacred trust. In the theology of creation, Christianity speaks of humanity as the steward of creation. Humanity is given a responsibility for the good of the entire created realm. Far from turning us away from our responsibility in and for the world, the belief that we together with the world are called to an eternal destiny with God should turn us to the world with a care and concern which befits the world in as far as it is the object of God's creative knowledge and love.

Both the Hebrew and the Christian Scriptures speak of a "new heaven and a new earth." These metaphors imply a fundamental renewal on a cosmic scale. The transformed world is the sphere in which God's rule is finally realized. If the metaphors of Scripture give any indication of what that may mean, it would have to be expressed in terms such as reconciliation, justice, love, truth, and fullness of life. These are not only a biblical language for a hoped-for future. Indeed, they are the language of the human heart itself as it struggles to find a home for itself in a world that seems hostile to its efforts. The word that God addresses to us through history is directed to the deepest

[15]Rahner, *Theological Investigations*, 2, p. 212.

roots of our human nature and opens to human hope the prospect of an absolute future in which all the good, the true, and the beautiful brought forth in history is brought to fulfillment and crowned with eternal significance in the life of God. In the darkness of historical experience, faith holds open this prospect of hope. The word of God, then, is an invitation to a radical, trusting hope that, indeed, the ground of reality is a power of creative, forgiving, accepting love. Trusting in that power, the Christian hopes for an absolute fulfillment of created existence without knowing precisely how this will be brought about or what it will be like.

While we have no precise information about this future, the person of Jesus remains a source of insight and hope during our earthly journey. He remains for all ages the model of radical trust in the life-giving power of God's creative love. From the life and destiny of Jesus, we may conclude that humanity can never realize its true fulfillment from its own resources alone. Neither does God bring about this fulfillment without an appropriate human response to God's love. Though we have no concrete image of the future, and though we do not understand how God acts in and through human actions, yet we work actively in the service of God and humanity to create within history that condition which is necessary for the realization of God's Kingdom by building the earth and contributing to the enrichment of human life and love. Speaking of Christian hope, Vatican Council II urges that Christians not keep this hope "hidden in the depths of their hearts." On the contrary, hope ought to be expressed in the programs of the secular life which Christians must be engaged in simply because they are human beings (*Lumen gentium*, IV, #35). It is precisely because we believe that the world has a future of ultimate significance that Christian hope ought to turn us actively to the world with deep love and concern for the gift of God which it is.

READINGS

Badham, P., *Christian Beliefs about Life after Death* (New Era Books, London/N.Y., 1976).

Head, J. & Cranston, S.L., ed. *Reincarnation: The Phoenix Fire Mystery* (Julian Press/Crown Publ. Inc., N.Y., 1977).

Hick, J., *Death and Eternal Life* (Harper & Row, N.Y., 1976).

Küng, H., *Eternal Life?* (Doubleday, N.Y., 1984).

MacGregor, G., ed., *Immortality and Human Destiny: A Variety of Views* (Paragon House, N.Y., 1985).

Pendergast, R.J., *Cosmos* (Fordham University Press, N.Y., 1973).

Robinson, J.A.T., *In the End God* (Fontana Books, London, 1968).

INDEX OF NAMES

INDEX OF TOPICS

INDEX OF SCRIPTURE REFERENCES

Old Testament

New Testament